SHAPING HISTORY
100 GREAT LEADERS

SHAPING HISTORY
100 GREAT LEADERS

BRIAN MOONEY

Capella

Contents

Statesmen

Military Commanders

Contributing Editors

Michael Fowke, Peter Jenkins, Neil Edward John, Emma Maurice, Marina Mooney, Felix Pryor, Dim Robbins, Richard Shaw, Barry Simpson, Benita Stoney, Richard Tames, Gail Turner, John Whelan, Paul Whittle.

This edition published in 2006
by Arcturus Publishing Limited
26/27 Bickels Yard,
151–153 Bermondsey Street,
London SE1 3HA

ISBN-13: 978-1-84193-559-1
ISBN-10: 1-84193-559-X

Printed in China

Religious Leaders

Reformers

National Liberators

Revolutionaries

Explorers

Industrialists

SHAPING HISTORY
100 GREAT LEADERS

HATSHEPSUT

Queen Hatshepsut was the first Queen of Egypt (c1509–c1469 BC) and one of the greatest Egyptian pharaohs. She was the first powerful woman ruler in recorded history, and governed Egypt at a time of peace and commercial expansion. She sent a voyage of discovery down the Red Sea and erected two unsurpassed obelisks at the Temple of Amun in Karnak – events recorded in beautiful reliefs on her terraced temple at Deir el-Bahri.

FROM VERY EARLY TIMES, women in Egypt were held in high esteem. In the early 18th Dynasty there was a strong matriarchal tendency. Hatshepsut was the daughter of the great warrior king Tuthmosis I. Her half-brother, Tuthmosis II, succeeded Tuthmosis I after her two brothers died prematurely. Portrait busts show Tuthmosis II as a soft yielding boy, while Hatshepsut, several years his senior, has an erect head, bold aquiline nose, firm mouth, and chin projecting considerably to give an air of vigour and resolution. She married her half-brother, reducing him to a cipher, and became the major influence in government.

After only a few years, their joint reign ended with the murder of Tuthmosis II, perhaps through a conspiracy. Hatshepsut then became regent for his son, Tuthmosis III, born of a minor woman in the harem, and, while he served as a priest of the god Amun, she took control of the throne and was accepted as pharaoh.

In inscriptions on her monuments, masculine and feminine designations of her person alternate. She is both son and daughter of Amun, the state god. Statues and reliefs show her with false beard and male dress. Though in the inscriptions masculine and feminine forms are inextricably mixed up, the personal and possessive pronouns which refer to her are feminine for the most part, with sometimes perplexing expressions such as 'His Majesty herself'.

As pharaoh, Hatshepsut's reign was largely peaceful, and this enabled her to carry out grand schemes of foreign commerce. Her expedition to the Land of Punt (probably modern-day Somalia) down the Red Sea can be seen as a parallel with the voyages of discovery of the European Renaissance. Her beautiful terraced mortuary temple at Deir el-Bahri has reliefs showing this expedition. It is rare that any single event of ancient history is so profusely illustrated as Hatshepsut's expedition. The various phases are recorded, from the gathering of the fleet on the Red Sea coast to the triumphant return to the capital Thebes.

Five large ships for the voyage were built in sections and transported overland and assembled

Hatshepsut's ambitious building programme far exceeded that of her predecessors

Chronology

c1509 BC Born, daughter of King Tuthmosis I
c1490–1468 BC Rules as pharaoh in the 18th Dynasty
YEAR 7 OF REIGN Grandiose scheme for temple at Deir el-Bahri started
YEAR 9 Expedition to Punt
YEARS 15–16 Quarrying and erection of a pair of obelisks at Karnak
YEARS 20–21, (c1469 BC) Kingship reverts to Tuthmosis III; Hatshepsut disappears from history

on the Red Sea coast. One of the main objectives of the expedition was to obtain incense trees; these only grow in southwest Arabia and Somalia. From reliefs on the temple at Deir el-Bahri, which show round huts on stilts accessed by ladders with coconut palms and incense trees, frankincense and myrrh, beside a copious stream with a great variety of fishes, it is believed that Punt is Somalia. Also shown are giraffes, hippopotami, apes and dogs. The expedition was received by the prince of Punt, Parehu, and his huge sway-backed wife, Eti.

Freedom of trade was established. Egyptian goods were traded for thirty-one living incense trees, sacks of incense resin, gold, silver, ivory, ebony, cassia, kohl, apes, baboons, dogs, slaves and leopard skins. The Queen of Punt and several chiefs accompanied the expedition back to Egypt. The arrival back in Thebes was a grand gala day. Hatshepsut offered the produce to Amun, and the incense trees were planted in the forecourt of her temple at Deir el-Bahri.

Hatshepsut's ambitious building programme was far in excess of that of her predecessors. She built all over Egypt and as far as Nubia. Thebes received the most attention. The temple at Deir el-Bahri was called 'Holy of Holies' and was Hatshepsut's most complete statement in material form about her reign. She cut a tomb for herself in the Valley of the Kings, and the Temple of Amun at Karnak was expanded.

The pride of her work at Karnak was two obelisks of red granite, carved from the quarries at Aswan in seven months, which are unexcelled in form, colour and beauty of engraving. Reliefs on the temple at Deir el-Bahri show the giant barge built of sycamore wood with the two obelisks on board being towed down the Nile by numerous boats. It is astounding that these obelisks, which were almost 100 feet tall, were taken on and off the barge and moved into position in the temple at Karnak. The obelisks are covered with the most delicately finished hieroglyphics in which Hatshepsut declares that they are erected to the glory of Amun and to the memory of Tuthmosis I, each 'one block of hard granite, without seam, without joining together'. The entire shafts and summits of the obelisks were gilded.

Meanwhile, Tuthmosis III had grown to be the energetic head of the army. Somewhere about Year 18 of Hatshepsut's reign several of her most prominent supporters disappeared from view, and sometime in Year 20 or 21, c1469 BC, Hatshepsut herself vanished from history. She was about forty years old and had ruled for twenty-two years.

A Master Builder

- *Hatshepsut attained unprecedented power for a queen. Her reign was mainly peaceful, with little war, allowing her to concentrate on improving the lot of her people. She inaugurated building projects that far outstripped those of her predecessors, including the magnificent temple at Deir el-Bahri. The temple is Hatshepsut's supreme achievement and her most enduring monument, containing scenes and inscriptions of important projects and events in her life.*
- *Although one of the obelisks at the Temple of Amun has fallen, the one to the north is still in its original position, the tallest standing obelisk in Egypt.*

PERICLES

Pericles (c495–429 BC) was an Athenian statesman and general under whose rule Greek civilization reached its zenith. So great an influence did he wield over Greek life that the time of his rule is known as the Age of Pericles.

HE WAS BROUGHT UP in the shadow of war in a military household; he was only three years old when the Persians made their first bid to conquer the Greeks and were soundly defeated at Marathon, and his father was the army commander Xanthippus, who overwhelmed the Persians at Mycale in 479 BC after they had invaded Greece for the second time and sacked Athens. The Persians were beaten off again seven years later at Salamis in 472 BC. It was this battle that indirectly gave Pericles, by now a young, cultured intellectual, his first break.

In 472 BC, Pericles sponsored a hugely successful dramatic production for the festival of Dionysus – a major annual event in Athens. It was the play *The Persians* by Aeschylus, the first of the great tragic playwrights, and it won first prize and brought Pericles to widespread public prominence.

His first real involvement in politics began a decade later, in 461, when he joined forces with a radical politician called Ephialtes to organize a vote in the popular assembly that would deprive the Areopagus, the old noble council, of its remaining power. It was a defining moment in Athenian democracy, one that is as relevant today as it was then; henceforth laws would be determined by the votes of the people, rather than by hereditary powers.

The move sparked a backlash in which Ephialtes was assassinated, and thrust Pericles into the centre of Athenian politics. In 458 BC, he was elected *strategos*, effectively master of the city-state – a position he held on and off for much of the next thirty years. During his time in office, he forged Athens into a 'superstate', extended her empire and expanded her sea power – sometimes at the head of his own forces – negotiated a final peace with Persia, and introduced payment for jury service. This allowed poorer people, who could otherwise not afford to leave their work, to take part in public life. In 451 BC Pericles introduced a new citizenship law which barred the children of non-Athenian parents from becoming full citizens. Pericles also instigated a great rebuilding programme of temples and public buildings, which transformed Athens into the most magnificent city of the ancient world.

CHRONOLOGY

c495 BC	Born in Athens
472 BC	Produces *The Persians*
461 BC	Leads vote against the Areopagus
451 BC	New citizenship law
431 BC	Peloponnesian War
429 BC	Death of Pericles

Pericles was always his own man. He commanded the popular assembly with his superb oratory but remained aloof from society and shunned social gatherings; he is reported to have attended only one in his adult life – and then he left early. He refused to accept 'gifts', as was the normal custom for politicians. But he did what he wanted in his own private life. He divorced his wife and scandalized polite Athenian society by taking up with a beautiful foreign hostess, Aspasia. What shocked most was that Pericles treated Aspasia as an equal – even though they were not married. Socrates described her as one of the most intelligent and witty women of her time.

His last years were dogged by war, which was partially of his own making; the splendour and power he had achieved for Athens had sparked the jealousy of the other Greek city-states, especially Sparta, and the Peloponnesian War broke out in 431 BC. The countryside around Athens was ravaged, and plague swept the city, shattering Athenian confidence. Pericles was deposed from office and subjected to a sham trial, but he was re-elected in 429 BC.

Pericles died of plague soon after – a year before the Parthenon was inaugurated. But his real

During his time in office, Pericles expanded the city-state of Athens into a superstate

monument was to have created an intellectual and cultural environment which nurtured the disparate geniuses of Anaxagoras and Socrates, Euripides, Aeschylus and Sophocles, Pindar and Pheidias, Antiphon and Aristophanes, Democritus and Hippocrates, Herodotus and Thucydides. They all lived in or came to Athens in the Age of Pericles, and many were his friends.

A Greek Orator

Extracts from Pericles' funeral oration for the dead of the first year of the Peloponnesian War:

- *'The man who can most truly be counted brave is he who best knows the meaning of what is sweet in life and what is terrible; and then goes out undeterred to meet what is to come.'*
- *'Our love of what is beautiful does not lead to extravagance; our love of the things of the mind does not make us soft.'*
- *'We regard wealth as something to be properly used, rather than as something to boast about.'*

ASHOKA

Ashoka (300–232 BC) was first of the great rulers of India. After renouncing violence and embracing Buddhism, Ashoka reigned over his empire with an unwavering respect for the sanctity of human life. He in effect introduced a completely new social philosophy.

ASHOKA WAS THE THIRD KING of the Maurya dynasty, which ruled much of the Indian subcontinent from its northern capital in Pataliputra, modern Patna. He lived lavishly and self-indulgently until he went to war to conquer the east-coast kingdom of the Kalingas, the modern Indian province of Orissa. The horrors of the war in which, by his own accounts, 100,000 were slain made such an impact on him that he renounced violence and became a Buddhist monk. For the next three decades, as monk and king, he ruled benignly over a peaceful and prosperous empire.

Our knowledge of Ashoka comes down to us in a series of edicts in which he sets out the theory and practice of a new social ethic. The edicts, in Prakrit for the Indian population and in Greek and Aramaic for the people in the northwest of his empire, were inscribed on rock surfaces or pillars.

The Dhauli stone near Bhibaneswar records the king's 'profound sorrow and regret' at the slaughter of the war against the Kalingas. The edicts are underpinned by his complete acceptance of the Buddhist dharma, the law of piety, right living and morality; he promoted what he called 'conquest by dharma' (Universal Law). 'The law of piety; to wit, obedience to father and mother; liberality to friends, acquaintances, relatives, Brahmins, and ascetics; respect for sacredness of life; avoidance of violence and extravagance and violence of language.'

Ashoka all but eliminated the unnecessary slaughter of animals, even curtailing fishing. He appointed ministers to ensure that the dharma was observed, and sent missionaries abroad as far as Syria and Egypt to preach its message – .

In a blueprint for his provincial officers Ashoka states: 'There are, however, certain dispositions which render success impossible, namely, envy, lack of perseverance, harshness, impatience, want of application, idleness, indolence. You therefore should desire to be free from such dispositions.'

CHRONOLOGY

300 BC	Born
273 BC	Ashoka accedes to the throne
269 BC	Ashoka crowned king
264 BC	War against the kingdom of the Kalingas
260 BC	Ashoka becomes a Buddhist monk
232 BC	Dies

He had similar strictures for himself: 'I have accordingly arranged that at all hours and in all places – whether I am dining or in the ladies' apartments, in my bedroom or in my closet, in my carriage, or in the palace gardens – the official reporters shall keep me constantly informed of the people's business, which business of the people I am ready to dispose of at any place' and 'Work I must for the public benefit.'

This was not just pious propaganda. The edicts have a refreshing ring of frankness and sincerity, and Ashoka practised what he preached. He went on frequent tours around his empire to spread his teaching. He looked after the welfare of his subjects by building an extensive network of road communications, planting the sides of the roads with shady banyan trees, providing roadside wells, setting up free rest houses, cultivating medicinal plants and founding hospitals – both for sick people, his subjects, and for animals.

Ashoka seemed to be particularly aware of the needs of women and the plight of the rural poor. He upheld the principle of religious freedom, saying he had achieved more by persuasion than by commands. Few leaders since him – perhaps none – have ruled with such a record of tolerance.

While Ashoka's rule of piety did not last long after his death, he himself gave India an unprecedented time of peace and prosperity and helped ensure that Buddhism and its teaching spread throughout the world.

Ashoka's edicts, far from being simply pious propaganda, have a refreshing ring of sincerity

The Edicts

- *The Major Rock Edicts and the Pillar Edicts are the more comprehensive of all the Buddhist doctrines of Ashoka, and stress the importance of religious and ideological tolerance, non-violence, justice, and harmony in relationships.*
- *The Minor Edicts relate Ashoka's commitment to Buddhism.*
- *Ashoka's full name was Ashokavardhana. In most inscriptions he is called King Priyadarsin.*
- *The lion capital of the Ashoka Pillar (pictured left) found at Sarnath is India's national emblem.*

QIN SHI HUANGDI

Qin Shi Huangdi (259–210 BC) unified China's warring states under the Qin or Ch'in dynasty, founded the Chinese Empire and became its first Emperor.

A ruthless dictator, before he was forty Qin had unified the warring Chinese states in a single empire

THE FUTURE EMPEROR was born in 259 BC in the state of Ch'in, in northwestern China. His name was Ying Zheng, and he was officially the son of Zhuang Xiang, the future king of Qin, one of China's seven feudal states. His father became king in 246 BC when Zheng was thirteen but died soon after, and for the next seven years his mother and a wealthy merchant Lü Puwei served as regents. In the wake of a sex scandal involving his mother and a lover who had pretended to be a eunuch, and an attempted revolt, Zheng took control of his kingdom and set about expanding it. His first act on becoming king was to execute his mother's lover and exile Lü.

He was a ruthlessly brutal dictator, and, with the help of good generals, bribery and bullying, before he was forty he had unified the warring states of China and forged them into a single empire; in 221 BC he took the title Qin Shi Huangdi – 'First Emperor of Qin'.

By most accounts, Qin Shi Huangdi was a nasty piece of work. He would mete out cruel punishments, and he organized one of history's first public book burnings in 213 BC when all works outside the imperial library of a 'non-technical' nature were ordered to be burnt – a brutal attempt to eliminate the teachings of Confucian scholars, who opposed the emperor's reforms. Thousands of dissenting scholars were buried alive. In later life, having survived three attempted assassinations, he lived in terror of death. He would travel with two identical carriages and never sleep the night in the same place. He made extensive tours of his empire but otherwise shut himself up in his palaces, increasingly remote from his people. He sent out agents and went, himself, in search of elixirs of eternal life, and he turned to alchemists with the same hope.

CHRONOLOGY

259 BC	Born Ying Zheng
246 BC	Inherits throne on death of his father
238 BC	Becomes king
221 BC	Takes title Qin Shi Huangdi, 'First Emperor'
210 BC	Dies of natural causes

But he also achieved many remarkable things for China; above all he established the structures of a modern state. He abolished territorial feudal power, and divided the country into thirty-six separately governed states; he gave his empire a single currency, standardized weights and measurements, a uniform legal system and a common written language. He also fostered religion. He built a network of roads and canals and, to protect the country against marauding Huns, he set up defensive military forces, and he ordered the construction of the major portion of the Great Wall of China.

His proclaimed that his dynasty would last 10,000 generations, while in fact it only survived four years after his death; but the centralized state he set up was the basis of Imperial China until its end in 1911, and in many respects lives on in another guise today.

A TERRACOTTA ARMY

- *Apart from the legacy of the name of China, named after the Ch'in or Qin dynasty, another of Qin's legacies lay undiscovered for more than 2,000 years. In 1974 farmers digging a well outside the present-day capital, X'ian, near the First Emperor's tomb, stumbled across the gravesite of an entire army made of terracotta. Archaeologists subsequently discovered four underground chambers containing some 7,000 life-size soldiers and horses – buried there to protect the emperor in the afterlife.*
- *Shi Huangdi was responsible for the construction of the major section – some 1,900 kilometres (nearly 1,200 miles) – of the Great Wall of China, one of the largest man-made objects in existence.*

Augustus

Augustus, the first Emperor of Rome (63 BC–AD 14) restored unity and order to Rome, and founded an empire that was to last longer than any other in European history. His reign bridged two epochs, and brought a period of unrivalled peace, prosperity and culture – the Augustan age.

GAIUS OCTAVIUS, AS HE WAS BORN, was an unknown twenty-year-old soldier, scholar and religious official when he received the alarming news that his great-uncle Julius Caesar had been assassinated, and the even more disturbing news that Caesar had nominated him as his successor. It would take seventeen years of fighting and intrigue to consolidate his power.

He changed his name to Julius Caesar Octavianus, to draw on popular support for his great-uncle and adoptive father, became Consul and initially fought and then formed an alliance with Mark Antony, Caesar's ambitious colleague, and his ally General Marcus Lepidus. This three-man military junta, the Second Triumvirate, began, with brutal violence, a proscription in which thousands of opponents, among them 200 senators and the orator Cicero, were killed. It was a fractured peace. After putting down a challenge from Pompey's surviving son, Sextus, Octavian then drove out Lepidus. Mark Antony, in the East, always posed the ultimate challenge, which came to a head after he married Cleopatra, Queen of Egypt. Octavian defeated their joint forces at the naval battle of Actium in 31 BC and consolidated his hold by taking control of the East.

The Senate conferred the title Caesar Augustus on Octavian in 27 BC, and, with more powers and honours to come, he spent the next forty-one years as the virtually undisputed ruler of Rome and her huge territories. But he was careful never to take on the trappings of a monarch, cleverly masking his dictatorial powers through various constitutional settlements, deals with the Senate and proconsular arrangements; with an abuse of language that would not have been out of place in Stalin's Russia, Augustus referred to himself as 'first citizen'.

Chronology

63 BC	Born in Rome, 23 September
47 BC	Raised to College of Pontifices
44 BC	Nominated heir to Caesar
43 BC	Second Triumvirate
31 BC	Battle of Actium
27 BC	Senate confers on him title Caesar Augustus
AD 14	Dies at Nola, Italy, 19 August

He was a complex character: ruthless at the outset and harsh, even to his own children – 'a chill and mature terrorist', said one opponent – but also magnanimous, tolerant, tactful, approachable, upright and hard-working. In the final analysis, he was a skilfully manipulative politician and a master of propaganda.

A great builder, Augustus literally transformed Rome. 'I found Rome brick and left it marble,' he said. He also left behind an impressive network of roads. He was a patron of the arts, and a friend of the poets Ovid, Horace and Virgil, as well as the historian Livy.

He strategically shifted the focus of the empire to the west, and pushed roads, garrisons and troops to the borders of the provinces, which benefited enormously from his reign. The resulting *Pax Romana*, based on easy communications and flourishing trade, and underpinned by what was now a professional army, was to provide western Europe, the Middle East and the North African seaboard with the longest period of unity, peace and prosperity in their entire recorded history.

'I found a Rome built of brick, and left a Rome of marble'

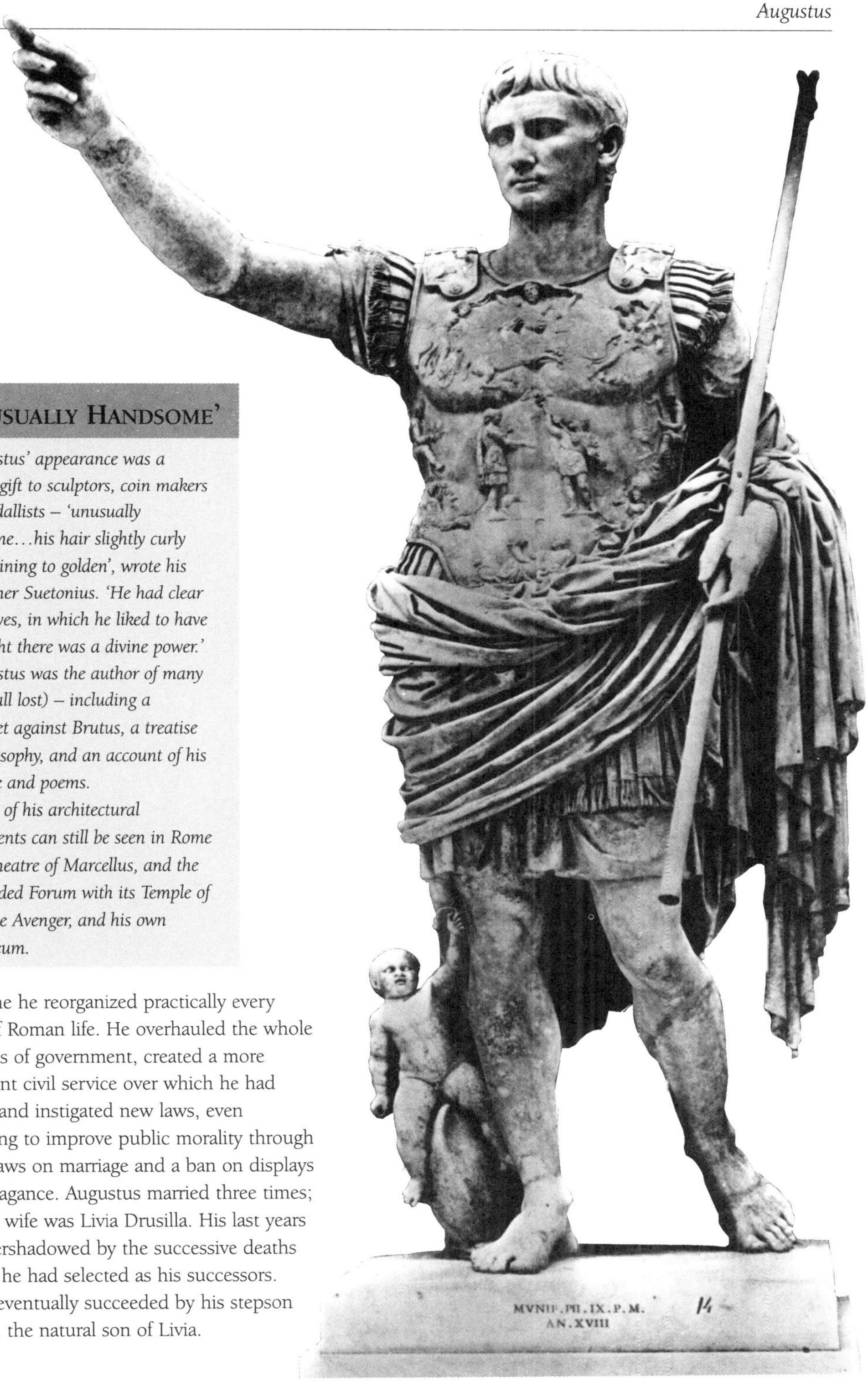

'Unusually Handsome'

■ *Augustus' appearance was a natural gift to sculptors, coin makers and medallists – 'unusually handsome...his hair slightly curly and inclining to golden', wrote his biographer Suetonius. 'He had clear bright eyes, in which he liked to have it thought there was a divine power.'*

■ *Augustus was the author of many works (all lost) – including a pamphlet against Brutus, a treatise on philosophy, and an account of his early life and poems.*

■ *Some of his architectural monuments can still be seen in Rome – the Theatre of Marcellus, and the colonnaded Forum with its Temple of Mars the Avenger, and his own mausoleum.*

At home he reorganized practically every aspect of Roman life. He overhauled the whole apparatus of government, created a more permanent civil service over which he had control, and instigated new laws, even attempting to improve public morality through stricter laws on marriage and a ban on displays of extravagance. Augustus married three times; his third wife was Livia Drusilla. His last years were overshadowed by the successive deaths of those he had selected as his successors. He was eventually succeeded by his stepson Tiberius, the natural son of Livia.

Constantine the Great

Constantine the Great (280–337), Roman emperor, was the first Roman ruler to convert to and legalize Christianity, and he was also the founder of Constantinople (present-day Istanbul). He laid the foundations of Christian European civilization.

The Holy Sepulchre

- *Constantine's mother Helena made a pilgrimage to Jerusalem in 326; in a tradition more cherished than trustworthy she is revered for unearthing the cross on which Christ was crucified at a spot where her son founded the Basilica of the Holy Sepulchre. The basilica is still there – down the centuries the object of endless feuds between different Christian churches.*
- *Did the Christian Church ever regain its purity after being legalized by Constantine? The church lost the independence it had previously enjoyed, and it became an instrument of imperial policy and part of the establishment – an awkward status that has haunted it for centuries and that remains even today in some countries, including England.*

BORN IN NAISSUS, the modern Nish in Serbia, Flavius Valerius Constantinus was the son of a military commander, Constantinus Chlorus, who rose to be co-emperor, and of a woman of humble background, Helena, who was canonized a saint. Constantinus died in 306 in York, England, where he had been campaigning against the Picts, accompanied by his son, who was immediately proclaimed co-emperor in his place. It would take Constantine eighteen years, however, before he finally established himself as sole ruler in 324.

Constantine's conversion to Christianity was almost certainly a gradual process, but the trigger was what he believed was a vision he had in 312 on the eve of the Battle of the Milvian Bridge in which Christ told him to inscribe the first two letters of his name (XP in Greek) on the shield of his troops. Constantine obeyed the vision, and took his subsequent decisive victory over his rival Maxentius as a sign from 'the God of the Christians'. Persecution of Christians was ended, and Constantine and his co-emperor Licinius issued what has come to be called the Edict of Milan, an edict of 'tolerance' in 313, which de facto legalized Christianity throughout the Roman Empire. Constantine became a Christian, though not Licinius.

An armed struggle for power soon began between Licinius and Constantine, from which Constantine emerged victorious in 324, as Emperor of both East and West, and as champion of Christianity. He involved himself more and more in ecclesiastical affairs, and convened the Council of Nicaea in order to get the Church Fathers to agree on a unified teaching. Out of Nicaea came the Nicene Creed, still a primary prayer for all Christian believers. A lavish builder, Constantine founded the basilicas in Rome of St Peter's and St John Lateran, and, in a momentous decision, he built a monumental new capital for the empire at the small town of Byzantium. It was called Constantinople in his honour, and is today's glorious Istanbul.

Constantine was only baptized into the church on his deathbed, a sign, his critics say, of a cynical, half-hearted approach to Christianity. In fact there is abundant evidence that he was sincere in his faith: he had enforced the observance of Sunday as a day of rest, he had his children educated as Christians, and surviving letters concerning the church in North Africa attest to a deep personal commitment. Moreover late baptism was quite normal in the early Christian Church.

But Constantine was also a product of his age and he could be both brutal and cruel. Even after his conversion, he had his brother-in-law, Licinius, executed, and Licinius's son, Licinianus, flogged to death. Constantine also had his wife, Fausta, suffocated in a superheated bath, and their son, Crispus, put to the sword. He maintained a certain ambivalence towards pagan practice, both as an expedient and a sign of genuine tolerance; he was also generous and did much for children, women and slaves.

In other fields, Constantine was not a great innovator, but he restored the empire's economy to a modicum of prosperity; he introduced a new gold coinage and imposed an unpopular new tax. He reformed both the civil administration and the professional army; his reign was marked by unbroken military success. But Constantine's lasting achievements were Christian Europe and the Eastern Empire.

CHRONOLOGY

280	Born at Naissus on 27 February
306	Proclaimed co-emperor
312	Battle of the Milvian Bridge
313	Edict of Milan de facto legalizing Christianity
325	Council of the Church at Nicaea
326	Constantinople founded
337	Dies on 22 May, two weeks after being baptized

Constantine's lasting achievements were Christian Europe and the Eastern Empire

JUSTINIAN I

Justinian I (483–565) was a Byzantine emperor who earned the title Great by re-establishing the old Roman Empire in the West, but his lasting achievement was to codify Roman law. His Codex Justinianus *remains the basis for the law of most European countries.*

BORN FLAVIUS PETRUS SABBATIUS of poor peasant stock in what is today Serbia, Justinian owed his advancement to his uncle, Emperor Justin I, after whom he took his name. Educated in Constantinople, capital of the Eastern Empire, he became Justinian's administrator and was nominated his successor in 518. He was elected Emperor on his uncle's death in 527.

The energetic Justinian set himself an ambitious goal – to recover the territories lost to invaders and restore the tattered Roman Empire and revive its glory. Italy, Spain and Rome's former North African provinces were in the hands of Vandal and Gothic tribes, the Slavs were encroaching from the north and Persia pressing from the east. Justinian was fortunate in his choice of military commander: General Belisarius was commander in chief for most of Justinian's reign, and he was more than a match for the new emperor's ambitions.

Heading a force of just 18,000 men, Belisarius recaptured North Africa from the Vandals in 533. He next landed in southern Italy and retook Rome from the Ostrogoths in 536 but, although most of the peninsula was back under Roman rule by 540, it would take until 552 before the last Gothic strongholds were overrun. Southeastern Spain fell more easily, and by the end of Justinian's reign the Mediterranean was, for most part, once again a Roman sea. Campaigns against the Persians checked their advances, and the Roman frontier was pushed back so the shores of the Black Sea were once again secured. Justinian was no less successful at home; in 532, Belisarius had bloodily put down the so-called Nika revolt, sparked by rival teams of chariot racers – the Blues and Greens – who staged a major insurrection.

Justinian's vision of strong empire called for a uniform legal system. He appointed an imperial commission, headed by the jurist Trebonian, to collect and systematize a thousand years of Roman laws. The task took ten years and resulted in the *Codex Justinianus* – the Justinian Code – which was published in four separate collections and then promulgated in its entirety in 534. The resulting work, which included a manual for law students, meant that for the first time Roman laws were logically arranged, so that every citizen could find out easily the law of the empire on any subject. The codification was Justinian's great work.

Justinian was also a prodigious builder and, more than any others, he refined and perfected the style that is Byzantine architecture. He covered the empire from Ravenna to Damascus with superb monuments, pride among them the Church of Our Lady in Jerusalem, which is now the Al-Aqsa Mosque, and the great Basilica of St Sophia (Hagia Sophia) in Constantinople. The emperor himself shines out in a portrait, standing in his toga and surrounded by his court, in the magnificent mosaics in San Vitale at Ravenna.

Justinian married a beautiful former dancing girl, Theodora, in 523. Scandal and salacious gossip pursued her, but Theodora provided crucial support to the emperor in times of crisis, notably the Nika revolt in 532.

Although Justinian's great conquests were not sustained by his successors, and his reunification of the Roman Empire proved fleeting, his legacy in law and Byzantine architecture would live on.

CHRONOLOGY

483	Born in Tauresium, Dardania (Serbia)
518	Named as Justin's successor
527	Justinian elected Emperor
532	Nika insurrection put down
533	North Africa recaptured
534	*Codex Justinianus* promulgated
536	Rome retaken
540	Gothic capital of Ravenna falls
565	Dies at Constantinople, 14 November

Justinian was a prodigious builder: more than any other he refined and perfected Byzantine architecture

A Jealous Emperor

■ *Belisarius, who rose to prominence fighting against the Persians, recaptured Rome from the Vandals for Justinian on two occasions. He held the city for a year and nine days (536–37) against a far larger Gothic force, famously defending the Aurelian walls by breaking statues and dropping them on the attackers.*

■ *Justinian was jealous of Belisarius. Afraid that his general would seize the throne, he recalled him early from Italy. In 542 he accused him of disloyalty and stripped him of his command. Belisarius was reinstated and sent back to Rome, but was jailed again for conspiracy in 562. He was, however, quickly released and allowed to live peacefully in retirement. The general died in 565, the same year as the emperor.*

■ *Justinian's reign was marked by a succession of earthquakes and other natural disasters. The bubonic plague, that was to ravage Europe in future generations, first appeared in Constantinople in 542.*

CHARLEMAGNE

Charlemagne (742–814) was the first ruler of Europe. King of the Franks and later Holy Roman Emperor, during forty years of military campaigns he expanded an empire that stretched from the Atlantic to the Danube, and from the Netherlands to Provence.

CHARLEMAGNE WAS A GIANT of a man: over six feet tall, strongly built with lively eyes, a long nose, long moustaches and fair hair. His father, Pepin the Short, had difficulty maintaining the Frankish empire which Charlemagne's grandfather, Charles Martel, had reunited. Pepin had deposed the Merovingian King of Gaul and made himself King of the Franks, and on his death in 768 the kingdom was shared between Charlemagne and his older brother Carloman.

Carloman died in 771 and Charlemagne reunited the kingdom, ignoring his nephews' rights. Charlemagne was primarily a great warrior leader, who in fifty-three campaigns extended the Frankish empire over most of present-day Europe and established Christianity over the pagans of central Europe. Wars gave him power because he distributed land and booty to his followers. Thus rewarded, his vassals were appointed as regional governors. Envoys checked that they were not oppressive, and because most of society was illiterate many clerics were employed as officials. In 774 Charlemagne invaded Lombardy (northern Italy) whose king supported Carloman's widow, and in 775 he began his campaigns against the Saxons, which lasted over thirty years. In 778 he besieged Zaragoza, to help Arab rebels of the Caliph of Cordoba. He deposed his cousin the Duke of Bavaria in 788, and began subduing other German tribes before taking on Hungary and Austria.

Charlemagne strengthened the alliance between the Roman papacy and the kingdom of the Franks. He considered himself to be appointed by God to look after the temporal and spiritual well-being of his people. He held the papacy in high regard, and protected it from territorial incursions. All churches in his kingdoms used the same Roman liturgy, a strong unifying factor. He therefore reacted angrily to the 787 Council of Nicaea decrees settling the iconoclast heresy. He had not been invited to attend the council, so he held his own synod in Frankfurt to decide the matter. In 800 Pope Leo III was deposed and escaped to Charlemagne's court. Later that year Charlemagne restored the pope, who in return crowned him first Holy Roman Emperor on Christmas Day. Not until 812 did the Byzantine Emperor Michael I recognize Charlemagne's title as Emperor of the West, maintaining that the Eastern Empire was the true heir of Rome.

Charlemagne spoke Latin and some Greek, and was a great patron of learning, although he was himself probably illiterate. Alcuin, a noted Northumbrian scholar, was persuaded to preside over the palace school where both girls and boys were taught. Illuminated manuscripts in Carolingian minuscule and ivory carvings reflect his patronage of the arts. He was a pioneer of Romanesque architecture, although his great chapel at Aachen reflects the Byzantine church of San Vitale in Ravenna, which he had visited and admired. He built a bridge over the Rhine, and a canal linking the Rhine and Danube rivers. He died in 814 aged seventy, leaving Europe with a dream of unity. Shortly after his death the Treaty of Verdun split Charlemagne's empire three ways: future France and Germany, and the 'Middle Kingdom' (Alsace Lorraine) which became a persistent problem well into the twentieth century.

CHRONOLOGY

742	Born in Aachen, now Germany, 2 April
768	Becomes joint ruler with brother of Frankish kingdoms
773	Invades and conquers Lombardy
775	Begins campaigning in Saxony
787	Holds own Synod of Frankfurt when not invited to Council of Nicaea
788	Conquers Bavaria
796	Campaigns in Hungary
800	Crowned first Holy Roman Emperor
814	Dies in Aachen, 28 January

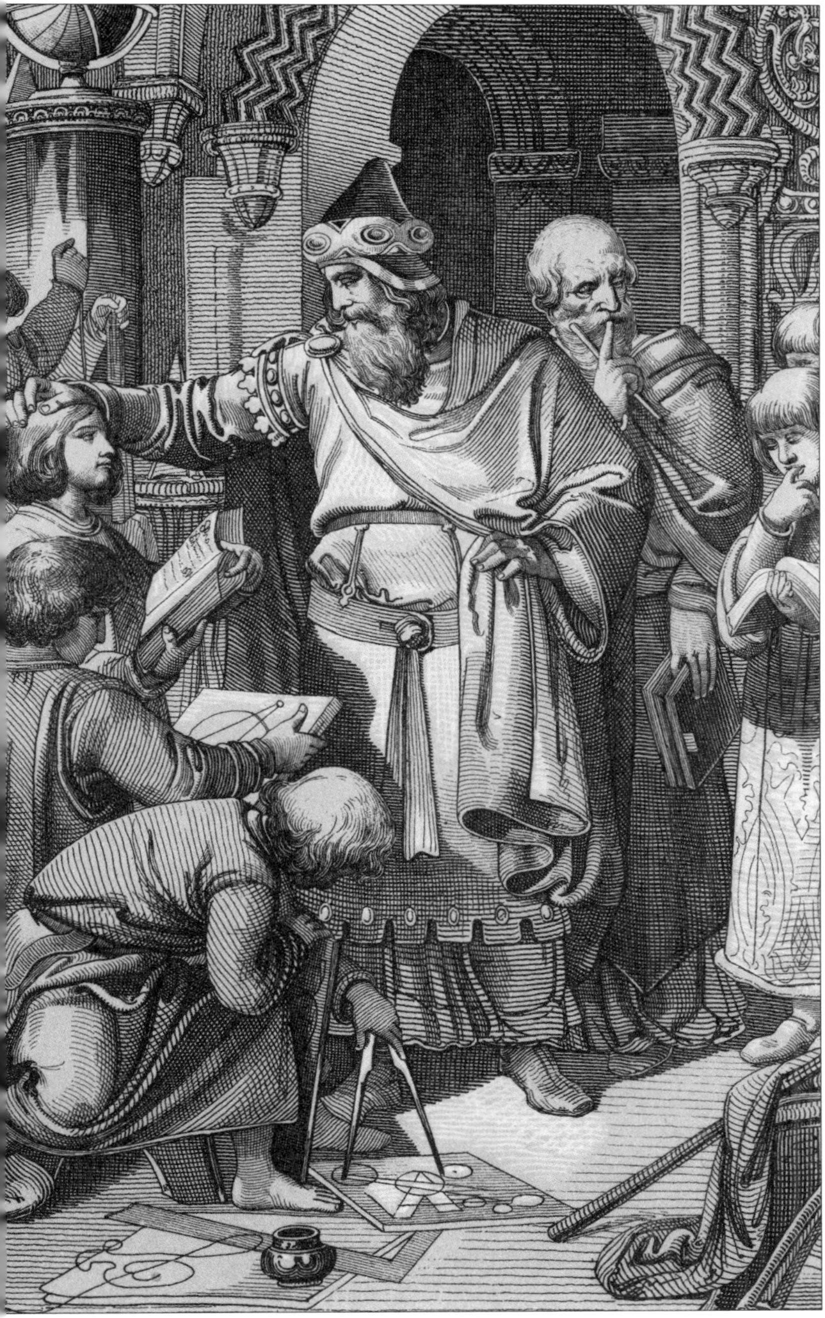

Carolingian Minuscule

■ *Carolingian minuscule was a clear and manageable script, intended to be recognizable throughout Charlemagne's Holy Roman Empire.*

abcd
klmno
uvw

It was designed by the Northumbrian scholar Alcuin. One of the foremost men of letters of his day, Alcuin had been headmaster of the cathedral schools of York and Aachen before becoming Abbot of St Martin's at Tours. Under Alcuin's guidance, this abbey would become the centre of a literary and spiritual renascence. Although Carolingian minuscule was to an extent discarded in favour of Gothic scripts after the break-up of the empire, this beautiful script was rediscovered during the Italian Renaissance and became the basis of the Roman alphabet of today.

Charlemagne established a Christian Frankish empire over the pagan peoples of Europe

MEHMED II

Mehmed II (1432–81), the conqueror of Constantinople and Sultan of Ottoman Turkey, was the true founder of Ottoman imperial power which lasted more than 400 years.

THE TURKISH OTTOMANS, originally nomads from Central Asia, had already conquered large swathes of the eastern Mediterranean and Balkans by the time of Mehmed's birth in 1432. The fourth son of Murad II and a slave girl, he was set on the throne in 1444, aged only twelve. But the Ottomans were still vulnerable to attack from Christian Europe; Mehmed's father had to come out of retirement to beat off a Crusader army at the battle of Varna. He then took back the throne until his death in 1451.

Mehmed, meanwhile, had nurtured an ambition to take Constantinople, a strategic stronghold on the shores of two seas and the crossroads between two continents, which had been the outpost of the Eastern Roman Empire since it was founded by Constantine the Great in 324, and the headquarters of the Eastern Christian Church. The Ottomans had their capital in a far more humble setting at Edirne, 200 miles northwest of the Golden City.

The twenty-year-old sultan prepared for the siege and assault with single-minded determination and remarkable skill – he reinforced his army and bought off Venice and Hungary with favourable treaties. He erected a fortress on the edge of the city's great walls at Rumeli Hisar, cast the largest-calibre cannons that had ever been fired, and built a fleet to control the Bosporus. The siege lasted from 2 April to 29 May 1453, and in the end neither the huge cannon nor the sight of impaled Christians broke the defenders but Mehmed's orders for the fleet to be dragged overland behind Pera and into the Golden Horn. It was a masterstroke; the city lost its harbour. On the day of the final attack Mehmed personally directed his crack soldiers, the janissaries, through one of the breaches in the city wall. The city was looted, and contemporary chroniclers spoke of rivers of blood. The last Roman emperor, Constantine XI, died fighting; it was the end of the Roman Empire. Mehmed, himself, went straight to the cathedral of Hagia Sophia, the mother church of Eastern Christendom, and converted it into a mosque.

The capture of Constantinople bestowed immense glory and prestige on Mehmed: he was the champion of Islam, heir to Alexander the Great and the Roman Caesars, and Padishah, 'Sovereign of the Two Lands and the Two Seas'. Mehmed gave back to Constantinople in equal measure: he established a truly cosmopolitan and multi-national city, tolerant of Jews and Christians alike. He built mosques and colleges, codified laws, and made foreign merchants, scholars and artisans welcome; and thus the imperial Byzantine traditions, with their Greek and Roman legacies, were opaquely distilled into a new Turkish Ottoman reality.

For the rest of his reign, Mehmed continued the expansion of Ottoman rule in a series of successful military expeditions, as far afield as the Crimea and southern Italy. He sealed Ottoman domination of Anatolia and the Balkans in a decisive victory over the Turkmen leader Uzun Hasan at the Battle of Bashkent in 1473, and he was planning to invade Italy when he died.

CHRONOLOGY

1432	Born in Edirne, 30 March
1444	Child Sultan
1446	Murad II takes back crown
1451	Mehmed becomes Sultan on father's death
1453	Captures Constantinople
1473	Battle of Bashkent
1481	Dies near Constantinople, 3 May

Chroniclers of Mehmed's seizure of Constantinople spoke of 'rivers of blood' during the city's capture

A Cultured Tyrant

■ *Although he was cruel and meted out dreadful punishment, Mehmed was a man of great culture, and he was remarkably broadminded. He read widely and also wrote poetry.*

■ *He asked the patriarch Gennadios Scholarius to write a treatise on the Christian faith and had it translated into Turkish.*

■ *He invited the artist Gentile Bellini from Venice to decorate the walls of his palace with frescos. Bellini painted a portrait of Mehmed which is in the National Gallery in London.*

■ *Mehmed's janissaries were the elite footsoldiers, the shock troops, who won the Ottoman Empire. The word comes from yeni ceri, Turkish for 'new troops'.*

SÜLEYMAN I

Süleyman I, the Magnificent, (1494–1566) was the greatest of the Ottoman sultans. He extended Ottoman rule from Baghdad to central Europe and set new standards for Ottoman civilization in law, literature, art and architecture.

THE SON OF SULTAN SELIM I and a slave girl, Süleyman gained experience as a provincial governor before succeeding his father as sultan in 1520. He inherited a crack army and he used it to good effect for much of his reign. He carried Ottoman arms far into Europe: Belgrade was captured in 1521 and the Hungarians defeated at the Battle of Mohács in 1526, after Süleyman crossed the Drava River on a bridge of boats, which he burnt behind him. Süleyman's armies went back and forth into Hungary many times during his reign to settle dynastic rivalries in the conquered land. In 1529, Süleyman unsuccessfully laid siege to Vienna, the East European capital of his Habsburg rival Emperor Charles V. But Süleyman eventually extracted tribute from Emperor Charles and he forged a close alliance with France; he made the Ottomans count in Europe.

Süleyman waged three major campaigns against Persia, and took Iraq, adding the dazzling Muslim city of Baghdad to his empire. Under Süleyman, the Ottomans became the leading power in the Mediterranean. Early in his reign he seized Rhodes from the Knights of St John of Jerusalem but soon realized that he needed a navy to match his ambitions. He built one with the help of Algerian corsairs under the leadership of Khayr ad-Din, known in the west as Barbarossa, who was made admiral of the Ottoman fleet in 1534. The Ottoman fleet overcame the combined fleets of Venice and Spain in 1538 and helped extend Ottoman rule through most of North Africa. Barbarossa died in 1546, but his mighty navy continued to pluck prizes – Tripoli in 1551 and Djerba in 1560. There were just two major setbacks: they failed to take Oran and were repulsed from Malta by the Knights of St John.

At home, Süleyman appointed a succession of able grand viziers, and employed architects to embellish Constantinople and cities like Baghdad with mosques, bridges and aqueducts. His chief architect Sinan built the Süleymaniye Mosque and its complex of colleges, libraries, shops and hospitals, and the Shehzade Mosque, buildings which transformed classical Constantinople into Muslim Istanbul. Sinan built or restored 477 buildings, of which 319 were in Constantinople. Süleyman's court was famed for its splendour and for its elaborate oriental rituals, and his gilded and bejewelled throne room left visitors in awe. Grand public celebrations to mark the circumcision of his sons in 1530 lasted fifty-five days. Poetry also flourished during his reign, and many new laws were enacted, earning Süleyman the posthumous title of the 'Law Giver'. It was in every respect a golden age.

CHRONOLOGY

1494	Born in Trabzon (Trebizond), 6 November
1521	Captures Belgrade
1520	Becomes Sultan
1526	Defeats Hungary at battle of Mochas
1529	Lays siege to Vienna
1538	Ottoman fleet defeats Spanish and Venetians
1566	Dies in Szigetvár, Hungary, 6 September

Under Süleyman, the Ottoman Turks would become the leading power in the Mediterranean

THE WARRIOR POET

- *Süleyman was an accomplished poet, leaving behind no fewer than 2,000 ghazals, short poems, most of them to his Polish-born wife Hürrem, to whom he remained devoted and faithful. She was a power in the palace.*
- *One of his verses to her starts: 'The green of my garden, my sweet sugar, my treasure, my love.'*
- *Baqi (1520–99), the sultan of poets, was Süleyman's favourite.*
- *The main business of the Ottoman state was war. Its governing class was known as soldiers (askeris), and the army was a dominant institution. The Ottomans employed mercenaries and slaves like the janissaries, who, on merit alone, could rise to high rank.*
- *'Day and night our horse is saddled and our sabre is girt,' Süleyman once boasted. This was no idle boast: Süleyman died in 1566 on his thirteenth campaign, and seventh in Hungary, while besieging the Hungarian fortress of Szigetvár.*

TOKUGAWA IEYASU

Tokugawa Ieyasu (1543–1616), samurai war lord and statesman, founded Japan's Tokugawa dynasty of shoguns that ended more than a century of feuding and lasted more than 250 years.

IN THE EARLY SIXTEENTH CENTURY, Japan was an anarchy of feuding clans, in which the future shogun was caught up as a child. Matsudaira Takechiyo was born into the Matsudaira military clan in Mikawa near the modern city of Nagoya, and at the age of seven he was sent as a hostage to cement an alliance with the neighbouring Imagawa family, who were headquartered at Sumpu (Shizuoka).

He grew up at Sumpu, receiving an education and military training; he also developed a love of falconry. Later, he started leading military expeditions for Imagawa Yoshimoto; over the years he was to become a fearless samurai warrior. He also married and fathered the first of many sons.

Imagawa Yoshimoto was killed in battle with the Nobunaga clan in 1560 and Ieyasu seized the opportunity to escape and return to his family lands in Mikawa. He made an alliance with the Nobunaga family, changing his name to Tokugawa Ieyasu, and started building up a home power base and his army. Ieyasu gradually expanded his territory, taking some of Nobunaga's land on his death in 1582, and also grabbing former Imagawa lands. He moved his headquarters to Sumpu, the city where he had been held hostage, and by 1583 he was master of five provinces.

For a decade he lived in the uneasy shadow of Japan's dominant warlord, Nobunaga's successor Toyotomi Hideyoshi, and keeping in with him even managed to share in some of his spoils when he took over part of the Hojo domains. These included the fishing village of Edo (modern Tokyo). Avoiding involvement in Hideyoshi's two disastrous military expeditions to Korea, Ieyasu built up a productive and well-governed state, and, by the time Hideyoshi died in 1598, Ieyasu had the largest and most efficient army and the best-run domains in Japan. There was a final clash between Hideyoshi's former lieutenants and Ieyasu in 1600 at Sekigahara, some eighty kilometres northeast of Kyoto, in which Ieyasu's eastern army triumphed. He was now undisputed master of Japan.

CHRONOLOGY

1543	Born in Okazaki, Japan, 31 January
1550	Sent as hostage to Imagawa family at Sumpu
1560	Imagawa killed, Ieyasu returns home
1586	Ieyasu establishes new headquarters at Sumpu
1600	Ieyasu triumphs in battle at Sekigahara
1603	Appointed Shogun
1605	Retires and passes title to his son
1616	Dies in Sumpu, 1 June

Ieyasu was a great organizer and he now set about rearranging his domains, redistributing land, switching warlords round and placing his most trusted vassals in control of central Japan. The powerless but prestigious imperial court confirmed his position in 1603, appointing him Shogun.

He retired from the post two years later and the title passed to his son, Hidetada, thus establishing the Tokugawa hereditary right. But as elder statesman, he retained great personal authority, and direct responsibility for foreign affairs.

He also had unfinished business and, to be absolutely certain of his son's inheritance, in 1614 and 1615 he mobilized his armies for two final assaults on the Hideyoshi stronghold. He reduced their great castle at Osaka and butchered the last of the Toyotomi. He died in 1616, having secured his family's dynasty and lasting peace.

Ieyasu built the largest castle in the world in its day – Edo – on the site of present-day Tokyo

A Test of Loyalty

■ *Ieyasu was forced to kill his first wife and order his son's suicide as proof of loyalty to Nobunaga. This demonstration of the low value of human life compared with honour clearly had an impact on Ieyasu: he once had a prisoner executed because he had insulted him when he was a child.*

■ *In his foreign affairs role, Ieyasu welcomed the new European traders; but he remained deeply suspicious of the Christian missionaries, and in 1614 he banned them.*

■ *By the time of his death, Ieyasu had built the largest castle in the world at Edo – a sprawling network of moats, stone walls, barbicans and warehouses.*

■ *The Shogun rule of Japan, (1600–1868), is named the Edo period, after the Tokugawa capital Edo (Tokyo).*

Charles V

Charles V (1500–58) was Europe's greatest ruler after Charlemagne. As Holy Roman Emperor and King of Spain, this Habsburg monarch ruled over the first empire 'on which the sun never set' – in Europe, North Africa, Spanish America and the Far East. His achievement was to hold this vast and disparate empire together for more than forty years against a rising tide of Protestant insurgency, French hostility, papal antagonism and Islamic incursions.

CHARLES V inherited his Burgundian and Austrian kingdoms, and his drooping jaw, from his grandfather, the Habsburg Holy Roman Emperor Maximilian, and his Spanish empire from his deranged mother, Joanna, daughter of Spain's joint monarchs Ferdinand and Isabella. He was brought up by his aunt Margaret of Austria in what is now Belgium, and his tutor was Adrian of Utrecht, a theologian who later became pope.

He began his reign as Charles I of Spain in 1516, and from then on his life was one of almost ceaseless travel. He went to Spain for the first time in 1517, but had to leave two years later to be crowned King of Germany and Holy Roman Emperor-elect. But the problems of his reign had just begun; the Spanish rebelled against their foreign king and the German Protestants started fomenting trouble in northern Europe.

Charles responded harshly to the 'Comuneros' rebels in Spain, but he was forced to be more pragmatic with the Protestants in Germany. His vision was to restore religious unity to Europe and, though initially he rejected Martin Luther's attempts to reform the Catholic Church, later he was forced to grant the Protestants some rights.

Territorial squabbles with France over Burgundy and Italy dominated much of Charles's reign, involving him in five wars. Charles's Spanish and German troops shocked Europe by marching on France's ally, Pope Clement VII, and sacking Rome in 1527. The Peace of Cambrai in 1529 brought compromise: Charles gave up claims to Burgundy, Francis I to Milan and Naples. Peace was made with the pope, who crowned Charles as Holy Roman Emperor in Bologna.

A resurgent Islamic Turkey, under Süleyman the Magnificent, posed a grave threat to Charles's empire in the east, and he took up the struggle against it on land and at sea. In the 1530s he dispatched an army to defend Vienna against a possible Turkish invasion, and he sent fleets to capture Tunis and Algiers.

Charles took special interest in Spain's South American possessions. A source of immense wealth, in his eyes they were a challenge to his Christian duty. He accepted the arguments of the Jesuit theologian Bartolomé de las Casas against slavery.

Charles tried to ensure his succession by preparing for his son Philip to marry Mary I of England, but the English refused to crown Philip, and Mary was childless. In 1555, in a moving speech in Brussels, Charles announced his decision to abdicate and give his lands in the Netherlands, Spain and the Indies to his son Philip, and the imperial crown to his brother Ferdinand. His attempts at universal unity had failed. The empire he had held together for more than four decades was broken up. Suffering from gout and insomnia, he left for Spain accompanied by two of his sisters, and died in his palace at Yuste in Extremadura in western Spain in 1558.

Chronology

1500	Charles born in Ghent, 24 February
1507	Crowned Duke of Burgundy
1516	Becomes King of Castile and Aragon
1517	Travels to Spain for first time
1518	Elected Holy Roman Emperor
1519	Revolt of 'Comuneros' in Spain
1525	Francis I of France prisoner in Madrid
1527	Sack of Rome by imperial armies
1535	Capture of Tunis
1556	Abdicates, and retires to Spain
1558	Dies in Yuste, Spain, 21 September

'There are those who say I wish to rule the world, but my thoughts and deeds demonstrate the contrary'

A Life in the Saddle

■ *Charles V spent one out of every four days travelling during his forty-three-year reign. He went to Germany nine times, seven times to Spain, seven times to Italy, four times to France, and twice to England and Africa. He spent twelve years in the Netherlands. He said, 'My life has been one long journey.'*

■ *Charles was also a great patron of the arts. He commissioned many portraits from the Italian artist Titian who was duly created Count Palatine and a Knight of the Golden Spur. One day when in Titian's studio, Charles bent down to pick up his brushes from the floor – an extraordinary gesture for a monarch at that time.*

■ *Charles said, 'There are those who say I wish to rule the world, but both my thoughts and my deeds demonstrate the contrary.'*

PHILIP II

Philip II (1527–98), King of Spain, ruled over the first global empire: his dominions stretched from Europe to the Americas to the Far East. He had a genius for bureaucracy and was said to have governed his empire from 'two inches of paper'.

PHILIP II was the eldest son of the Holy Roman Emperor and King of Spain, Charles V, and his wife Isabella of Portugal. His father was abroad for much of Philip's youth, and he was educated by tutors. He married four times. In 1543 he wed his cousin Maria of Portugal, and became de facto regent of Spain. Maria gave birth to a son Don Carlos, who was later accused of plotting against his father and who died in mysterious circumstances. His second wife was Mary Tudor, and Philip lived briefly as her consort in England. By the time of his father Charles V's abdication in 1556, Philip was already Duke of Milan, King of Naples and Sicily, and ruler of the Netherlands, and he was soon to inherit lands in the Americas and the Far East.

He fought in the battle of Saint Quentin against the French in 1557, achieving a victory which paved the way for the Treaty of Cateau Cambrésis in 1559 that ended sixty years of war with France. Philip then married for the third time to Isabelle de Valois of France. They had two dearly loved daughters, Isabella, who later became joint Governor of the Netherlands with her husband, and Catalina. His fourth marriage in 1570 was to his Austrian cousin, Anne, who gave birth to the future Philip III.

Philip was in the vanguard of the Catholic Church's attempt to regain its ascendancy after the Protestant Reformation; he was fanatically Catholic, and the Inquisition was his principal weapon. His harsh repression of rebellion in the Netherlands sparked an eighty-year war, which resulted in a split between the northern (Protestant) Netherlands, and the southern (Catholic) Belgium. In Spain, Philip's religious orthodoxy led him to oppress Christianized Moors (Moriscos). Many thousands were exiled after 1571.

Philip took the war against infidels to the Mediterranean where his half-brother, Don John of Austria, led a Christian alliance to victory over the Ottoman Turks at the naval battle of Lepanto. Religion underpinned his decision to send his 'Invincible Armada' to unseat Queen Elizabeth I in 1588, and return England to Catholicism, but the great fleet was scattered and destroyed by violent storms. Philip also came to the aid of the Catholic Holy League in France, which was fighting the Huguenot (Protestant) King Henri IV from 1590 until 1598. He claimed his rights to the throne of Portugal in 1580.

For all his war-making, Philip was a tender, loving father and husband. While in Lisbon, pursuing his claim to the Portuguese throne in 1580, he wrote delightful letters to his daughters. Philip loved art, and like his father was a patron of Titian. He also developed a passion for the ghoulish work of Dutch master Hieronymus Bosch, but he found the originality of El Greco too much. He built and expanded palaces around Madrid. His major artistic achievement was the construction of El Escorial (1563–84), a monastery, palace and royal mausoleum filled with paintings, books and holy relics. Philip died peacefully in his bedchamber at El Escorial, clasping his father's crucifix, looking on to the High Altar of the church.

CHRONOLOGY

1527	Born in Valladolid, Spain, 21 May
1543	First of four marriages
1549–51	First trip to Italy and Netherlands
1553–59	Second trip to northern Europe and England
1559	Treaty of Cateau Cambrésis with France
1563	Monastery palace of El Escorial begun
1568	Revolt of the Netherlands begins
1571	Ottoman Turks defeated at Lepanto
1580	Conquers Portugal
1588	Sends 'Armada' fleet to fight against England
1598	Dies at El Escorial, Spain, 13 September

Philip's palace complex at El Escorial was described as the 'Eighth Wonder of the World'

A Bibliophile King

■ *Philip had a mania for collecting: he owned thousands of coins and medals, precious stones, and arms and armour. He left more than 10,000 books in the library at El Escorial, and thousands of holy relics, including a supposed hair from Christ's beard, and the entire bodies of several early Christian martyrs.*

■ *Philip governed his global dominions from the centre of Spain in Castile. Distrusting his advisers and secretaries, he insisted all important decisions be referred to him. 'What his father gained by the sword, Philip keeps by the pen,' a contemporary commented.*

■ *His youthful trips to northern Europe led him to create Flemish gardens for his palaces near Madrid and Segovia. Unfortunately many of his plants and trees (those imported from the Netherlands, France and America) died because his Spanish gardeners forgot to irrigate them.*

■ *El Escorial was regarded by contemporaries as the 'eighth wonder of the world' and by Philip as 'the lady of his heart'.*

■ *The Philippines, conquered in 1565, are named after Philip II.*

ELIZABETH I

Elizabeth I (1533–1603), Queen of England, is widely regarded as the greatest of Britain's monarchs, who brought stability to the country after the tumult of previous reigns and who laid the political foundations of the English-speaking world.

ELIZABETH WAS THE ONLY CHILD of the marriage of Henry VIII to Anne Boleyn, from whom he had hoped for a male heir. For the sake of this marriage, he had divorced Catherine of Aragon and split with Rome. Anne Boleyn was, in her turn, executed. Henry then married Jane Seymour, who gave him a son, the future Edward VI. Princess Elizabeth received a superb humanist education, but her position at court was often fraught. During the reign of her brother Edward VI she became entangled with the over-ambitious Lord Seymour, and during the reign of her sister Mary she became the natural rallying-point of Protestant opposition.

By the time she ascended the throne on 17 November 1558, Elizabeth had acquired a thorough knowledge of statecraft, guided from the beginning by her adviser Sir William Cecil, later Lord Burghley. Her first and perhaps longest-lasting achievement was the establishment of the Church of England, alienating Roman Catholics, who had a champion in her cousin the Catholic Mary Queen of Scots (mother of her successor James I), while her moderation made her unpopular with the more earnest Protestant brethren.

Cecil apart, the dominating figure early in her reign was Lord Robert Dudley, whom she created Earl of Leicester and who was, it seems, the real love of her life. But Leicester had been accused of murdering his wife and was an unsuitable match; and so, throughout the first decades of her reign, Elizabeth conducted a series of fantastically elaborate and protracted courtships with a string of foreign suitors, the most famous being the Duke of Alençon, brother of the French king. Later on, when it became plain that she would never marry, the cult of the Virgin Queen blossomed; and when Sir Walter Raleigh attempted to establish the first colony in America, it was named Virginia in her honour: it was these later years that have given us the archetype of the Virgin Queen surrounded by doting poet-courtiers. The last decade of her reign was dominated by the Earl of Essex, young enough to be her son; but this foundered when he attempted a rising in 1601 and was executed.

CHRONOLOGY

1533	Born at Greenwich Palace on 7 September
1554	Imprisoned in the Tower of London by her half-sister Queen Mary
1558	Ascends throne on Mary's death
1568	Her cousin Mary Queen of Scots flees to England
1570	Excommunicated by Pope Pius V
1584	Sir Walter Raleigh granted a patent for colonizing America
1587	Mary Queen of Scots executed
1588	Defeat of the Spanish Armada
1601	Her favourite the Earl of Essex rebels and is executed
1603	Dies at Richmond on 24 March

At home and abroad, Elizabeth's policy was characterized by caution and thrift and a notable reluctance to squander human life. She gave reluctant support both to Henri IV, the Protestant King of France, and to the Protestants in the Netherlands, fighting against the rule of Philip II of Spain. At sea, she tolerated, and sometimes profited handsomely from, the exploits of privateers such as Sir Francis Drake. Eventually Philip II was goaded into launching the ill-fated Spanish Armada of 1588. It was on this occasion that Elizabeth made the speech that has come to define her both as a woman and as a ruler: 'I know I have the body of a weak and feeble woman, but I have the heart and stomach of a king and of a king of England too...'

The last decade of Elizabeth's reign was marked by something akin to a sense of weariness, brought about partly by an economic downturn, by a series of bad harvests and by the ruinous expense of the English campaign to subdue Ireland.

'I may have the body of a weak and feeble woman, but I have the heart of a King, and a King of England, too'

The Elizabethan Age

■ *Elizabeth was extremely erudite, and a brilliant linguist. Elizabethan England has become seen as a golden age. But she showed little interest in drama, and stories linking her to Shakespeare are for the most part apocryphal: most of his plays were written after her death.*

■ *The popular image is of Elizabeth gleefully ordering executions. This may have been true of her father, Henry VIII, but Elizabeth never used execution as a tool of policy: only one of her servants was even dismissed (a secretary suspended on full pay), and none executed, and it took her twenty years before she decided to have Mary, Queen of Scots executed.*

■ *Pope Sixtus V, sponsor of the Spanish Armada, said of her: 'She certainly is a great Queen and were she only a Catholic she would be our dearly beloved. Just look how well she governs! She is only a woman, only mistress of half an island, and yet she makes herself feared by Spain, by France, by the Empire, by all.'*

Oliver Cromwell

Oliver Cromwell (1599–1658) was a country squire who rose through Parliament to challenge royal authority, provoking two civil wars in which the New Model Army he helped forge triumphed over the Royalists. He had King Charles I tried and beheaded, but himself ended up a virtual dictator as Lord Protector of England, Scotland and Ireland.

BORN IN HUNTINGDON, and educated at Cambridge University, and for a short time in law at London, Cromwell was a gentleman farmer and in adult life a Calvinist puritan. He became a Member of Parliament for his local Huntingdon constituency in 1628, and later for Cambridge, but continued running his fenland estates until he emerged as one of the main protagonists in a row between Parliament and King Charles I. The king had summoned Parliament in 1640, after an eleven-year break, to raise taxes for his wars against Scotland, and Cromwell became one of his most outspoken critics. The parliamentarians disliked the king's Catholic sympathies, but above all they demanded constitutional reform and more power. Royalists stood defiantly behind their king, insisting he had a divine right to rule, with or without Parliament.

With political deadlock, civil war broke out in 1642. Cromwell immediately seized Cambridge Castle and raised a local troop of cavalry. He was to prove a master at deploying horsepower in battle, training his cavalry so well that they could charge in battle and then regroup without scattering. He had no previous military experience, but he quickly started winning victories against the Royalists in eastern England, and was promoted colonel in 1643 and lieutenant general in 1644. Cromwell's cavalry won the parliamentary forces a decisive victory at Marston Moor, and he was put in charge of the cavalry in the New Model Army, which crushed the Royalists in its first major test, Naseby in 1645. Cromwell had proved to be both an innovative field commander and a brilliant organizer, and by the end of the first Civil War he was field commander of the parliamentarian army, and in fact the most powerful man in the country.

There was a lull before a second Civil War erupted in 1648 in which Cromwell put down a rebellion in Wales and defeated an invading army of the king's Scottish supporters. King Charles was handed over, and he was tried and executed in London on 30 January 1649. Cromwell, by then de facto head of state, had not at first sought the king's execution, but he was one of 135 commissioners who signed the death warrant, and he could have stayed it.

Chronology

1599	Born in Huntingdon, 25 April
1620	Married Elizabeth Bourchier
1628	Elected to Parliament as MP for Huntingdon
1640	Represents Cambridge in Short and Long Parliaments
1642	Civil war breaks out
1644	Victorious at Marston Moor
1645	Victorious at Naseby
1649	Execution of Charles I and Siege of Drogheda
1650	Defeats future Charles II at Dunbar and Worcester
1653	Declared Lord Protector
1654	Summons his first Protectorate Parliament
1658	Dies in London, 3 September
1661	Body exhumed from tomb and hanged at Tyburn

'I had rather have a plain captain that knows what he fights for, than what you call a gentleman'

Cromwell dealt with rebellions in support of the king's son in Ireland and Scotland with crushing force, twice defeating the future Charles II: similarly he put down a mutiny in his own army. Cromwell earned his reputation for cruelty in Ireland, above all for his massacre of the surrendered garrison at Drogheda and of both soldiers and civilians at Wexford in 1649. The slaughter shocked even at the time, but Cromwell justified it as revenge for similar massacres of Protestant English by the Irish, and he wrote that it would 'tend to prevent the effusion of blood for the future'

With the Royalists defeated, a Commonwealth was established to unite England, Scotland and Ireland, a republic in all but name. Cromwell was offered the crown, which he refused. Instead, from 1653, he ruled as Lord Protector, with the powers of a military dictator without the accountability of a king. As Lord Protector, Cromwell dealt confidently with foreign wars and restored Britain's status as a leading European power, but he turned on Parliament, proroguing it on two occasions, and governing for a period through military commissars. He imposed some unpopular puritan measures, such as the closure of theatres. At odds with the hierarchy of the Church of England, he was tolerant to all religions except Catholicism, and he let Jews return to England after an interval of 365 years. Literature, science and education flourished under his protectorate.

Cromwell died of malaria during a great storm in London on the anniversary of his victories at Dunbar and Worcester on 3 September 1658.

'Warts and All'

■ *The expression 'warts and all' comes from Cromwell's instructions to the portrait painter Lely: 'to paint my picture truly like me and not flatter me...but remark all these roughnesses, pimples, warts and everything'.*

■ *Cromwell's first military engagement was against his old university when, after seizing Cambridge Castle, he led a small force to prevent the Cambridge colleges giving away their ceremonial plate in support of the king's cause.*

■ *His troops became known as Ironsides after his opponent Prince Rupert nicknamed him 'Old Ironsides'.*

■ *Cromwell disciplined his soldiers to pray, and made them pay fines for blasphemy and drunkenness. They charged at the enemy singing hymns and psalms.*

■ *Cromwell has no grave. In 1661, on the twelfth anniversary of King Charles's execution, his embalmed body was removed from its vault under Westminster Abbey and ritually hanged from the gibbet at Tyburn for regicide. His head was cut off and displayed on a spike on top of Westminster Hall for twenty-four years, until it blew away. There is, however, a statue of Cromwell in London close to Parliament.*

LOUIS XIV

Louis XIV (1638–1715), Sun King and absolute ruler of France, who brought great glory to his country and sought to dominate Europe through war. French culture flourished during his seventy-two-year reign, but Louis impoverished the country and sowed the seeds of the Revolution.

LOUIS INHERITED HIS FATHER'S THRONE when he was only four. His mother, Anne of Austria, acted as regent with her minister, Cardinal Mazarin, who helped to educate the boy-king. After two rebellions against the Crown, known as the Fronde, in 1648 and 1653, Louis was suspicious of the nobility, and longed for France to have order, stability and strong government. He married his Spanish cousin Maria Teresa, and in 1661, after Mazarin's death, Louis shocked France by deciding to rule alone. He regarded himself as God's representative. One result of this was his withdrawal of French Protestants' (Huguenots) religious freedom in 1685, with the revocation of the Edict of Nantes. The Huguenots refused to convert to Catholicism, and over 200,000 went into exile.

In his prime Louis worked energetically, usually eight hours a day, and developed two powerful instruments of power: a professional diplomatic corps and a permanent army. As a result France became a model of bureaucracy for eighteenth-century Europe, and through the king's financial adviser, Colbert, a well-managed economy.

In 1682 Louis officially announced that the seat of government and the court would henceforth be at Versailles, where he had spent millions transforming a modest château into a grand palace. This palace, with its spectacular hall of mirrors and magnificent gardens, was an artistic statement, and also a means of bolstering France's prestige and a way of keeping an eye on the nobility. Louis had been inspired to build it partly out of jealousy at the magnificent palace and gardens at Vaux, a château belonging to an earlier finance minister, Fouquet. The king had reportedly been offended when he saw Vaux's exquisite furnishings, fountains and its thousand orange trees; Fouquet was tried for corruption and treason and sent into exile. Louis, meanwhile, took over Fouquet's decorator, architect and gardener – Le Brun, Le Vau and Le Nôtre – to work on Versailles. A keen patron of all the arts, including music and literature, Louis founded academies of painting, sculpture, science and architecture, as well as the Comédie Française.

CHRONOLOGY

1638	Born at Saint Germain-en-Laye, 5 September
1643	Aged four, succeeds his father Louis XIII
1660	Marries Maria Teresa of Spain
1682	Seat of government transferred to Versailles
1683	Wife dies; marries Mme de Maintenon
1685	Revocation of Edict of Nantes
1714	Treaty of Utrecht
1715	Dies at Versailles, 1 September

His aim was to glorify France, and transfer the European power base from the Habsburgs to the French Bourbons. He joined his armies on their military campaigns every spring, enjoying life under canvas and reviewing his troops. His thirst for glory and expansion led France into four major wars: in the Spanish Netherlands, Holland, the Rhineland and finally the War of the Spanish Succession (1701–14), against a coalition of European powers. In the Treaty of Utrecht, which ended this war, Louis's grandson, Philip, was recognized as heir to the Spanish throne, but France was left on the brink of ruin.

Louis was the patron of the writers Corneille, Molière and Racine, and the musician Lully. With his succession of mistresses, he disregarded the moral code of the time, but after his wife's death in 1683 he married the pious widow Madame de Maintenon, who encouraged his interest in religion. He began to carry around a prayer book and rosary. Disasters in war, and the deaths of several of his closest heirs were a cause of public and private grief. This absolute monarch, obsessed by grandeur and flattered by courtiers, was isolated from the ordinary people, and at his death in 1715 crowds jeered when his body was taken to St Denis.

Louis' thirst for expansion led France into four major wars, leaving the nation on the brink of ruin

The Pursuit of Glory

■ *He was christened Louis Dieudonné (gift of God) because his parents were grateful for his birth after a childless marriage of over twenty years. The name clearly had an impact on the young Louis, who would grow to be the embodiment of the absolute monarch. 'L'État c'est moi' (I am the State), he remarked on one occasion, and was also prone to calling himself 'le Grand Monarque' (the Great Monarch).*

■ *When he was thirty he wrote in his Mémoires, 'Beyond all doubt, my ruling passion is the pursuit of glory...Love of glory has the same subtleties as the most tender passions.'*

He did however leave this advice to his great-grandson, who would meet his death under the guillotine in the Revolution: 'Do not imitate my love for building and for war, and assuage the misery of my people.'

Peter the Great

Peter the Great (1672–1725), Tsar Peter I, turned Russia's eyes to the West and established his country as a European power. A giant of a man, capable of dreadful cruelty, Peter introduced European customs and technology and founded the city of St Petersburg.

THE SON OF TSAR ALEXIS, who died when Peter was four, Peter grew up in an atmosphere of bloody court intrigue, but spent a lot of his childhood carefree in a country village outside Moscow, safely away from the lurking dangers of the Kremlin. He became co-ruler with his half-brother Ivan in 1682, under the regency of his half-sister Sophia, and took full control of the throne in 1689.

As a young boy he had learned to drill his own 'army', to build houses, to hunt and to sail. Ever practical, he spent his entire life acquiring knowledge and skills. In 1697, he embarked on a Grand Embassy, a tour of European capitals, in which he worked as a shipbuilder in both Amsterdam and London, where he also visited Parliament and received an honorary law degree from Oxford. In addition to shipbuilding, he learned about navigation and clock making, took lessons in drawing and engraving, paper making, carpentry and masonry, cut up blubber, studied human anatomy and surgery, and became a keen gardener. More importantly, Peter engaged 800 craftsmen to work in Russia to help modernize his backward oriental country.

He rushed back to Moscow in 1698 to crush a rebellion by the Moscow streltsy, musketeers of the sovereign's bodyguard, and then turned his attention to his foreign policy ambitions. He had inherited a land-locked kingdom and he was determined to give Russia outlets to the sea. He built Russia's first navy and transformed a ragbag army into a modern fighting force. He moved first against the Turks in the south to forge a path to the Black Sea, and then prepared for war against Sweden with the aim of gaining control of the eastern part of the Baltic. The Great Northern War lasted from 1700 to 1721 and started with a devastating setback at Narva. But Peter went on to win one of the greatest military victories in Russia's history, crushing the Swedish army at Poltava in 1709. Under the ensuing Treaty of Nystadt in 1721, a humbled Sweden surrendered its Baltic provinces to Russia.

Peter underpinned the strategic shift to the west by founding St Petersburg on the Baltic coast in 1703; built at huge human cost, it became his 'window on Europe' and, in 1712, the Russian capital.

Peter was proclaimed emperor in 1721, thereby establishing the Russian Empire. On the domestic front, Peter consolidated the tsar's power, subordinating both nobles and church to the throne, and he reformed central and provincial government. He encouraged industry, implemented a new calendar, simplified the Russian alphabet and introduced Arabic numerals, and founded schools and an Academy of Sciences. Russia's first newspaper, *Vedomosti*, was published in his reign. But the lot of the peasant serfs remained pretty much unchanged, and several rebellions were cruelly put down. Although cast as a great reformer,

Chronology

1672	Born in Moscow, 9 June
1682	Becomes joint Tsar with his brother Ivan V
1689	Takes full control
1697	Grand Embassy tour of Europe
1700	Defeat at Narva
1703	Founds St Petersburg
1709	Victory at Poltava
1721	Treaty of Nystadt cedes Baltic coast to Russia
1725	Dies at St Petersburg on 8 February

In 1721, Peter was proclaimed Emperor, thus establishing the Russian Empire

in the end many of Peter's reforms lacked substance, and his lasting achievement was the territorial expansion of the Russian Empire, above all the conquest of the Baltics.

Peter was constantly on the move. He never stayed in one place more than three months. He died true to character. He had dived into the Gulf of Finland to help rescue some soldiers in danger of drowning, and contracted a fever from which he did not recover.

An Image of Humility

- *Peter liked to live humbly. He built and lived in a number of wooden cabins, and at court he would often deliberately 'dress down' in shabby clothes. He also set about imposing Western customs on his nobility with his own hands: demanding the Western, clean-shaven look, he personally cut off the beards of his boyars, and the skirts of their long caftan coats.*
- *Peter's appetite for learning never left him; during his lifetime he acquired fourteen specialist skills. Among the more unusual, he could pull a tooth, cast a cannon and cobble boots. He had boundless energy and was an astonishingly hard worker.*
- *Peter was also capable of exceptional cruelty. He personally inflicted sadistic torture on the rebel streltsy in 1698, and seemed unmoved by the sight of his son being racked to death. He was six and a half feet tall, and had an extraordinary capacity for drink, and a ferocious temper.*
- *His second wife Catherine, a former Latvian servant girl, was one of the few people who could stand up to him. They had twelve children, of whom only two daughters, Anna and Elizabeth, survived.*

John Sobieski

John Sobieski (1624–96) was the last great king of Poland, whose defining achievement was to break the Turkish siege of Vienna in 1683. But while as King John III he was Christian Europe's champion against the Ottomans, he left his own kingdom in a parlous state.

John Sobieski was born in a thunderstorm during a Tartar raid at Olesko, near Lwów, to an ancient noble family, and he was raised in a world accustomed to warfare: his maternal grandfather and his brother were both beheaded on the battlefield by Tartars and his uncle died in Tartar captivity. Southeast Poland, where he was brought up, was near the front line of the resurgent Ottoman Empire, which for years had been eating away at Europe's southern borders. Not surprisingly, Sobieski chose a military career from an early age, first entering the army in 1648.

He distinguished himself in the Polish–Swedish war of 1655–60 and in fighting against the Cossacks and Tartars in 1667, and was appointed first field commander and, in 1668, commander in chief of the Polish army. In 1673, by chance the day after the death of Poland's King Michael Wisniowiecki, Sobieski won an overwhelming victory over the Turks at Chocim on the Dniester (now in Ukraine), annihilating an entire Ottoman army. By now one of the country's most successful generals, the following year he was elected to succeed King Michael, as King John III of Poland. He remained a soldier king, and devoted a lot of time and energy to modernizing the Polish army.

Abroad, he at first befriended the French, who were allies of the Turks, so that he could concentrate on gaining territory in East Prussia. Encouraged in part by France, Sobieski attempted peace with the Turks, but he eventually returned to his instinctive view that the Ottomans posed mortal danger to Poland and Europe. He accordingly broke with France, and in 1683 entered into a mutual defence pact with the Holy Roman Emperor Leopold I, in which both sovereigns pledged to come to the defence of the other in the event of an Ottoman attack on their capitals. A few months later a huge Ottoman army, under Grand Vizier Kara Mustafa, marched on Vienna, Leopold's capital, intent on crushing Habsburg power.

Chronology

1624	Born at Olesko (Ukraine), 9 June
1666	Polish army field commander
1668	Commander in chief of Polish army
1673	Battle of Chocim
1674	Elected King
1683	Battle of Khalenberg, Vienna saved
1696	Dies at Wilanow, near Warsaw, 17 June

Sobieski rushed to Vienna's defence and, as the highest-ranking military leader, he took command of the entire relief force and achieved a brilliant victory over the Turkish army beneath the Vienna Woods at Kahlenberg on 12 September 1683. Sobieski and his Hussars led the spectacular charge at the grand vizier's tent which started the rout. It was one of the most decisive battles of European history, the beginning of an Ottoman retreat that continued for a further 200 years.

Despite an ungrateful reception from Leopold, Sobieski continued his campaign and pursued the Ottomans into Hungary, but over many more years of campaigning he failed to wrest from them the Romanian principalities of Moldavia and Walachia and failed to extend Polish sway to the shores of the Black Sea.

In the final analysis, Sobieski pursued the Ottomans at the expense of Poland's other interests nearer at home; he surrendered the Ukraine to the Russians for next to nothing, and let Lithuania slide into anarchy. Sobieski left behind a weak and divided kingdom to be carved up by its neighbours and rubbed off the map of Europe within a century.

Sobieski's defeat of the Ottoman Turks at Vienna was one of the defining battles of European history

A Passionate Husband

■ *Sobieski married one of the most sensational women of his day, a very beautiful French widow, Marie-Casimire de la Grange d'Arquien – Marysieńka. His correspondence with her has been preserved; it is a fascinating record of his reign, and deeply passionate.*

■ *'Our Lord and God, blessed of all ages, has brought unheard victory and glory to our nation. All the guns, the whole camp, untold spoils have fallen into our hands...enough powder and ammunition alone for a million men,' Sobieski wrote to his wife after the victory at Vienna.*

■ *In the same letter, Sobieski reckoned the Ottomans had been camped under 100,000 tents. Some of these tents, and the banners and trophies captured from the Ottomans are still on display at Wawel Castle in Kraków.*

Catherine the Great

Catherine the Great (1729–96), a usurper and profligate empress, reigned for thirty-four years, and completed the transformation of Russia into a great power and a modern and prosperous state.

Originally Sophie Fredericke Auguste von Anhalt-Zerbst, the future Russian empress was the daughter of a minor German prince. In 1745, she married Grand Duke Peter, heir to the Russian throne and grandson of Peter the Great, after being rebaptized into the Orthodox Church as Catherine. The marriage was not a success, but Catherine was ambitious and threw herself wholeheartedly into the court and her new life in Russia. She stealthily built up support in St Petersburg and, through the first of what would be a string of lovers, a dashing officer Grigory Orlov, secured the loyalty of the Imperial Guard. In 1762, just a few months after taking over as Tsar Peter III, her unpopular, alcoholic husband was overthrown in a palace putsch and was later murdered; the way was open for the former German princess to seize the Russian throne.

Catherine flirted with liberal ideas: she corresponded extensively with the great French philosophers Voltaire and Diderot, entertaining the latter at her court in 1773. But despite some promising initiatives, and a reform commission set up in 1767, her domestic policies served only to strengthen tsarist power, give the nobility greater clout and make government more efficient. Far from enacting the ideas of the Enlightenment and emancipating the serfs, Catherine in fact made their lot worse, and she used military force in 1775 to crush a great Cossack-led peasant uprising. She refilled her treasury by confiscating church lands.

It was in foreign policy, and her conquests, that she staked her claim to greatness. Under Catherine, Russia waged two wars against the Ottomans and expanded almost to the gates of Constantinople, taking over the Crimea and its Black Sea ports in 1783. Nearer to home, Catherine's Russia unashamedly partook of the territorial carve-up of Poland.

Russian and foreign culture flourished under Catherine. She was a great builder, and transformed St Petersburg into a stately granite capital, and left behind the nucleus of what is today the Hermitage Museum and one of the world's most priceless art collections. Catherine promoted both the arts and sciences, and founded Russia's first school for girls.

Catherine's greatest lover, Grigory Potemkin, was also her greatest adviser. A minor aristocrat who had distinguished himself in the war against Turkey, the one-eyed Potemkin became Catherine's lover in 1774. Their close relationship continued long after their passions had cooled. Catherine ruled Russia, it was said, while Potemkin ruled Catherine; he selected all but one of her next ten lovers. The annexation of the Crimea from the Turks in 1783 was his work. The Empress treated him as an equal until he died in 1791.

Catherine mourned him for many days but lived on until 1796, her last years darkened by the execution of her fellow monarch, King Louis XVI of France, and the march of the revolutionary armies.

Chronology

1729	Born in Stettin (Szczecin), Poland, 2 May
1745	Marries Grand Duke Peter
1762	Seizes throne after palace putsch ousts Peter
1783	Annexation of the Crimea
1795	Final partition of Poland
1796	Died in St Petersburg, 17 November

Rumours of Catherine's sexual excesses have been greatly exaggerated over the years

Catherine's Lovers

■ *Empress Catherine dealt with Poland with a deft hand: she installed one of her many ex-lovers, Stanislaw Poniatowski, as king, and he was obedient to her will.*

■ *Empress Catherine was far from pretty, and by her own description she had a mind 'infinitely more masculine than feminine'. She took young lovers up to the time of her death at the age of sixty-seven. It was rumoured that she died through failure of a machine called 'Catherine's Winch', while trying to make love with a horse, a rumour with seemingly little foundation.*

■ *In 1787 Field Marshal Prince Grigory Potemkin took Catherine, her court and ambassadors on a grand river tour to inspect Russia's new Crimean provinces. He arranged for gaily dressed peasants to wave at the royal party from a number of mobile villages, which he had assembled and dismantled as the party progressed downstream. The show of 'Potemkin villages' was designed to deceive the ambassadors.*

FREDERICK THE GREAT

Frederick the Great (1712–86), King of Prussia, waged war to expand his nation and make it a European power, and introduced liberal reforms at home, which earned him the title 'enlightened despot'.

FREDERICK WAS BROUGHT UP in two contrasting worlds. He was constantly beaten by his father, King Frederick-William I, and forced to watch the execution of his friend, Lieutenant Hans von Katte, with whom he had tried to escape to England, and was then imprisoned by his father. Encouraged by his mother, and in contrast to the strict Prussian military atmosphere of his father's household, Frederick had developed a taste for the arts and music and French literature. He corresponded with and met the leading French philosopher Voltaire, played the flute and wrote music and poetry, and he was homosexual; he also eventually applied himself to his father's business and became a brilliant soldier and administrator. And he was strong willed.

Within days of taking over from his father as King Frederick II, he plunged Prussia into war. He was determined to make use of the highly-trained army he had inherited from his father, and for a quarter of a century war was his prime instrument of policy. The first target was Habsburg-ruled Silesia, which Frederick seized from Austria's new Empress Maria Theresa. He fought two wars for possession of these strategically rich mining and agricultural duchies, in 1740–42 and 1744–45. His first battle, Mollwitz, was a near disaster; he fled the field before his disciplined army won the day. But from then on Frederick notched up a string of impressive victories, often overwhelming far larger armies through bold offensive action. The flute-playing intellectual had grown into a brilliant military campaigner.

In 1756, King Frederick launched a new war by invading Saxony, a move that historians liken to Germany's pre-emptive strikes in the European wars of the twentieth century. Frederick's justification was that he was encircled and threatened, that he had to attack to survive. The invasion pitted Frederick's Prussia against the armies of Austria, Russia, Sweden, Saxony and France, and dragged Europe into the Seven Years War. Frederick won most but not all the battles, and came out on top, if only by the skin of his teeth, thanks in large part to the timely death in 1762 of his arch-enemy, Empress Elizabeth of Russia. He had gained no new territory and exhausted his army and state, but he had emerged with a reputation for military greatness. Aided only by the British Treasury, he had established Prussia as the leading rival to Austria for the domination of German Europe, and in the diplomatic manoeuvring following the war he carved up Poland with Russia in 1772, and gained Polish Prussia and Torún. In 1779, he grabbed more land from Austria, the Franconian principalities of Bavaria. In the end he tripled Prussia's population and almost doubled its territory.

At home, he was an absolute ruler, but he also embraced the principles of the Enlightenment and exercised a large degree of tolerance, allowing a free press, freedom of speech and freedom of religion. 'My people and I have come to an agreement which satisfies us both,' he once remarked. 'They are to say as they please, and I am to do what I please.'

CHRONOLOGY

1712	Born in Berlin, 24 January
1730	Imprisoned by his father in Küstrin fortress
1740	Accedes to the throne as King Frederick II
1741	First victory, at Mollwitz
1756	Invades Saxony
1759	Defeated by Russia at Battle of Kunersdorf
1763	Peace of Hubertusburg ends Seven Years War
1772	First partition of Poland
1786	Dies at Sans Souci, 17 August

KINGSHIP AND THE STATE

FREDERICK THE GREAT'S WRITING FILLS THIRTY VOLUMES. IN THIS TRACT WRITTEN IN 1752, HE SETS OUT HIS VIEWS OF KINGSHIP AND GOVERNMENT:

- *'Politics is the science of always using the most convenient means in accord with one's own interests.'*
- *'A well-conducted government must have an underlying concept so well integrated that it could be likened to a system of philosophy. All actions taken must be well reasoned, and all financial, political and military matters must flow towards one goal, which is the strengthening of the state and the furthering of its power.'*
- *'The sovereign is the first servant of the state.'*
- *'Catholics, Lutherans, Reformed, Jews and other Christian sects live in this state, and live together in peace...It is of no concern in politics whether the ruler has a religion or whether he has none. All religions, if one examines them, are founded on superstition, more or less absurd. It is impossible for a man of good sense, who dissects their contents, not to see their error; but these prejudices, these errors and mysteries, were made for men, and one must know enough to respect the public and not to outrage its faith, whatever religion is involved.'*

Frederick continued the work of his predecessors in modernizing the Prussian state administration. He issued a new code of Prussian law, the *Codex Fridericanus*, made judges sit stiff exams, outlawed torture and curtailed the death sentence, but, fearful of the reaction of his powerful Junker landlords, he stopped short of abolishing serfdom. The king also patronized the arts and encouraged science and learning, laying the groundwork for universal primary education. But in the end it was the army that counted in Frederick's Prussia: it took 50 per cent of the state budget and increased from 80,000 to 190,000 in the course of his reign. Frederick died in 1786 at Sans Souci, the rococo palace he built near Berlin.

'I have an agreement with my people: they are to say as they please, and I am to do as I please'

GEORGE WASHINGTON

George Washington (1732–99) commanded the army of America's rebel colonies fighting for independence from Great Britain and became the first President of the United States.

BORN IN VIRGINIA in 1732, the son of a tobacco farmer and grandson of an immigrant from Northamptonshire, George Washington merely wanted to be rich, but was destined to be revered. With more ambition than formal education, he became a skilful surveyor and avid land speculator. Initially modelling himself on his cultured older half-brother, Lawrence, who had married into Virginia's elite, Washington succeeded to his Mount Vernon estate following Lawrence's early death from TB. Militia service brought Washington further social advancement and invaluable experience in fortification, finance and frontier diplomacy. Retiring from active service at twenty-seven to marry a wealthy widow, Martha Custis (1731–1802), the slave-owning squire then busied himself with estate improvement and the Virginia House of Burgesses. British attempts to limit land acquisition in the interests of frontier security caused Washington much personal aggravation, embroiling him in opposition politics. The outbreak of the revolutionary war brought him command of the rebel army, partly in deference to his previous military experience, partly in recognition of the need to bind Virginia to the rebel cause.

As a general Washington proved a dogged survivor of defeats rather than an architect of victories. No military genius but an excellent administrator, he held together a patchwork force of fractious patriots despite chronic shortages of supply and arms and recurrent uncertainties of support from the Continental Congress and state governments. Successfully forcing the British from Boston, he abandoned New York adroitly to regroup at White Plains and gain tactical successes at Trenton and Princeton, which proved vital in lifting morale and acquiring much-needed stores. Following major defeats at Brandywine and Germantown, Washington's success in simply maintaining his force through a terrible winter at Valley Forge in 1777–78 proved crucial to final victory, but thereafter his command was limited to strategic direction, as campaigning in the south took priority and the intervention of French forces finally proved decisive in defeating the divided commands of the British. In September 1781 Washington left his New York headquarters to assume personal command of the Franco-American forces which successfully forced the surrender of the besieged British at Yorktown, effectively ending the war.

CHRONOLOGY

1732 Born at Wakefield, Westmoreland County, Virginia, 22 February

1755–59 Commands Virginia Regiment

1775–83 Commander in Chief of the Continental Army

1789–97 Serves as first President of the United States

1799 Dies at Mount Vernon, Virginia, 14 December

Denied a longed-for rural retirement, Washington was pestered into serving as president, first of the constitutional convention of 1787 and then of the new nation itself. As such he established an efficient civil service and financial stability. Re-elected to a second term of office, in 1794 Washington also assumed personal command in suppressing the 'Whiskey Rebellion' against the taxing powers of the Federal government. When war broke out between Britain and France, he maintained US neutrality against pro-French pressures from Jefferson and his supporters. Emerging factionalism at home made Washington grateful to decline a third presidential term, thus establishing a convention which endured until Franklin D. Roosevelt won four terms.

Washington explained this decision in a farewell presidential address (another precedent) deploring

Washington's success in the terrible winter at Valley Forge proved vital to the final American victory

the growth of political parties and warning against entanglements in foreign affairs. Returning briefly to nominal command when war threatened with France in 1798–99, Washington died on 14 December 1799 at Mount Vernon and was buried there. When news of his death reached England, his old enemies honoured him with a 20-gun salute fired by the Channel fleet.

AN 'ENGLISH' GENTLEMAN

■ *Ironically, the father of the great republic epitomized the qualities of an English country gentleman, reluctant for office but dutiful in its performance, jealous of personal honour but indifferent to public regard, more content on his broad acres than in the counsels of power. Fittingly the Stars and Stripes flag which symbolized the independence of his country is based on the heraldic coat of arms of his English ancestors.*

■ *Washington's iconic stature as the personification of American virtue was rapidly enhanced by the appearance of Mason Locke Weems's* Life and Memorable Actions of George Washington *(1806), which first circulated the legend of the cherry tree. Subsequent biographers of note included Washington Irving (1855–59) and future President Woodrow Wilson (1896).*

■ *Thomas Paine, who had served in Washington's army, dedicated his* Rights of Man *to him, but said that he was 'treacherous in private friendship ..and a hypocrite in public life'.*

■ *Historian Samuel Eliot Morison summarized Washington's career as that of 'a simple gentleman of Virginia who so disciplined himself that he could lead an insubordinate and divided people into ordered liberty and enduring union'.*

Abraham Lincoln

Abraham Lincoln (1809–65) was the 16th President of the United States. Although he was responsible for the abolition of slavery, Lincoln pursued the bloodiest conflict in American history not to right an historic wrong, but to preserve an historic principle, the unity of a nation.

ALTHOUGH FEW BURNISHED Lincoln's legend more assiduously than Lincoln himself, he really was born in a log cabin and really was almost entirely self-educated. After qualifying as a lawyer, he entered politics as a Whig in the Illinois legislature (1834–41) before moving up to Congress (1847–49), where he proposed a bill for the gradual and compensated emancipation of slaves.

Abandoning politics for a thriving legal practice, Lincoln returned to the fray when the Kansas–Nebraska Act (1854) opened western territories to slavery. Entrusting his fortunes to the new Republican Party, Lincoln established a national reputation in 1858 through debating the slavery issue with his Democratic (and successful) opponent for the US Senate, Stephen A. Douglas. In 1860 Lincoln attained the presidency in a four-way contest which gave him only 39 per cent of the popular vote. By the time he succeeded to office, seven southern states had already seceded from the Union to form the Confederacy. Lincoln used his inaugural address to pledge acceptance of slavery where it already existed but also to confirm his determination to uphold the solidarity of the Union. Four more states then seceded but Lincoln successfully retained the loyalty of a further four potential recruits to the rebellion.

Although possessed of far greater industrial and manpower resources than the Confederacy, Lincoln was initially hampered in his prosecution of the war by inadequate generals. When the over-cautious George B. McClellan (1826–86) failed to pursue Robert E. Lee after defeating his incursion northwards at Antietam in September 1862, Lincoln was, however, able to capitalize on this limited success to issue an Emancipation Proclamation. This freed slaves in rebel areas and welcomed freedmen into military service, although slavery did not end officially until the passage of the Thirteenth Amendment in 1865.

'That government of the people, by the people, for the people, shall not perish from the Earth'

Following further defeats at Fredericksburg and Chancellorsville, the Union finally prevailed in repulsing a second Confederate advance at Gettysburg in July 1863. The brief but brilliant valedictory address proclaimed by Lincoln on that bloody field on 19 November that same year was subsequently hailed as a milestone of American oratory, but was inaudible to many there and scarcely mentioned in the press coverage of the event.

After Ulysses S. Grant took Vicksburg, splitting Confederate forces in the West, Lincoln appointed him to supreme command. Grant delegated the western campaign to Sherman, set Sheridan on a hugely destructive raid through Georgia, and

Chronology

1809 Born Hodgenville, Kentucky, 12 February
1834 Enters Illinois state legislature
1847–49 As Congressman opposes Mexican War and proposes emancipation
1858 Lincoln–Douglas debates
1860 Elected President
1863 January First Emancipation Proclamation comes into force
1864 Re-elected President
1865 9 April, Robert E. Lee surrenders at Appomattox Courthouse, Va.15 April, Lincoln assassinated by actor John Wilkes Booth at Ford's Theatre, Washington, DC

himself enveloped Lee's forces in Virginia, although unable to rout him decisively in the field. Union successes proved sufficient, however, to secure Lincoln's re-election in 1864 with 55 per cent of the vote. The far-sighted vision for the post-war reconstruction of a defeated South sketched in Lincoln's masterly second inaugural address ('With malice toward none, with charity for all...') proved too lenient for a vengeful Congress, but the issue remained unresolved when an assassin's hand struck down the president within a week of Lee's surrender.

Gifted with humour and an unadorned eloquence, Lincoln was criticized in his lifetime as wily, calculating, vacillating and a demagogue – 'fox populi' as Vanity Fair put it in 1863. To become president he had sometimes to sound more radical than he was; to survive as president he was compelled to act more cautiously than he might have wished.

Lincoln's Address

■ *Lincoln's speech at the dedication of the Gettysburg National Assembly on 19 November 1863 followed a two-hour oration by Edward Everett, one of the most famous speakers of the time. 'I wish that I could flatter myself that I had come as near to the central idea in two hours as you did in two minutes,' Everett wrote afterwards to Lincoln.*

The Gettysburg Address

■ *'Four score and seven years ago our fathers brought forth on this continent, a new nation, conceived in Liberty, and dedicated to the proposition that all men are created equal.*

■ *'Now we are engaged in a great civil war, testing whether that nation or any nation so conceived and so dedicated, can long endure. We are met on a great battlefield of that war. We have come to dedicate a portion of that field as a final resting place for those who here gave their lives that that nation might live. It is altogether fitting and proper that we should do this.*

■ *'But, in a larger sense, we cannot dedicate – we cannot consecrate – we cannot hallow – this ground. The brave men, living and dead, who struggled here, have consecrated it, far above our poor power to add or detract. The world will little note, nor long remember what we say here, but it can never forget what they did here. It is for us the living, rather, to be dedicated here to the unfinished work which they who fought here have thus far so nobly advanced. It is rather for us to be here dedicated to the great task remaining before us –that from these honoured dead we take increased devotion to that cause for which they gave the last full measure of devotion – that we here highly resolve that these dead shall not have died in vain – that this nation, under God, shall have a new birth of freedom – and that government of the people, by the people, for the people, shall not perish from the Earth.'*

VICTORIA

Queen Victoria (1819–1901) presided for sixty-three years over a glittering and expanding empire. Although as a constitutional monarch she had no formal power, Victoria gave her name to an age, and was one of the best-known figures in the world in the nineteenth century.

PRINCESS VICTORIA was the daughter of George IV's brother, Prince Edward, Duke of Kent, and Princess Victoria of Saxe-Coburg. She was born in England – but only just, her mother travelling from Germany by coach when eight months pregnant. After the death of her father, Victoria was closely brought up by her mother, who dreamed of power through her daughter, but almost the first thing that Victoria did on her accession at just eighteen was to assert her own authority and independence.

Though she believed it was a job no woman should hold, the young Queen set out to take an active part in ruling her country, and she learned her role from her elderly, conservative-minded Prime Minister, Lord Melbourne, a Whig, whom she 'loved like a father'. When his government fell to the Tories, she precipitated a serious constitutional crisis by refusing to appoint Tory ladies to her household. Melbourne's influence waned when Victoria married her first cousin Prince Albert of Saxe-Coburg-Gotha. It was a passionate love match, at least on Victoria's side, and together they set an unprecedented example of sedate, respectable, royal family life. They had four sons and five daughters.

Victoria was at her most active as a ruler in collaboration with her 'beloved Albert'. She ardently supported all his projects, from the rebuilding of their holiday palaces of Osborne House on the Isle of Wight and Balmoral in Scotland, to the resounding success of the vast public project, the Great Exhibition, held at the Crystal Palace in 1851.

The diminutive 5-foot-tall Victoria was blessed with a robust constitution, but not Albert, who wore himself out with being, in effect, her private secretary. The shock of his death at the age of forty-two in 1861 drove the Queen, as passionate in grief as in love, into deep seclusion for many years. An iron sense of duty kept her involved privately in overseeing the business of government but she neglected her public royal duties, such as the Opening of Parliament, and grew very unpopular. One of the few people she allowed near her was, famously, one of her Scottish servants, John Brown. He treated her with a brusque, comforting directness that shocked others. Lurid and jealous speculation flourished round the friendship, no more than that, which cut across accepted norms.

Her popularity returned as she began to come out of seclusion, encouraged by the charm and flattery of her Prime Minister Benjamin Disraeli, whom she preferred to his predecessor William Gladstone (because, said Disraeli, Gladstone treated her less like a woman and more like a government department). In 1876, Disraeli persuaded Parliament to proclaim Victoria Empress of India and, with her Golden and Diamond Jubilees, this small, black, dumpy, revered figure became a symbol of imperial power, and regained her popularity.

Queen Victoria combined the figure of monarch and matriarch, and she had a great zest for life. In Albert's day she danced, travelled by the new railways in Germany and France, and revelled in their holidays together at Osborne and Balmoral. An acute and interested observer, she recorded

CHRONOLOGY

1819	Born in Kensington Palace, London, 24 May
1837	Succeeds to throne, 20 June
1838	Crowned
1840	Marries Prince Albert, 10 February
1861	Prince Albert dies, 14 December
1876	Declared Empress of India
1887	Golden Jubilee
1897	Diamond Jubilee
1901	Dies at Osborne House, Isle of Wight, 22 January

Queen Victoria combined the roles of monarch and matriarch with a great zest for life

Victoria's Legacy

- *Victoria's children and grandchildren married far and wide into the royal houses of Europe, with important diplomatic and dynastic implications. Her eldest daughter Vicky was married to the German heir in the hopes of steering Germany in a liberal direction; an intent thwarted through personalities, illness and death.*
- *Queen Victoria's most catastrophic legacy was the transmission of her haemophiliac gene to the Romanovs.*
- *The famous 'we are not amused' statement reputedly arose from her stern reaction to a joke told to her by some of her grandchildren.*

everything in her journal, parts of which were published as *Leaves from the Journal of my Life in the Highlands*. Her sketchbooks were filled with fresh little watercolours of her baby children and favourite views. In later life, she frequently travelled to Europe, but she never visited India.

Queen Victoria was truthful, strong-willed, stubborn, emotional, tough, susceptible to beauty in men and women, commonsensical, uncompromising, shy, hot-tempered, rich in contradictions, headstrong and alone: after Albert, there was no-one on level terms who could truly help and advise her. This makes her lonely transition into a legendary queen, who gave her name to an age, all the more remarkable.

This longest-reigning of British monarchs died at Osborne House on 20 January beneath the photograph of Albert on his deathbed which had been pinned to the bedhead forty years before, and was succeeded by her son, Edward VII.

Otto von Bismarck

Prince Otto von Bismarck (1815–98) was a Prusso-German statesman who used war and diplomacy to re-unify Germany and become the first chancellor of the new German Empire. He was one of Europe's greatest nineteenth-century statesmen.

BISMARCK WAS THE SON of a prosperous Prussian Junker landowner and a well-educated mother. He studied law in Göttingen and Berlin, leaving an account of himself as a dueller and drinker, and entered government service in 1836. But he resigned soon after to look after his estates and came back to Berlin in 1847 as a delegate to Prussia's United Diet (Parliament). He first made his mark in politics as a trenchant landowning conservative during the nationalist liberal revolutions that swept Europe in 1848, fanned by demands for greater democracy and self-rule. Three years later, in 1851, Bismarck came face to face with the realities of nationalism when he was posted to Frankfurt to represent Prussia at the German Confederation, a league of the thirty-nine German states. They were all divided, some under the sway of Prussia, most in the south dominated by Austria, which he began to think of as a 'wormy old warship'. It was Bismarck's achievement to exploit the conditions that made it possible to unite these disparate states into a unified Germany, under Prussian and not Austrian control.

He moved to St Petersburg in 1859 as ambassador to Russia, and to Paris, for a few brief summer months, in 1862 as ambassador to France. Conservative landlord, soldier, lawyer, government servant and ambassador, he was perfectly placed when a dispute broke out between the Prussian Parliament and King William I over military budgets, which Parliament wanted to reduce. The King would not agree. Bismarck was recalled from Paris and named prime minister and foreign minister in 1862, and broke the deadlock by continuing to apply the old budget.

'The great questions of the day will not be settled by speeches and majority decisions', he said, 'but by blood and iron.'

Over the next ten years, Germany was re-united in three lightning wars: in 1864 Bismarck attacked and defeated Denmark, and laid claim to the Danish duchies of Schleswig and Holstein. When Austria quarrelled over these spoils in 1866, he attacked and defeated her and her German allies at Königgrätz, incorporated some southern German states and set up a Prussian-led North German Confederation. The reality of growing Prusso-German power sent shockwaves through Europe, which Bismarck skilfully exploited by tricking Louis Napoleon into war against the German states. When the French Emperor, outraged he had not been ceded Luxembourg and that a German prince had been offered the Spanish throne, made bellicose noises, Bismarck invaded France in 1870, and won a decisive battle at Sedan. In the euphoria of victory, the southern German states joined a united Germany, and the following year, in 1871, the new German Empire was proclaimed in the Palace of Versailles. Germany annexed Alsace-Lorraine and exacted a five-billion franc indemnity from France – sanctions the French would not forget.

Chronology

1815	Born at Schönhausen, near Berlin, 1 April
1847	Enters politics as delegate to Prussia's Diet
1859	Ambassador to St Petersburg
1862	Ambassador to Paris
1862	Appointed Minister-President of Prussia
1864	Defeats Denmark, claims Schleswig and Holstein
1866	Defeats Austria, annexes southern German states
1870	Defeats France, annexes Alsace-Lorraine
1871	German Empire declared, Bismarck Chancellor
1890	Dismissed from office
1898	Dies at his estate near Hamburg, 30 July

'The great questions of the day will be settled not by speeches and majorities, but by blood and iron'

The Iron Chancellor

■ Bismarck came to be known as the Iron Chancellor because of his use of the phrase 'blood and iron' in speeches, although they were about budgets, not wars.

■ 'You can do everything with bayonets', he said, 'except sit on them.'

■ Bismarck knew the limitations of power; he did not seek to 'control the current of events, only occasionally to deflect it'. He was a master of the limited war.

Bismarck governed Germany as an autocratic chancellor for the next two decades. He applied the same tactics to domestic policy as he had to the maps of Europe. With no party power base, he demanded and exacted absolute loyalty and, when he did not get it, he waged war, first against the Catholics on whom he imposed financial penalties and onerous burdens and then against the Poles and the Socialists. He outlawed the Social Democratic Party and, fearful of revolution, he tried to outflank them by introducing accident and health insurance and pensions. He bribed and bludgeoned the press. Abroad, he pursued a largely cautious and peaceful foreign policy, based on interlocking alliances, which kept the European peace for more than half a century but which were ultimately to prove fatal for all parties in the 1914–18 war.

Like many great leaders, Bismarck was a man of contradictions: a landlord who industrialized Germany, a conservative who gave Germany both universal male suffrage and social security, a monarchist who despised his emperor, a victor in wars who knew all too well the limitations of military power, a blustering, fearsome man in public beset by hysteria and insomnia in private, keeping himself going in later years on morphine.

After he was dismissed by the Emperor William II, Bismarck retired to his estate near Hamburg, where he died in 1898.

Winston Churchill

Soldier, journalist, historian, painter, Nobel-prize winning author, and politician, Sir Winston Churchill (1874–1965) gambled with destiny and led Britain through the darkest days of World War II to eventual victory over Nazi Germany.

BORN IN BLENHEIM PALACE, the seat of his ancestor the Duke of Marlborough, Churchill was the son of a prominent Tory politician and an American heiress. He was educated at Harrow and trained as an army officer at Sandhurst. He saw action in two colonial spats, on the Northwest Frontier and in Sudan, and began writing about his exploits; *The Story of the Malakand Field Force* was the first of fifteen books. Leaving the army he reported the Boer War for the *Morning Post*, further enhancing his reputation when he was captured and escaped.

In 1900 he was elected Conservative Member of Parliament for Oldham, but he lost faith in the Conservatives over free trade, and joined the Liberals. With meticulous preparation and endless rehearsal, Churchill mastered a speech impediment and developed into a skilled and effective orator.

He entered Cabinet in 1908 as President of the Board of Trade, one of several ministerial posts he held before and during World War I. As First Lord of the Admiralty from 1911, he pushed hard to build new battleships to match Germany. In 1915 he was held responsible for the abortive naval attack on the Dardanelles and the bungled landings in Gallipoli. He resigned and left for France to fight in the trenches. In 1917, he was recalled to office by Lloyd George as Minister for Munitions, where he threw himself behind the roll-out of the new battle-winning tank, and from 1919 to 1920 as Secretary of State for War, when he supported the Allied campaign in Russia against the Bolsheviks. As Colonial Secretary from 1921 to 1922, he ordered mass bombings of rebel Iraqis and even proposed using chemical weapons against them. In 1924 he became Chancellor of the Exchequer in a Conservative government, and exacerbated his already poor relations with the trade unions by helping to break the 1926 General Strike.

For most of the next decade, Churchill was in the political wilderness, increasingly isolated as he warned of the rising threat of Nazi Germany; few would listen. He also alienated people over his support for the King in the abdication crisis and by his opposition to Indian nationalists. But his hour came when war broke out. Brought back to head the Admiralty, where he managed to avoid blame for the failure in Norway, he was called to replace the discredited Neville Chamberlain as Prime Minister in May 1940. 'I felt as if I were walking with destiny', he said, 'and that all my past life had been but a preparation for this hour and this trial.'

In fact he gambled with destiny. With continental Europe in Hitler's grasp, Churchill took an enormous risk and chose to fight on alone in 1940,

Chronology

1874	Born in Blenheim Palace, Oxfordshire, 30 November
1895	Leaves Sandhurst as cavalry officer
1897	Action on Northwest Frontier
1899	Reports Boer War, captured and escapes
1900	First elected to Parliament
1908	President of Board of Trade
1910–11	Home Secretary
1911–15	First Lord of the Admiralty
1919–20	Secretary of State for War
1924	Chancellor of Exchequer
1940	Prime Minister
1945	Loses post-war general election
1951–55	Prime Minister
1963	Made honorary US citizen
1965	Dies in London, 24 January

'Never in the field of human conflict has so much been owed by so many to so few'

Quotes

AMONG HIS FAMOUS SAYINGS:

- *'We shall fight them on the beaches, we shall fight on the landing grounds, we shall fight on the fields and in the streets, we shall fight in the hills; we shall never surrender.' 4 June 1940.*
- *'Never has so much been owed by so many to so few.' About the pilots who fought in the Battle of Britain.*
- *Accused by a hostile lady of being drunk at dinner, he replied: 'And you, madam, are ugly, but I shall be sober tomorrow.'*
- *Nancy Astor told him: 'Winston, if I were your wife I would put poison in your coffee', to which Churchill replied: 'If you were my wife, I would drink it.'*

without knowing that the following year Japan would attack Pearl Harbor and that Germany would declare war on the US – events that ensured America would once again come to the rescue.

His unflinching determination in the face of the Axis powers during the Blitz and the Battle of Britain won massive support. He promised nothing more than 'blood, toil, tears and sweat', but through his speeches to Parliament, his radio broadcasts and his public displays of defiance – scrambling over bombed-out sites dressed in a boiler suit giving his trademark 'V' salute – he mobilized and inspired an entire nation. Once America joined the war and President Roosevelt started to take centre stage, with Russia's Stalin, in shaping the final victory and the post-war world, Churchill began to fade from the picture. He was attending the last 'Big Three' summit in Potsdam when he was voted out of office.

Churchill remained a challenging if bored opposition leader but, in his 'Iron Curtain' speech in Fulton, Missouri, in 1946, he used his position as a world statesman to masterful effect when he warned of the growing Soviet threat. He had a final stint as Prime Minister in 1951 but illness, following strokes, forced him to resign in 1955.

Churchill retired to Chartwell, his country house in Kent, and spent his last years writing, painting and holidaying. In his lifetime he was regarded as the greatest living Englishman, a reputation that has declined little since his death in 1965.

Charles de Gaulle

General Charles de Gaulle (1890–1970) was a military leader and statesman who led France through two major crises – World War II and defeat of Nazi Germany, and the birth of the Fifth French Republic and independence of Algeria.

BORN CHARLES ANDRÉ JOSEPH MARIE de Gaulle in Lille, northern France, he grew up in Paris where his father worked as a teacher at a Jesuit school. Graduating from Saint-Cyr military academy, he fought in World War I at Verdun and was wounded three times and three times mentioned in dispatches. He was captured by the Germans in 1916, and spent two and a half years as a prisoner of war, attempting to escape five times.

After the war, and in between teaching and further training at the War College, he was sent on missions to Poland, the Rhineland and the Middle East, and, on promotion to lieutenant colonel, he joined the National Defence Council. De Gaulle also wrote books and articles on military subjects, displaying talent as both a writer and a thinker. In *The Army of the Future* (1934) he criticized France's reliance on the static Maginot line for defence against Germany, calling instead for a small, highly mechanized mobile army. He was delivering the same message to politicians as late as January 1940, but his advice went unheeded, and, in May and June 1940, Nazi German forces swiftly and easily overran France.

De Gaulle was commanding a tank brigade at the outbreak of war, and on 6 June 1940, now a temporary brigadier general, he was called into the beleaguered government as Under-Secretary of State for Defence. When Marshal Pétain took over ten days later with the intention of suing for peace, de Gaulle moved to London and, on 18 June 1940, he announced the formation of a French government in exile. He became head of the French Committee for National Liberation, the body which directed the Free French Movement, but was sentenced to death in his absence by a French military court. At first he ploughed a lonely furrow; he was unknown and had no political status. But he had absolute belief in his mission and obstinate determination. His relations with the British were never easy, and in 1943 he moved his headquarters to Algiers.

De Gaulle was given a hero's welcome on his return to Paris in August 1944 in the wake of the Allied Normandy landings. He assumed power as President of a provisional government, and guided France through the drafting of a new constitution. Seeking to avoid the political instability of the Third Republic, which had ended in the humiliating collapse of 1940, de Gaulle argued for a strong executive presidency and a subordinate parliament. When his wishes were ignored, he resigned, but over the next decade he remained in the political limelight, as leader of the Rally of the French

Chronology

1890	Born in Lille, northern France, 22 November
1913	Graduates from Saint-Cyr as 2nd lieutenant
1916	Wounded and captured at Verdun
1940	Appointed Under-Secretary of Defence
1940	De Gaulle escapes to London, issues call to French Resistance 18 June
1943	Transfers headquarters to Algiers
1944	Triumphal return to Paris
1945	President of the provisional government
1958	Elected President of Fifth French Republic
1965	Elected President for second term
1969	Resigns after losing referendum on reform
1970	Dies, Colombey-les-Deux-Églises, 9 November

'How do you govern a nation that has 246 different kinds of cheese?'

Quotes

- *De Gaulle was a master of the explosive short phrase.*
- *In June 1940 de Gaulle proclaimed from London: 'France has lost a battle, but France has not lost the war.'*
- *'Je vous ai compris,' he told Algerians in June 1958. 'I have understood you.'*
- *'Vive le Québec libre,' he said in 1967 on the balcony of Montreal City Hall. 'Long live Free Quebec.' The statement caused a diplomatic uproar with Canada.*
- *At home, de Gaulle could be equally diplomatic. 'How do you govern a country that has 246 different kinds of cheese?' he once asked.*

People, and he also wrote his memoirs.

As he had predicted, the Fourth Republic soon ran into trouble; by 1958 a revolt in French-held Algeria, combined with runaway inflation and financial instability at home, had brought France once again to the brink. There was real threat of civil war. De Gaulle came out of retirement, and this time he got his way. On 21 December 1958 he was elected President of the Fifth Republic under a new constitution that gives the president executive authority and which prevails today.

De Gaulle used the new presidential powers to face down a revolt by right-wing generals, determined to hang on to Algiers. He gave Algeria full independence in 1962 and unravelled the remainder of France's colonies. Egotistical and strongly nationalist, de Gaulle set about strengthening France both financially and militarily. He developed France's own nuclear deterrent and withdrew French forces from NATO, and he famously vetoed the entry of pro-American Britain into the European Common Market. De Gaulle served two terms as President, ruling France like a general on a battlefield, with the referendum his mandate.

Violent demonstrations by university students rocked France in 1968 and a general strike followed. De Gaulle responded by moving troops towards Paris, and by promising reform. A year later, de Gaulle resigned the presidency after losing a referendum on his reform proposals. He retired to Colombey-les-Deux-Églises, where he died from a heart attack in 1970.

Franklin D. Roosevelt

Franklin Delano Roosevelt (1882–1945), elected President of the United States an unprecedented four times, led the nation out of the Great Depression and through most of World War II. Patrician, controversial and inconsistent, 'FDR' transformed Federal government and paved the way for the US to become a twentieth-century superpower.

BORN TO A WEALTHY FAMILY of Dutch origin on an estate overlooking the Hudson River, Roosevelt had a classic patrician East Coast education – Harvard University and Columbia Law School. After working briefly as a lawyer, he plunged into a political career, following in the footsteps of his fifth cousin, President Theodore Roosevelt – only as a Democrat. He was elected to the New York Senate in 1910, became Assistant Secretary to the Navy in 1913, and by 1920 he was Democratic nominee for Vice President.

That same year, aged thirty-nine, Roosevelt was stricken with poliomyelitis. He fought back to regain the use of his legs, particularly through swimming, but for the rest of his life he was confined to braces and wheelchairs.

In 1928 he became Governor of New York, and in November 1932, at the height of the Great Depression in a contest of hope over despair, Roosevelt was elected President. He had offered confidence and a promise of action – a New Deal. 'The only thing we have to fear', he said in his inaugural address, 'is fear itself.' When he took over there were 13 million unemployed and virtually every bank had closed its doors. Congress enacted a sweeping programme to bring recovery to business and farming; the nation quit the gold standard, and millions were poured into public works and emergency relief. Capitalist America even embarked on an experiment in public ownership in the Tennessee Valley hydro-electricity scheme. By the end of his first term, he had introduced social security, unemployment benefits, banking controls, higher taxes and an end to prohibition. But despite renewed optimism, sustained recovery did not kick in until the economy went on to war footing in 1940.

Chronology

1882	Born in Hyde Park, New York, 30 January
1903	Graduated Harvard
1907	Columbia Law School
1910	Elected to New York Senate
1913	Assistant Secretary to the Navy
1921	Stricken with polio
1928	Governor of New York
1932	Elected President for first term
1936	Elected for second term
1940	Elected for third term
1941	Pearl Harbor, US enters World War II
1944	Wins unprecedented fourth term
1945	Dies in Warm Springs, Georgia, 12 April

Through the New Deal, Federal authorities significantly, and irreversibly, extended their power over American society. This mirrored what was happening in Europe and Russia and, although in America it was democratically implemented, conservatives claimed that Roosevelt had undermined rights of states and individual liberty. They also disliked the rise of organized labour.

Roosevelt was re-elected in 1936 with an even larger majority and he set out to extend Federal authority by seeking to enlarge the Supreme Court which had been blocking some of his New Deal. He lost the court battle but he established the right of government to regulate the economy.

Roosevelt was a pragmatist in foreign policy. He pledged the United States to a 'good neighbour' policy, a promise not to intervene in the internal affairs of countries in the region. He bowed to isolationism, conscious that most Americans blamed the depression on their involvement in the First World War, and he accordingly applied strict neutrality over Europe. He recognized the Soviet

'We have nothing to fear but fear itself'

A Way With Words

- *Roosevelt was one of the first politicians to exploit radio. He started broadcasting 'fireside' chats as Governor of New York, and used radio to rally America during World War II. He began the custom of weekly presidential broadcasts.*
- *He coined 'The New Deal' at his nomination 'I pledge you, I pledge myself, to a new deal for the American people.'*
- *Roosevelt called the day of the attack on Pearl Harbor – 7 December 1941 – 'a date which will live in infamy'.*

Union in 1933, and America at first did little as Adolf Hitler grabbed power, unleashed war on Europe and set about the mass extermination of Jews and Gypsies. When Poland, France and Belgium fell to Hitler and Britain came under siege, Roosevelt, constrained by Congress, could provide only non-military assistance. He did eventually give substantial 'non-neutral' aid to both Britain and Russia, including warships, but he won re-election in 1940 with a pledge that American boys would not fight foreign wars.

That changed, however, when the Japanese attacked and nearly destroyed the US Pacific fleet in Pearl Harbor on 7 December 1941. Roosevelt immediately geared the nation for global war, and he became one of the principal architects of the defeat of Germany and Japan, presiding over a sometimes strained alliance with Britain and Russia at a succession of international summits He concentrated on shaping the post-war world through the embryonic United Nations, and in particular on drawing Soviet Russia into it. He saw Russia as a vital ally in the defeat of Fascism, but in the end he was duped by Soviet leader Joseph Stalin who after the war imposed Communist dictatorship over half of eastern Europe. Re-elected in 1944, Roosevelt died on 12 April 1945, less than a month before Nazi Germany surrendered.

David Ben-Gurion

David Ben-Gurion (1886–1973) dedicated his life to establishing a Jewish homeland in Palestine, and was the first Prime Minister and founding father of Israel.

Born David Gruen in 1886 in Plonsk, then part of Russia and now in Poland, Ben-Gurion was educated in a Hebrew school founded by his father, a lawyer and ardent Zionist. Inheriting his father's passionate belief in the Zionist goal of a Jewish return to their original homeland, became a teacher in a Warsaw Jewish school aged eighteen, and joined a socialist-Zionist group, Poale Zion (Workers of Zion). Always learning and writing, he was a lifetime scholar.

In 1906, he emigrated to Palestine, which was then part of the Turkish-ruled Ottoman Empire; convinced that Jews had to start cultivating the land there again, he set up the first agricultural workers' commune which evolved into the kibbutz movement. He also helped establish the Jewish self-defence movement, Hashomer (The Watchman), and became editor of the Hebrew-language newspaper *Achdut* (Unity). In Palestine, he adopted the surname Ben-Gurion, Hebrew for 'son of the young lion'.

He was deported to Egypt by the Turks in 1915, soon after the outbreak of the First World War, and travelled on behalf of the socialist-Zionist cause to New York, where he married a Russian émigré, Paula Munweis. When Britain took control of Palestine from the crumbling Ottomans and issued the Balfour Declaration, which boosted Zionist hopes for a Jewish 'national home', Ben-Gurion enlisted in the British army's Jewish Legion and rushed home to fight. But the war was over by the time he reached Palestine.

Under the British Mandate, he threw himself into labour union politics, founding in 1920 the Histadrut national confederation of Jewish workers. The Histadrut was effectively a 'state within a state', and Ben-Gurion was de facto the local authority. Ten years later, Ben-Gurion founded the Israeli Workers Party and in 1935 he was elected executive chairman of the World Zionist Movement and head of the Jewish Agency in Palestine. Ben-Gurion cooperated with the British until 1939, but fell out with them when, yielding to Arab pressure, they started cutting back the flow of Jewish immigrants. From then on he was increasingly in the vanguard of the fight against the British, and after the 1939–45 war he called openly for insurrection and authorized guerrilla attacks.

It fell to Ben-Gurion to proclaim the State of Israel from the balcony of a Tel Aviv apartment in May 1948, and then to weld the underground forces into an army and lead the young nation as Prime Minister and Defence Minister through its first war with its Arab neighbours. The war was costly for

'What matters is not what the Gentiles say, but what the Jews do'

Architect of a Nation

- *Israeli poet Amos Oz said of him: 'Part Washington, part Moses, he was the architect of a new nation state that altered the destiny of the Jewish people – and the Middle East.'*
- *Always a man of action, Ben-Gurion used to say: 'What matters is not what the Gentiles will say, but what the Jews will do.'*
- *One of Ben-Gurion's most controversial acts as Prime Minister was to establish diplomatic relations with West Germany – a move bitterly contested at the time.*
- *Ben-Gurion's home in Kibbutz Sde Boker, near Beersheba, was in the heart of the Negev Desert, which he loved. His house looked out over a dramatic desert landscape, and his tomb faces the same view.*

both sides – one per cent of the Jewish population died as well as thousands of Arabs, and more than half a million Palestinians lost their homes. After the war, Ben-Gurion presided over the rapid development of the country – its kibbutz movement, the construction of new towns, the creation of a unified public education system, the establishment of a national water supply, the 'greening' of the land, and the absorption of a huge influx of immigrants. During his thirteen years as premier, Israel's population tripled from half a million to 1.5 million.

He quit government in 1953 to live in his kibbutz home in Sde Boker, a pioneering settlement in the Negev Desert, but came back to government two years later, initially as Defence Minister and then again as Prime Minister. He led Israel through the 1956 Suez War, during which Israel joined Britain and France in their abortive invasion of Egypt, and briefly occupied the Sinai Peninsula.

Ben-Gurion resigned as Prime Minister in 1963, but remained active in politics as a member of the Knesset (Parliament) for splinter parties which he founded until June 1970. His hallmark silvery hair now reduced to two wild bushes sprouting from his bald scalp, he retired for the last time to Sde Boker to write, and died three years later in the shadow of the 1973 Yom Kippur War.

Chronology

1886	Born Plonsk, Poland, 16 October
1906	Emigrates to Palestine
1914	Deported by the Turks, travels to New York
1917	Returns to Palestine
1948	Proclaims State of Israel, Prime Minister
1953	Quits government
1955	Prime Minister again
1963	Resigns
1970	Retires from political life
1973	Dies in Sde Boker, 1 December

Gamal Nasser

Gamal Abdel Nasser (1918–1970) rose from humble origins to be the first President of Egypt. He nationalized the Suez Canal and became a hero of the Arab world, but his reputation suffered after he was defeated by Israel in 1967.

GAMAL ABDEL NASSER, the son of a postman, was born in a mud-brick house and raised in and around Alexandria and Cairo. After finishing his schooling in Cairo, he entered military college in 1936 and graduated two years later as an officer in the Egyptian army. Egypt was still under British rule, with a puppet King Farouk on the throne, and Nasser helped forge a clandestine nationalist group that sought independence – The Free Officers, El-Dhobatt El-Ahrar. He fought as a major in the first Arab–Israeli war in 1948, when neighbouring Muslim countries tried, without success, to knock out the new Jewish state. Nasser was an officer in one of three battalions surrounded for weeks by the Israelis in a group of Arab villages called the Faluja Pocket.

Defeat in the war and general disaffection with the widespread corruption in government sparked an almost bloodless coup d'état in July 1952. Nasser was the leader, although he remained in the shadows for two more years. The rebel officers, nominally headed by General Mohammed Naguib, forced King Farouk to abdicate, and his son Ahmad Fouad was declared king in his place. The British agreed to pull out by 1954, but before that the army rebelled twice more – first to depose the young boy king and proclaim a republic under General Naguib, and then to depose Naguib and make Nasser head of state. He officially became president in 1956, and proclaimed Egypt an Arab socialist state, with Islam as the official religion.

Chronology

1918	Born in Alexandria, 15 January
1936	Enters military college
1938	Graduates as officer in Egyptian army
1948	First Arab–Israeli war
1952	Bloodless coup overthrows King Farouk
1954	Nasser assumes power
1956	Egypt nationalizes Suez Canal
1967	Egypt defeated by Israel in Six Day War
1970	Dies in Cairo after heart attack, 28 September

Nasser now bared his nationalist teeth; Egypt unilaterally took over the Suez Canal, a vital waterway linking the Mediterranean and Arabian seas over which Britain had maintained control. Nasser nationalized the canal after Britain and the United States withdrew funding from his Aswan High Dam project. The move triggered a crisis, and the British and French, together with Israel, launched an air and ground invasion to retake the canal. The Americans, instinctively opposed to what they saw as the final fling of British imperialism, sided with Nasser and forced the invaders to pull back. British Prime Minister Anthony Eden resigned in humiliation, while, in the Arab world and in other nations still ruled by European powers, Nasser, even though he had lost part of the Sinai to Israel and had been blooded in the fighting, was elevated to the status of a post-colonial hero. Egypt's takeover of the Suez Canal

Damming the Nile

- *The Aswan High Dam was Nasser's most controversial legacy. Designed to harness the vast waters of the Upper Nile for hydropower and to irrigate thousands of acres of dry desert, it flooded many monuments that could not be rescued by UNESCO and had a damaging effect on the River Nile's water levels.*
- *The 1956 Suez War still evokes strong emotions – but in retrospect, except in the context of the Cold War, it is hard to justify the armed intervention.*
- *The scars of the 1967 war are still visible in the Sinai Desert – the burnt hulks of Egyptian tanks litter the landscape.*

Charming and personable as an individual, as a politician Nasser ran a repressive police state

was a defining moment in Arab nationalism.

Nasser introduced socialist reforms throughout Egypt – nationalizing land and banks – although the effect was at times more symbolic than economically beneficial. He did however break decisively with Egypt's near-feudal past, and attempted to modernize and industrialize the country, raising educational standards and significantly enhancing the role of women. Charming and personable as an individual, as a politician Nasser kept all opposition at bay by running a repressive police state.

He achieved unprecedented popularity throughout the Arab world and became one of the founding leaders of the Non-Aligned Movement of countries that were supposedly free from either East or West, even though in the final analysis he was closely allied to the Soviet Union. Fiercely anti-Israel, he attempted to unite the Arab world, setting up a federation of Egypt and Syria and forming the United Arab Republic under his presidency. But the union broke down in 1961, following a military coup in Syria.

Nasser led Egypt into a disastrous war against Israel in 1967 when his army was completely routed, and he never fully recovered from the shattering blow. He resigned but was persuaded to stay on. He died from a heart attack three years later, after struggling to rebuild the army and national morale.

RONALD REAGAN

Ronald Reagan (1911–2004), a former movie star who became the 40th President of the United States, was known as the 'great communicator'. A Republican, he re-established conservative politics at home and won the Cold War.

BORN IN TAMPICO, Illinois, the son of an Irish-American alcoholic shoe salesman, Reagan attended high school in nearby Dixon, and worked his way through Eureka College, where he earned a degree in economics and sociology, played football and acted. After college he became a radio sports announcer, and took a screen test in 1937 to win a contract at Warner Brothers in Hollywood. During the next two decades he acted in fifty-three films, mostly B movies. He also appeared in training films for the army during World War II. His wartime marriage to actress Jane Wyman failed, and he married another actress, Nancy Davis, in 1952.

Reagan became involved in politics as president of the Screen Actors Guild, which was then embroiled in the issue of Communism in the film industry. He shifted from liberal to conservative, and toured the country as a television host and public relations speaker, becoming an increasingly popular spokesman for the Republican right. In 1966, he was elected governor of California by a margin of a million votes, and he was re-elected in 1970. He established his own style as governor, delegating most day-to-day business and

CHRONOLOGY

1911	Born in Tampico, Illinois, 6 February
1932	Graduates from Eureka College, first job on radio
1937	First Hollywood film contract
1966	Elected governor of California
1970	Re-elected governor
1980	Wins presidential election, beating Jimmy Carter
1981	Takes office as 40th President of the United States
1984	Wins second term as US President
1989	Leaves office
1994	Withdraws from public life with Alzheimer's

'Surround yourself with the best people you can, delegate authority and don't interfere'

concentrating only on the larger policy issues. He also learned how to exploit television to marshal popular support.

Ten years later, and after two failed bids for the nomination, Reagan swept into the White House on a conservative platform, winning 51 per cent of the vote to beat Jimmy Carter, mainly due to Carter's poor management of the economy and bungling of the crisis over the American hostages in Iran. Reagan and his vice-president George Bush trounced the Democrats again in 1984, winning 59 per cent of the vote to earn a second term.

On the domestic front, Reagan stuck to his election promises; he cut taxes and government spending, and persuaded Congress to vote in measures to stimulate the economy. His opponents lambasted his economic policy as 'Reaganomics'; unemployment initially soared as did the budget deficit, but in the end his policies delivered a decade of growth. He was tough with unions – in a typical move he had the nation's air traffic controllers sacked for striking.

Abroad, Reagan sought to achieve 'peace through strength', and he upped the ante in the Cold War by increasing defence spending by 35 per cent over his eight years in office, and by embarking on his 'Star Wars' programme to create a defence shield in space. Reagan struck up a special relationship with British Prime Minister Margaret Thatcher, and working in close harmony they in turn threatened and wooed the Soviet Union, which Reagan had denounced early in his presidency as 'an evil empire'. Reagan's summits with Soviet President Mikhail Gorbachev led to a major nuclear arms treaty in 1987 and ultimately fostered the climate which resulted in the peaceful dismantling of the Soviet Empire. Reagan also took his war on Communism to Central America, and in characteristic style he tackled the perceived source of terrorism by bombing Libya.

As in some of his cowboy film roles, Reagan kept things simple. He had clarity of vision – whether on government spending or getting rid of Communism – and he was able to communicate his message well and, with few exceptions, keep it consistent.

Reagan survived an assassination attempt on his sixty-ninth day in office, an event which gave the actor his first major role on the world stage. He said he had forgotten to duck, a joke in keeping with his affable, folksy charm. 'I hope you're all Republicans,' he said as he was wheeled into the operating theatre. Reagan's broadcasts to the nation at times of crisis, and on occasions such as the Challenger Shuttle disaster in 1986, were brilliant performances that seemed to come straight from the heart. They more than justified his reputation as the 'great communicator' and perhaps enabled him also to become the 'great escaper' when, for example, he managed to dodge responsibility for the arms-for-hostages Iran-Contra Affair.

Reagan retired to his Los Angeles home and wrote his autobiography, *An American Life* (1990). In a poignant letter to the American people in 1994 announced that he was withdrawing altogether from public life because he was suffering from Alzheimer's disease. Reagan died in 2004, aged 93.

Memorable Quotes

- *'Mr Gorbachev, open this gate. Mr Gorbachev, tear down this wall!'*
- *'There are no such things as limits to growth, because there are no limits on the human capacity for intelligence, imagination and wonder.'*
- *'Surround yourself with the best people you can find, delegate authority and don't interfere.'*
- *'Welfare's purpose should be to eliminate, as far as possible, the need for its own existence.'*
- *'It is the Soviet Union that runs against the tide of history... (It is) the march of freedom and democracy which will leave Marxism-Leninism on the ash heap of history.'*

Margaret Thatcher

Baroness Margaret Thatcher of Kesteven (1925–) was British Prime Minister for an unbroken eleven years, during which she won a war in the South Atlantic, helped bring down Soviet Communism and reasserted the triumph of capitalism at home and abroad. She was Britain's first woman prime minister.

BORN HILDA MARGARET ROBERTS, Thatcher was the daughter of a shopkeeper from Grantham. She took a degree in chemistry at Oxford University and became a barrister specializing in tax law, married a wealthy businessman, Denis Thatcher, and was elected to Parliament for the London constituency of Finchley in 1959.

Thatcher first entered the Cabinet as Education Secretary in 1970 in the government of Edward Heath, and she challenged Heath for the party leadership after he lost two general elections in 1975. To the surprise of many, and the lasting bitterness of the centrist Heath, the crusading anti-socialist Thatcher won.

She swept to power in the general election in 1979 and had an uneasy start; her policy of rolling back the frontiers of the state, freeing up business and industry from government interference and subsidies, while clamping down on public expenditure, produced spiralling interest rates and high unemployment. The number out of work peaked at three million. But she stuck defiantly to her belief that market forces alone would create lasting prosperity.

She bolstered her reputation by leading the country in a war against Argentina to recover the Falkland Islands, a remote British dependency in the South Atlantic, which Argentina had invaded in pursuit of long-standing territorial claims. The war was highly risky; but it showed the world and Britain that Thatcher had steel. Soon after recovering the Falklands, Thatcher won a landslide election victory over a weak and divided opposition for a second term.

Her second government pursued a more radical programme of privatization and deregulation, reform of the trade unions to curtail their power once and for all, tax cuts and introduction of free market mechanisms into health and education. In 1984–85, she won a major confrontation with striking coal miners, who staged nation-wide protests in their bid to keep the pits open with state subsidies. The sale of state-owned enterprises continued apace until virtually nothing but health, education and defence was left on the state payroll – telecommunications, aerospace, television, radio, gas, electricity, water, the state airline, British steel and public housing were all sold off. The number of individual shareholders in Britain tripled, while one and a half million people purchased their state-owned homes. Her policy of privatization caught on around the world, and by the end of the decade more than fifty countries had started similar programmes.

A bomb planted by the Irish Republican Army (IRA) almost killed Thatcher at a Conservative Party conference in Brighton in 1984 – attempted revenge for her refusal to negotiate with Republican hunger strikers, ten of whom starved themselves to death in British jails in Northern Ireland.

Thatcher demonstrated her steely will again in 1986 when she abolished London's governing body – the Greater London Council; she had no time for its socialist leader Ken Livingstone.

Thatcher won a record third term in 1987. She

Chronology

1925	Born in Grantham, Lincolnshire, 13 October
1959	Entered Parliament
1975	Tory leader
1979	Prime Minister
1982	Falklands War
1983	Wins second general election
1987	Wins third general election
1990	Loses party leadership

'The lady's not for turning'

had by now become a world leader and had struck up an especially close relationship with US President Ronald Reagan, which had paid dividends in American support during the Falklands conflict. Both leaders openly set out to bring down what they saw as the 'evil empire' of Soviet Communism, earning Thatcher a backhanded compliment from Soviet leader Mikhail Gorbachev, who dubbed her the 'Iron Lady'. Thatcher vigorously supported Reagan's policy of rearming, which brought the Soviets to the negotiating table, set off perestroika and eventually led to the collapse of Communism.

In 1989, Thatcher introduced a widely unpopular community 'poll tax', sparking angry riots. Meanwhile, her heavy-handed dealings with her own Cabinet and her increasingly strident opposition to the European Union led to several stormy resignations – notably her Defence Secretary Michael Heseltine and, in 1990, her long-serving Foreign Secretary Geoffrey Howe. His resignation speech in Parliament set in train the events which led to Thatcher's downfall a few weeks later. Heseltine challenged her for the leadership and, while he failed to win, he gained enough votes to persuade her that a crucial minority of the party favoured change. She resigned, and two years later Thatcher quit front-line politics and took a seat in the upper House of Lords as Baroness.

The Wisdom of Thatcher

Some legendary quotes:

- *'Economics are the method; the object is to change the soul.'*
- *'It will be years before a woman either leads the Conservative Party or becomes prime minister. I don't see it happening in my time.'*
- *'I am extraordinarily patient, provided I get my own way in the end.'*
- *Margaret Thatcher was the longest consecutively serving prime minister for more than 150 years (since Lord Liverpool). Her total time as prime minister was 11 years, 209 days.*
- *Her hardline, uncompromising approach and combative style of government acquired its own name – Thatcherism.*
- *'You turn if you want to. The lady's not for turning.'*

MIKHAIL GORBACHEV

Mikhail Gorbachev (1931–) was the last Soviet leader. He ushered out Communist rule in Russia and East Europe and helped end the Cold War. Hailed in the West as a great liberator, he was reviled by many in his own homeland for the collapse of the Soviet Empire.

THERE WAS LITTLE in his early career to suggest that Mikhail Sergeyevich Gorbachev would become the leader to dismantle the Soviet Empire. He was born into a peasant family near Stavropol in southwestern Russia in 1931, joined the Communist Party and drove a combine harvester at a state farm for four years before leaving for Moscow where he took a degree in law at the State University. He worked his way up the party apparatus in his home region of Stavropol and, under the wing of two senior Politburo members, Mikhail Suslov and Yuri Andropov, he was elected on to the Communist Party's Central Committee in 1971. In 1978 he was put in charge of Soviet agriculture. He already knew about the inefficiencies of the collective system from his own family background, but he now had to grapple with it.

In 1980 Gorbachev became a full member of the Politburo, the Soviet Union's highest policy-making body, and two years later his mentor, Andropov, succeeded Leonid Brezhnev as Soviet leader. Andropov continued to push Gorbachev, who was now building a reputation as an enemy of corruption and inefficiency. Brimming with self-confidence, Gorbachev took over as Soviet party leader in March 1985, and became President of the USSR in 1988.

From the outset, he was a man in a hurry. He strove to reform the highly inefficient and now stagnant state-run economy; glasnost (openness) and perestroika (restructuring) became the keynotes of his six-year rule. Realizing that the Soviet economy was virtually bankrupt and that the capitalist West had far outstripped it in terms of new technology, Gorbachev also began to argue for an end to the costly arms race with the West.

It is always said that the most dangerous moment for a dictatorship is when it begins to liberalize, and Gorbachev soon found himself caught between the party establishment, who saw its privileges threatened by a free press, elections and market economy reforms, and the radicals who wanted to do away at once with the one-party state and the command economy. Gorbachev introduced a new partially elected parliament, the Congress of People's Deputies and, in 1989, was duly elected its chairman. But he never quite dared go all the way in freeing the economy from state control, and in the resulting chaos and confusion he all but lost control at home. He had also unleashed forces of nationalism in the Baltics and other Soviet republics, which were to prove unstoppable. The success he achieved in negotiating new arms control agreements with the United States and in withdrawing Soviet troops from Afghanistan led to the peaceful breakaway of the former Communist countries of Asia and eastern Europe, and to the re-unification of Germany – all welcomed in the West as the start of a new era. At home, and to hardline Communists, it all appeared a sell-out.

CHRONOLOGY

1931	Born in Privolnoye near Stavropol, 2 March
1955	Graduates in law from Moscow University
1971	Elected to Central Committee
1978	Party Secretary in charge of agriculture
1980	Joins Politburo
1985	General Secretary of Soviet Communist Party
1987	Agreement with US to scrap intermediate-range nuclear-tipped missiles
1988	President of the USSR
1990	Fall of the Berlin Wall
1990	Awarded Nobel Peace Prize
1991	Survives attempted coup against him
1991	Gorbachev resigns as President of defunct USSR

Mikhail Gorbachev changed the world, but lost his own country while doing so

Hardliners and their military supporters struck back in August 1991 and staged a coup while Gorbachev was on vacation in the Crimea. The coup collapsed, in large part because of the courage of Moscow street demonstrators and of the President of Russia, Boris Yeltsin. Gorbachev was restored to office, but he no longer had any power. This now belonged to the leaders of the various republics, above all to Yeltsin. On 25 December 1991, Gorbachev resigned and the Soviet Union ceased to exist. He had changed the world, but lost his own country.

AN 'ACCIDENTAL' HERO

- *Did Gorbachev plan the break-up of the Soviet Union? Almost certainly not from the start. Gorbachev zigzagged through history, but his lasting achievement was that his – probably unintended – dismantling of one of the most heavily armed empires in history was achieved without major bloodshed.*
- *Gorbachev remained active in politics but got nowhere in the new Russia of Boris Yeltsin. He stood in the 1996 presidential elections, but failed to attract much support. He was a hit on the American and European lecture circuit, and even used his popularity to sell a pizza brand in a US television spot.*
- *Gorbachev was the first Soviet leader to 'market' his wife. The strikingly attractive Raisa would accompany him on visits, bringing him admirers in the West, but the Russians, unaccustomed to 'First Ladies', resented her. Raisa died of leukaemia in 1999, and Gorbachev won great sympathy for his display of grief at her death.*

Alexander the Great

Alexander the Great (356–323 BC), King of Macedonia, was one of the great military leaders: he conquered half the known world in thirteen years, and never lost a battle. His achievement was to spread Hellenic culture from Gibraltar on the Atlantic seaboard to the Punjab in India.

ALEXANDER BECAME KING of Macedonia in 336 BC after his father, King Philip II, was assassinated. Not yet twenty, he inherited a prosperous kingdom with a professional standing army that dominated Greece's city-states. Alexander, who had been raised in the art of warfare by his father and tutored by Aristotle, swiftly consolidated his hold on Greece, with a combination of force and diplomacy, and was elected supreme commander of the Greek forces for a war against Asia. He spent the next year putting down regional rebellions and crushing a revolt in Thebes.

Alexander led one of the world's greatest military machines. Well-trained infantry, deployed in phalanx formations and supported by cavalry,

Chronology

356 BC	Born in Pella, ancient capital of Macedonia
336 BC	King of Macedonia
334 BC	Leads Greek invasion of Persia
334 BC	Battle of Granicus
333 BC	Battle of Issus
331 BC	Battle of Gaugamela
327 BC	Enters India
324 BC	Returns to Persia
323 BC	Dies in Babylon on 13 June

Alexander was a master of all kinds of warfare, but above all he led his men from the front

provided the cutting edge and backbone of the Macedonian army; Alexander's success often derived from the careful coordination of light horse and foot soldiers by which he would surprise and outmanoeuvre far larger forces. Alexander was also a master of siege. Above all, though, he led his men from out front. He was wounded in battle at least seven times, most seriously when an arrow pierced his lung in India.

He crossed the Dardanelles in 334 BC, and went straight to Troy – now in modern Turkey and the site of the great victory of the Greeks over Asia – and it was near here that he won a major victory against the Persians at Granicus River. The following year Alexander overwhelmed a far bigger force of Persians, led by their King Darius, at Issus in what is now northeastern Syria. Alexander now knew he could take Persia, but first he secured the eastern Mediterranean – invading Syria and then capturing Tyre after a seven-month siege, brilliantly executed by building a causeway to the island fortress. Gaza and Egypt fell without a fight and, after a suitable spell among his new Egyptian subjects and a pilgrimage to their shrine of Amon-Ra in the Libyan desert, Alexander reassembled his forces in Tyre and set out for Babylon. Crossing the Tigris and Euphrates, he met King Darius on the plains of modern-day northern Iraq and inflicted a crushing defeat on him at Gaugamela in 331 BC. Darius fled but was later slain. Over the next three years, Alexander subdued the whole of Persia and set about creating an eastern empire, appointing local officials and even, to the consternation of his own Macedonians, going native, adopting Persian dress and marrying a Persian, Roxana.

Alexander now spent two years fighting in what is modern-day Afghanistan, pressing as far north as the Oxus River, before announcing his intention of conquering India. He crossed the Indus River in 326 BC and invaded the Punjab as far as the river Hyphasis. By now he had realized that the subcontinent was bigger than he had been led to believe; his fellow Macedonians refused to go on, and their iron-willed leader halted the push into India. Alexander notched up one more victory, defeating a force led by King Porus in 326 BC after his men had overcome their terror of facing elephants in battle, and his army then returned home by land and sea.

Back in Persia, Alexander set about organizing his empire. He imposed a bizarre mix of potentate central control – executing bad governors and introducing a single currency – with the fostering of a looser federation based on co-existence and racial equality, something his fellow Macedonians did not like at all. He was in the end full of contradictions – driven and yet flexible, a dreamer and a strategist, cruel and kind, and given to murderous fits of rage, often directed at those closest to him. Immensely good looking, he seems at times to have believed in his own divine origins. He was preparing an invasion of Arabia when he died of fever in Babylon in 323 BC, most probably after another of his notorious drinking bouts, although some sources suggest he was poisoned.

Cutting the Gordian Knot

■ *The Gordian knot was fiendishly difficult and had no open ends. Legend had it that he who loosed it would conquer Asia. With characteristic decisiveness, Alexander was said to have taken one look and sliced it through with a sword. 'What difference does it make how I loose it?' he asked. To cut the Gordian knot has come to mean slicing through a problem that appears hopelessly complex by some simple, bold stroke.*

■ *Alexander is said to have tamed the wild black stallion Bucephalus when he was aged only ten. Bucephalus was his favourite mount and he named a city in India after the horse when it died with him on his 327 BC campaign throughout that country.*

■ *Alexander and his successors founded some seventy cities, most famous among them Alexandria, at the mouth of the Nile, in Egypt, in 332 BC.*

HANNIBAL

Hannibal, a Carthaginian general (247–183 BC), spent almost his entire adult life fighting Rome, most of it with unparalleled success. His great achievement was to invade Italy through the back door – over the Alps.

HANNIBAL WAS THE SON OF Hamilcar Barca, the general who commanded the Carthaginian forces in Sicily during the first of the three great Punic Wars, a struggle for mastery of the Mediterranean between an aggressively expansionist Rome and the seafaring state of Carthage. After he was defeated by the Romans and driven from Sicily, Hamilcar set about repositioning Carthage, by building up its power in Spain.

Aged only nine, Hannibal accompanied his father to Spain, and before he left he swore a solemn oath of enmity to Rome. He remained true to that vow all his life.

Hannibal grew up to fight successful campaigns in Spain, and in 221 BC, on the death of his brother-in-law Hasdrubal and aged only twenty-six, he was appointed commander in chief of the Carthaginian forces. He was a brilliant tactician, using intelligence to the utmost, sending scouts into enemy camps and even at times going behind enemy lines himself. He always seemed to be able to second-guess the enemy; he became the master of the pincer movement. Within two years he had consolidated Carthage's hold on the Iberian Peninsula, with the exception of the Roman outpost of Sanguntum, which he overran after an eight-month siege. This sparked a new war between Rome and Carthage – the Second Punic War (218–201 BC).

Hannibal's daring would now win him an unsurpassed place in military history; he undertook one of the great outflanking movements of all times. Italy was too heavily defended by sea, so Hannibal decided to go the long way round. Hannibal's march on Rome began in 218 BC. He set out from New Carthage (now the Spanish city of Cartagena), at the head of a force of 40,000, including cavalry and elephants, and stormed over the Pyrenees through southern France, and then, in just fifteen days, he crossed the Alps, by either the Col de Grimone or the Col de Cabre. This was an extraordinary feat for an army used to operating in hot plains. How many men were lost to the hostile terrain, cold and guerrilla attacks remains a matter of conjecture, but Hannibal emerged on the other side with at least one elephant and a fighting force of foot soldiers and cavalry. His invasion of northern Italy was the equivalent of America's September 11: Rome was stunned. Hannibal pushed on south, cutting down whole armies of Romans in a string of punishing victories, culminating at Lake Trasimeno, where contemporary accounts say the water was turned red with the blood of Gaius Flaminius's army. Rome was probably, at that stage, his for the taking, but he hesitated.

CHRONOLOGY

247 BC	Born Carthage
221 BC	Hannibal appointed commander in chief
218 BC	Start of Second Punic War
218 BC	Hannibal invades Italy
217 BC	Defeats Gaius Flaminias at Lake Trasimeno
216 BC	Inflicts worst defeat on Roman army at Cannae
203 BC	Hannibal recalled to Carthage
202 BC	Hannibal defeated by Scipio Africanus at Zama
183 BC	Dies by taking poison

Hannibal's campaign in Italy continued for fifteen more years and, although he inflicted another crushing defeat on a Roman army in 216 BC at Cannae on the Aufidus (Ofanto) River, he never quite got the upper hand again – in part because of a change in Roman tactics. Rather than confront him in open battle, they harried him and ground him down. Also, reinforcements failed to arrive. Hannibal was progressively pushed back to the south.

In 204 BC, his nemesis Scipio seized the initiative

Far from the cruel, uncouth soldier he is sometimes portrayed as, Hannibal was a cultured Greek scholar

and landed in North Africa; Hannibal was ordered to return to Carthage. The two generals clashed at Zama in 202 BC, and Hannibal, let down by Numidian horsemen who changed sides, was finally defeated by Scipio. Carthage capitulated to Rome, and the Second Punic War ended, and Scipio returned in triumph bearing the title 'Africanus'.

Hannibal successfully set about restoring Carthage's fortunes, proving to be an effective peacetime leader, but, under pressure from Rome, he was driven into exile. He went on to fight the Romans from Syria, but when Syria fell into Roman hands in 190 BC, Hannibal moved further east. He was finally trapped in Bythnia, in northern Asia Minor, where he committed suicide by drinking poison from the casket on the ring he always wore – probably in the year 183 BC.

The Punic Wars

■ *The Punic Wars derive their name from Punica, the Latin for Phoenicia, from where the Carthaginians originally came. Rome won all three wars.*

■ *Livy's* History of Rome *highlights Hannibal's military successes as he swept through Italy after crossing the Alps. He called the battle at Lake Trasimeno 'one of the few memorable disasters to Roman arms'.*

■ *Although Livy painted Hannibal as a cruel and uncouth soldier, he was in fact a cultured Greek scholar who could compose state papers in Greek and who also wrote books.*

JULIUS CAESAR

Gaius Julius Caesar (100–44 BC), Roman general and statesman, extended Rome's rule into western Europe and laid the foundations of the Roman Empire. A superb and daring general, who inspired loyalty in his soldiers, he was also an enlightened administrator, a writer and a famous lover. His detractors saw him as a tyrant, who saw himself as a god and allowed Rome's republican system of government to collapse.

JULIUS CAESAR was born into the prestigious Julian clan and was always destined for high office. As a young man he acquired his first taste of power thanks to his aunt's husband, the great general Gaius Marius, who appointed him to the position of priest of Jupiter, the chief god of the Roman people. But Marius died soon after, and Caesar left Rome and travelled east to fight with the legions and gain his first experience of warfare. He later returned to Rome to study and practise law and then spent time in Rhodes learning oratory. On the way there he was kidnapped by and escaped from pirates, whom he later captured and crucified. Returning to Rome, he started working his way up the political ladder. Elected quaestor in 68 BC, he served time in southern Spain and, with a lavish lifestyle and new wife to support, began to enjoy the patronage of Rome's richest man, Marcus Licinius Crassus. By 60 BC Caesar was established with Crassus and Pompey as one of the three masters of Rome in what was known as the First Triumvirate. But instead of a military command, Caesar was assigned to the care of the roads and forests.

This unglamorous appointment was a turning point. With trouble brewing on the Rhine, Caesar lobbied hard to be given military command of the territories north of the Alps. Rome had hitherto concentrated most of her might on consolidating in the Mediterranean. The decision to send Caesar north would transform what was to become the Roman Empire and lay the foundations of modern Europe.

This was his brilliant period – the seven years of the Gallic Wars in which Caesar notched up a string of victories over the Helveti, Germans, Nervi and Belgae, as he gradually consolidated Rome's rule over central and northern Europe west of the Rhine. The achievement was all the more remarkable because the north European barbarians were on the whole an even match for the Romans. Caesar prevailed through his mastery of strategy and tactics and the discipline of his soldiers. He was at the same time a ruler of vision, respecting local customs and giving a system of government and rights of citizenship to the conquered. There were setbacks and defeats, too; two expeditions to England, in 55 BC and 54 BC, came to nothing, and the Gallic leader, Vercingetorix, forced his army off the field at Gergovia, near modern Clermont-Ferrand, in 52 BC. But Caesar's star was in the ascendant and, when in 52 BC Pompey seized control and ordered Caesar's army to disband, the battle-hardened and power-hungry general disobeyed, and marched on Rome. 'The die is cast,' he said, as he crossed the Rubicon, a small stream separating his province of Cisalpine Gaul from Italy.

The move sparked civil war, which lasted on and off for four years, even though Caesar swiftly overwhelmed Rome and proceeded to crush Pompey at the battle of Pharsalus, in Greece. Caesar then moved on to Egypt, where he fell into the amorous arms of Cleopatra. More campaigns

CHRONOLOGY

100 BC	Born in Rome on 12 or 13 July
60 BC	Member of the First Triumvirate
59 BC	Elected Consul
58 BC	Governor of Gaul
55 BC	First expedition to Britain
49 BC	Returns to Rome, crossing the Rubicon
48 BC	Defeats Pompey at battle of Pharsalus
44 BC	Murdered on steps of Senate on 15 March

Caesar notched up a string of victories as he consolidated Roman rule over Europe

Veni, Vidi, Vici

■ *Caesar was the author of several great works (most of them lost), including self-serving but brilliant accounts of his Gallic Wars and the civil war against Pompey.*

MEMORABLE STATEMENTS:

■ *'Veni, Vidi, Vici' (I came, I saw, I conquered), about his successful campaign against Mithridate's son, Pharnaces (a supporter of Pompey), in 47 BC.*

■ *'Et Tu, Brute' (You, too, Brutus), his last words, on realizing that even his closest companion, Marcus Junius Brutus, had betrayed him. They may, however, have been spoken in Greek.*

■ *The word Caesar lived on as Kaiser and Tsar.*

followed – in Asia Minor, North Africa and Spain – and when he returned to Rome for the final time in 45 BC he had been at war more or less without a break for thirteen years. Back in Rome, he became dictator for life, thus quashing the power of the now discredited Roman nobility. He used the title Imperator; in effect he was emperor of a republic. Ultimately it was this contradiction, combined with his magnanimity and vanity, which turned his friends against him; he was cut down in the Senate with twenty-three stab wounds on the Ides of March. The people had loved Caesar, and Romans rose in anger against the conspirators; the chaos that followed ultimately resulted in Caesar's great-nephew Octavius taking power. He, as Augustus, established the Roman Empire.

Caesar introduced the Julian calendar; the month of July is named after him. It began on 1 January 45 BC.

Attila The Hun

Attila, King of the Huns (404–53) and 'scourge of God', ravaged and all but finished off the Roman Empire. He is known as one of history's great destroyers: the name of his tribe has become synonymous with uncouth violence.

HIGHLY SKILLED HORSEMEN who had crossed from the Asian steppes, the Huns were the fastest and most furious fighters the world had seen. By the time of Attila's birth in 404, they had reached the banks of the Danube – close to the tattered frontiers of the decaying Roman Empire. Born into the ruling Hun family, Attila reputedly spent time in Rome as a teenager, but the experience seems to have left him with a burning ambition to conquer it.

He got his chance at the age of thirty-one on the death of his uncle King Roas; he and his brother inherited a huge territory, from the Alps and Baltic Sea in the west, to the Caspian Sea in the east. Described by contemporaries as a short, squat man, with a flat nose and thin beard, and as an irascible but tenacious negotiator, Attila consolidated his hold over the barbarian tribes of northern and central Europe, through conquest and alliances, and in 441 he turned on eastern Rome, ostensibly to extract unpaid tributes from the Emperor Theodosius. Over the next few years he proved to be an outstanding commander; he smashed his way to the gates of Constantinople, razing cities such as Belgrade and Sofia on the way, and then annihilated the remnants of the eastern army in Gallipoli. The ensuing peace treaty cost the Eastern Empire the unpaid tribute in full plus 2,100 pounds of gold a year. After murdering his brother Bleda in 445, Attila took full control of the kingdom, and again waged war on the Eastern Empire; he emerged from it in 449 with both tributes and large territorial gains.

He now turned his attention on the west, and invaded Gaul, and then the kingdom of the Visigoths. His declared objective was the hand of the emperor's sister Honoria, and he demanded half the Western Empire as dowry. Attila destroyed Metz, left Paris and almost took Orléans before turning south towards Châlons. Here, on the Catalaunian Plains, he met bloody defeat at the hands of Flavius Aetius and his Roman-led coalition of Gallic and Visigoth tribes. The Visigoth king, Theodoric I, was slain and, although General Aetius's forces prevailed, it would be the last victory in the name of the Western Empire.

'The grass will not grow again where Attila's horse has trod'

Chronology

404	Birth of Attila
435	Attila becomes King of the Huns
441	Attacks Eastern Empire
445	Attila murders his brother Bleda
450	Attila invades Gaul
451	Defeated at the Battle of Châlons
452	Attila invades Italy, sacks northern cities
453	Death of Attila on his wedding night

Unbowed, Attila turned on Italy itself in 452 and his marauding forces fell on Aquileia, Padua, Verona, Brescia, Bergamo and Milan, before something quite remarkable occurred. A force led by a man with a grey beard came out to meet him on the shores of Lake Garda. No one knows exactly what happened, but somehow Pope Leo I persuaded Attila to withdraw.

On his way home he picked up as booty a girl called Ildico, and he married her at a great wedding feast when he got back to Tisza. He had been married many times before and fathered countless sons, but the celebrations this time proved his undoing; Attila died on his nuptial night from a burst artery 'suffocated by a torrent of blood'. He was buried in a secret location along with a horde of treasure and a number of his cohorts.

The Huns

- *The Huns came from Asia and first appeared in Pannonia at the end of the fourth century. They built a tented capital on the plains of Tisza in 420.*
- *Their army was swifter and more mobile than any at the time, consisting primarily of mounted troops carrying 5-foot bows, with which they could inflict deadly onslaughts. Each man carried his own baggage.*
- *The Huns most probably brought smallpox to Europe, a killer disease that plagued the continent well into the nineteenth century and wrought havoc in the New World.*
- *The Huns were responsible for the foundation of Venice, driving the Veniti of northeastern Italy to take refuge in lagoons and islands at the head of the Adriatic Sea, which later became the state and republic of Venice.*

GENGHIS KHAN

Genghis Khan (1167–1227) was a Mongol leader who welded rival nomadic tribes into a nation, and then made that nation the heart of an empire that stretched from China to Russia, the largest the world has ever seen.

THE SON OF A CHIEFTAIN, Temüjin, as the future Genghis Khan was called, was born clutching a clot of blood in the palm of his hand. He was raised in a hostile world; in childhood he weathered his father's murder, captivity, the kidnapping of his wife, and the recurring threat of starvation. Trauma, and the stern climate of the steppe, tempered the man who would grow up to be a great conqueror into an inimitable, almost indestructible warrior.

Temüjin became leader of the remnants of his father's tribe in 1190; and through his charisma and daring he drew followers from around the region and, one by one, began to subdue the rival tribes. He ruthlessly exterminated all who stood in his way, and he virtually wiped out the Tartars, who had murdered his father, slaughtering all those taller than a cart axle. By 1206 he was master of the steppes, almost all the territory that is now Mongolia, and at a khuriltai, a traditional meeting of tribal leaders, he was proclaimed Genghis Khan – 'Universal Ruler', or 'Prince of All that Lies between the Oceans'.

This was a turning point in history; the nomadic tribesmen of the steppe, swift horsemen whose main weapon was the bow and arrow and whose principal dwelling was the yurt, were about to burst on to the world stage with terrifying force. Genghis Khan had the fortune to rule at a time of disarray in China, and he profited by first pushing into southern China and subjugating the Tangut kingdom of Xi Xia, and next by marching on the north and taking Zhongdu, capital of the Jing Empire, what is now Beijing. Provoked by the massacre of a caravan under his protection, Genghis Khan then turned on Khwarazm, the new Islamic empire to the west, capturing major cities such as Samarkand and Bukhara, encircling the Caspian Sea and slashing his way as far as the shores of the Black Sea; it was in fighting the Muslims that the Mongols earned a reputation for savagery and terror. To the north, his generals drove into Russia and, in the south, to Kabul and Peshawar.

CHRONOLOGY

1167	Born near Lake Baikal, Russia
1190	Chief of family tribe
1206	Elected Genghis Khan
1215	Captures Zhongdu (Beijing)
1219	Invades Khwarazm
1227	Dies 18 August

His enemies portray Genghis Khan as a cruel, avenging killer – 'they came, they sapped, they burnt, they slew, they plundered and they departed', said one Muslim – but he was at the same time a sophisticated and intelligent ruler, and an adroit statesman. He quickly adapted his cavalry-based army so that it could handle siege warfare, and even on one occasion divert a canal, in order to take big cities. He forged a unified Mongol nation, which has survived 800 years; he appointed a law lord, introduced record keeping, had the Mongol language reduced to a Turkic script, encouraged literacy, practised religious tolerance and learned, from the Chinese, the importance of cultivation and, from the Muslims, the value of towns as sources of wealth. He established a capital at Karakorum, and organized a network of post-houses to facilitate speedy communications over his vast empire. His military genius stemmed from an ability to adapt to rapidly changing circumstances. He combined physical strength and will power with flexibility, and he knew how to heed advice. His greatest weapon in the end was simple military

The stern climate of the steppe tempered Temüjin into an almost indestructible warrior

skill, combined with the sheer terror that his forces could unleash – both the psychological threat of it and its harsh reality.

Genghis Khan was campaigning in China when he fell ill and died. His body was carried back to Mongolia, where he was buried in utmost secrecy. Those who witnessed the burial were themselves killed, so that no one would discover the great conqueror's tomb. Genghis' final resting-place remains hidden to this day.

GENGHIS THE CONQUEROR

- *In terms of square miles conquered, Genghis Khan was the greatest conqueror of all time – greater even than Alexander the Great.*
- *Genghis's icy eyes grace Mongolian money; his people still cherish the legend that their great ruler will come again.*
- *The thirteenth-century European chronicler Matthew Paris called the Mongols a 'detestable nation of Satan that poured out like devils from Tartarus so that they are rightly called Tartars'.*
- *Genghis Khan told the Muslims. 'I am the punishment of God. If you had not committed great sins, God would not have sent punishment like me upon you.'*

WILLIAM THE CONQUEROR

William the Conqueror (1027–87), Duke of Normandy and King of England, led the last successful invasion of the British Isles. One of the great soldiers and rulers of the Middle Ages, William established England's Anglo-Norman dynasty, subdued the turbulent Welsh and Scottish borders, and left a monumental testament to royal administrative power and public record keeping, the Domesday Book.

WILLIAM THE BASTARD was appointed Duke of Normandy at the age of eight, the illegitimate son of Duke Robert I and Arlette, a tanner's daughter. With many of his father's family all too eager to profit from his death, and the legitimacy of his position tenuous as a bastard heir, his childhood was beset with danger: three of his guardians died violently and his tutor was murdered. His successful personal rule of the duchy began in 1042, consolidating the power of the ducal family over rebellious barons and asserting his independence from the French king, whose authority as royal overlord of Normandy was reduced to that of a nominal figurehead for the following 150 years.

William's claim to the English throne started taking shape from 1052, when he opened negotiations with his cousin Edward the Confessor to build an alliance in the face of rebellions on his eastern borders. Norman chroniclers, writing after the Conquest, went as far as to allege, improbably, that the heirless king of England had even promised the Norman duke the English throne, supposedly then confirmed by Harold, Earl of Wessex, during a trip to Normandy around 1064.

However, when Edward died childless in January 1066, Harold was himself crowned king, much to William's fury. Having successfully subdued his duchy, the duke had now set his sights on greater territorial riches: the wealth of the nearby isles presented an irresistible challenge. William's soldiers crossed the Channel in September of that year, met just in time by King Harold, who had rushed back to the south coast after fighting off another rival claimant to the throne, Harald Hardraada. After a 250-mile march from Stamford Bridge, near York, the English troops put up a strong fight at Hastings but they were outdone by the Normans' fresh troops and cavalry, and outwitted by their cunning tactic of feigned retreat. Harold was killed towards dusk on 14th October 1066, and William was crowned King of England at Westminster Abbey on Christmas Day. To show he was now in control, William ordered the construction of the Tower of London as his fortress.

William I was a king of his time, a man of iron will, who applied brutal methods of government to maintain peace and administer justice. The first three years of his reign were spent crushing localized rebellions, notably in the West and North, and in securing the historically turbulent Welsh and Scottish borders. He created the defensive marcher counties along these after his successful invasions of Scotland in 1072 and Wales in 1081. With the conquest complete, William selected loyal experts to run his new kingdom during his prolonged absences in Normandy; much of the successes of Anglo-Norman government can be attributed to his old friend Lanfranc, whom he made Archbishop of Canterbury.

In 1086, William ordered a full survey to be made of his kingdom, resulting in the compilation of the Domesday Book, a tribute to the sophisticated machinery of Anglo-Saxon local government and Norman efficiency in utilizing it. Abroad, William was threatened by an alliance of

CHRONOLOGY

1027	Born in Falaise, Normandy
1035	Duke of Normandy, 'William the Bastard'
1066	Defeats King Harold at Hastings and crowned King of England
1086	Orders the Domesday survey
1087	Dies at Rouen, 9 September

Having successfully subdued his own territory, the duke set his sights on greater riches

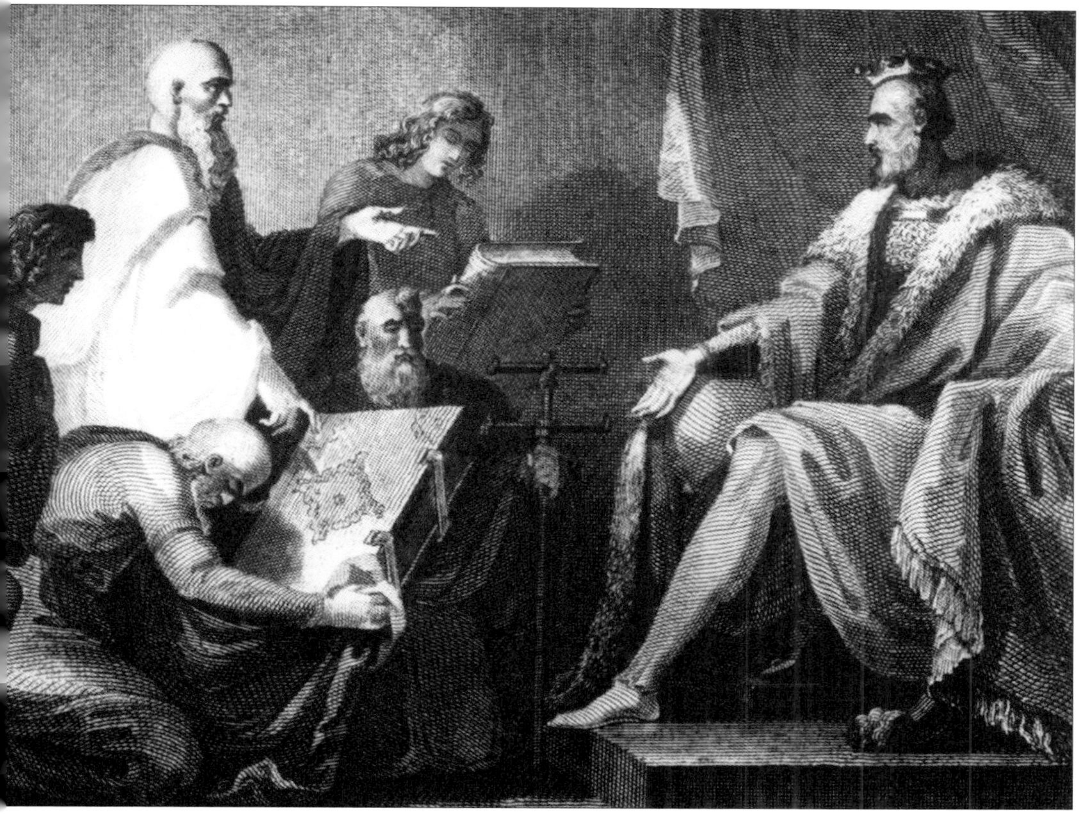

Philip I of France and his own son, Robert Curthose. This angered the king so much that on his deathbed in 1087, having been mortally wounded by the pommel of his horse's saddle in Mantes, he deprived Robert of his English inheritance and gave it instead to his second born, William Rufus, while Robert was left with Normandy.

Unprecedented Power

■ *Contemporaries regarded William as a more powerful king than any of his Anglo-Saxon predecessors; they were overawed by the almost merciless imposition of his royal power, and by his success in wiping out virtually all trace of the old English ruling class. Indeed, Williams's revolution was so complete that within 20 years, the entire ruling class of church and state spoke French. Church chroniclers glossed over what was an essentially violent life portraying William with a veneer of legitimacy and respectability; however the inscription on his tombstone at Caen presents a perhaps a more accurate summary of the life of this warrior king:*

He ruled the savage Normans; Britain's men
He courageously conquered, and kept them in his power
And bravely thrust back swords from Maine
And made them subject to his rule's laws
William the great king lies in this little urn,
So small a house serves for a mighty lord

SALADIN

Saladin (1138–93), Sultan of Egypt and Syria, reunited the Arabs and led a 'jihad', a holy war, against the Christian Crusaders, recapturing Jerusalem for the Muslims and successfully fending off the great counter-offensive of the Third Crusade.

SALAH AL-DIN YUSUF IBN AYYUB, or Saladin as he is popularly known, was born in 1138 in Tikrit, now in Iraq, and was of Kurdish descent. It was a time of disunity among Arabs, with much of Palestine, including Jerusalem, in the hands of foreigners from Western Europe – the Christian Crusaders. Saladin learned to fight them from an early age. He was only 14 when he entered into the service of his uncle, the Syrian military commander Asad ad-Din Din Shirkuh, with whom he fought with distinction on three expeditions to help the decadent Fatimid caliphate of Egypt against the Crusaders. On his uncle's death, in 1169, Saladin became commander in chief of the Syrian army and vizier of Egypt. He quickly established a power base in Cairo, and in 1171 he toppled the weak and unpopular Shi'ite Fatimid regime and brought Egypt back under the Abbasid caliphate and Sunni law; in the process he founded the Ayyubib dynasty.

He had to use his wits to survive the ensuing complex power struggles of the divided Holy Land, and he could well have met an inglorious end had it not been for the timely deaths in 1174 of the Syrian Emir Nur ed-Din, and of Amalric, the King of Christian Jerusalem. The way was now open for Saladin to take control of Syria, and from then on he worked tirelessly to bring the feuding Muslim territories of the Middle East under one banner with the single purpose of driving out the Crusaders. He consolidated his hold over Muslim lands from Egypt to the borders of Persia, engaging in an on-off frontier war with the Crusaders until finally, on 30 June 1187, he crossed the Jordan and launched an all-out invasion of the now weakened and internally riven Latin Kingdom.

The end came with unexpected swiftness. Saladin lured the Christians into a waterless trap on the Horns of Hattin, a rocky escarpment above the Sea of Galilee near Tiberias, and, on a scorching summer day, 4 July 1187, he inflicted a crushing defeat on their thirst-wracked army. Saladin was magnanimous to the defeated King Guy and to his lay barons, but he had the surviving Templar and Hospitaller knights beheaded, and the remaining soldiers sold into slavery. The price of a captive Christian in Damascus dropped to three dinars, and one prisoner was bartered for a pair of sandals.

CHRONOLOGY

1138	Born in Tikrit, modern Iraq
1169	Commander of Syrian army; Vizier of Egypt
1171	Seizes power in Egypt
1174	Seizes power in Syria; unites Muslims
1187	Battle of Horns of Hattin. Recaptures Jerusalem
1193	Dies in Damascus on 4 March

The mighty Crusader castles now fell to Saladin one by one – with the exception of Tyre – and less than three months later, on 2 October, he had taken Jerusalem, but in stark contrast to the way the Crusaders had entered the city 88 years before, this time there was no looting and no bloodshed.

The fall of Jerusalem provoked an angry response in Western Europe and no fewer than three monarchs set out at the head of a massive counter-attack – the Third Crusade. Led by Richard I, King of England, the Crusaders took back Acre in 1191, but they failed in their primary objective – Jerusalem. King Richard got the better of Saladin at the battle of Arsuf later the same year, but it was little more than an indecisive skirmish; the war itself was a stalemate. In 1192 Saladin concluded an armistice agreement with King Richard, which left the Crusaders in command of the coastal cities, and the bulk of Palestine, including Jerusalem, in the hands of the Muslims.

Saladin died the following year in Damascus, on 4 March, ill and worn out by years of warfare.

A military genius, he was honoured alike by his enemies and his own people for his chivalry

A Chivalrous Warrior

■ *Saladin was no great beauty – he was short and stout, red-faced and blind in one eye – but he exercised a fascination over his Christian contemporaries and remains a captivating figure even today. His chivalry challenged the Crusaders as much as his courage on the battlefield. There is even a suggestion by some sources that Saladin was secretly knighted by Humphrey of Toron; perhaps this was the Crusaders' way of explaining his chivalry. Although Saladin could be harsh, and he never hesitated to use the sword and even crucified some Shi'a opponents, there are countless accounts of his acts of chivalry towards the Crusaders; he once sent fresh fruit to the sick King Richard and snow from Mount Hermon to cool his drinks.*

■ *Jerusalem, a holy city to the world's three great monotheistic religions Judaism, Christianity and Islam, has been fought over for centuries. It remains a contested city to this day.*

ST JOAN OF ARC

Joan of Arc (1412–31) was an illiterate peasant girl, inspired by visions to expel the English from France during the Hundred Years' War. She did not succeed. Captured, tried and burnt at the stake, her bravery nonetheless rallied the French and their king at a critical moment.

JOAN OF ARC was born to a peasant farming family in the village of Domrémy near the borders of the province of Lorraine. As a young girl she claimed regularly to hear voices which she later identified as St Michael, St Catherine and St Margaret. In May 1428 her voices urged her to go to the King of France and help him reconquer his kingdom from the English. At this time the French king was still uncrowned, and known as the Dauphin. The English king, Henry VI, claimed the French crown and was supported by the Duke of Burgundy, the Dauphin's uncle, in campaigns to occupy large areas of northern France.

Joan went to the nearest French enclave in Vaucouleurs and demanded to see the king. She was only sixteen, and she and her visions were not taken seriously. The following year, 1429, dressed in men's clothes, she made her way to Chinon, where she immediately recognized the Dauphin, who had hidden among his courtiers. Charles was at first sceptical of Joan urging battle against the English, but changed his mind after she had been intensively examined by theologians. Her rallying cry gave new energy to the French. She was given a small military force, and adopted a suit of white armour, and a banner with the fleur-de-lys. Joan – who was only seventeen – gave new energy to the French and inspired them to a decisive victory over the English in May 1429 at the relief of Orléans. This led to parts of northern France, which had previously sided with the English, declaring their loyalty to Charles.

The Dauphin was crowned King Charles VII at Rheims on 17 July 1429, with Joan standing near him holding her banner. This was a daring move as Rheims, the traditional coronation site for French kings, was in enemy territory.

Charles was indecisive about attacking Paris, then in Burgundian hands, but Joan felt it was essential to take the city; she became impatient, and on 8 September 1429 she was waving her banner on the fortifications and urging the Parisians to surrender to the French troops. Wounded, she was hailed as a heroine who had put an end to English supremacy in France. She and her family were ennobled by the king.

But Charles vacillated and opposed all further plans to fight against the English and their Burgundian allies. Joan, independently, in May 1430, led a campaign against the enemy at Compiègne. She was unhorsed and taken prisoner by the Burgundians who handed her over to the English representative, Pierre Cauchon, Bishop of Beauvais, in exchange for 10,000 francs. For fourteen months Joan was tried as a heretic in a church court at Rouen. She recanted when faced with death by burning, but because she donned men's clothes when led away to begin life imprisonment she was once again accused of heresy. Her insistence over her 'voices' sent from

CHRONOLOGY

1412	Born at Domrémy, in Bar, France, 6 January
1428	Hears angelic voices telling her to go to the Dauphin and help him regain his kingdom from the English
1429	Meets Dauphin at Chinon. Rescued city of Orléans from being besieged by the English. Witnessed coronation of Dauphin as King Charles VII of France at Rheims. Urged Charles to attack Paris. He refused, but many towns in northern France surrendered to him. In September led troops to Paris but failed to take city
1430	Tries to repel the Burgundians from Compiègne but was captured by John of Luxembourg
1431	Tried for heresy by church court. Burnt at the stake, 30 May
1920	Canonized

Her insistence on her 'voices' from God was seen as heretical defiance: Joan was burnt at the stake

God, and her habit of wearing men's clothing were seen as heretical defiance, and Joan was sentenced to death and burnt at the stake on 30 May 1431. She was aged only nineteen. Charles VII, who totally deserted her, ordered an inquiry into her trial when he finally took Rouen in 1450.

Joan is also known as the Maid of France or La Pucelle. She is one of the patron saints of France.

Called by God

- *When Joan was burnt at the stake she asked a Dominican monk to hold up a crucifix, and shout out words of salvation so she could hear them above the crackle of the flames. After she died her body was shown to the crowds, before it was completely incinerated. Her ashes were scattered in the River Seine near Rouen*
- *Her youth, pious convictions, common sense and heroism have inspired plays, poems, films and biographies by German, French, English and American writers, including Schiller, Shaw, Anouilh, Voltaire and Twain.*
- *When not in a suit of white armour, Joan dressed in knightly attire of cloth of gold and silk trimmed with fur and a doublet and hose.*

GUSTAVUS ADOLPHUS

Gustavus Adolphus (1594–1632), King Gustav II of Sweden and leader of the Protestant forces in the Thirty Years' War, was one of the fathers of modern warfare and the founder of the modern Swedish state. He formed the first national conscript army in Europe, and planned his military campaigns on the basis that attack was the best form of defence.

THE SON OF CHARLES IX, Gustav was groomed in warfare and succeeded to the throne aged 16 with Sweden engaged in war on three fronts – against Denmark, Russia and Poland.

He made peace with Denmark, by agreeing to pay huge indemnities, but pursued Swedish campaigns against Russia and Poland, eventually securing big territorial gains in the Baltics, pushing back Russia and neutralizing the threat to his throne from his cousin, Sigismund III, King of Poland with the 1629 Truce of Altmark. By this time, Gustavus was known as the 'Lion of the North'.

At home, Gustavus laid the groundwork of the modern Swedish state, establishing a new supreme court, a permanent civil service with treasury and chancery in Stockholm, and a standing army and navy. He worked in tandem with a brilliant chancellor Axel Oxenstierna; their constitutional arrangements gave the council of state a permanent role in government and conferred new status to the Riksdag or parliament. Gustavus did much for education; he permanently funded Uppsala University in Sweden and founded the University of Tartu in Swedish-occupied Estonia, and created the Gymnasia to provide national secondary education. Under Gustavus, Sweden became the most efficiently run and modern state in Europe.

Gustavus was at his most innovative as a war leader.

Forming the first national conscript army in modern Europe, he emphasized officer education, strict discipline, rigorous training, and the combination of firepower and mobility, till he had forged a formidable fighting force that stands unrivalled between Caesar's legions and Napoleon's 'Grande Armée'. He always believed that attack was the best form of defence and he made a policy of making his wars pay for themselves.

CHRONOLOGY

1594	Born at Stockholm, 9 December
1611	Becomes King of Sweden 30 October
1613	Concludes peace with Denmark
1630	Sweden enters Thirty Years' War
1631	Victory over Tilly at Battle of Breitenfeld
1632	Victory over Tilly at Batle of Lech
1632	Victory and death, Lützen, 6 November

In 1630 Gustavus rescued the beleaguered Protestant cause in Germany from the Catholic League of the Holy Roman Emperor Ferdinand II, militarily led by the era's two other great captains, the Habsburg commanders Johann Tserclaes von Tilly and Albrecht von Wallenstein. Gustavus triumphed against them (twice defeating Tilly) in battles that are tactical masterpieces. His victory over Tilly at Breitenfeld in 1631 was a landmark in the art of war. Gustavus, seeing his left flank was routed by the imperial army, moved Swedish infantry into the breach, an unprecedented move for the times. In the ensuing months, Gustavus swept all before him as his army pushed into southern Germany, and the following year he beat Tilly again and left him mortally wounded at the Battle of the River Lech. His army was at first checked by Tilly's successor, Wallenstein, at Alte Veste in September 1632 but on 6 November Gustav attacked Wallenstein's entrenched positions at Lützen, near Leipzig, in Saxony, and again overwhelmed the imperial army. But Gustavus was shot and killed in a cavalry charge.

He died just a few weeks before his 38th birthday but he had made Sweden a major European power, and set new standards for warfare; his victories over the Catholic League assured Protestant survival in Germany and northern Europe.

Under Gustavus, Sweden became the most efficiently run and modern state in Europe

A New Model Army

■ *Gustavus' army was based on permanent conscripts and rigorous training. He was the first commander to use musketeers in three ranks, each firing in turn while the others reloaded.*

■ *At the Battle of Breitenfeld (1631), Gustavus set a new first in modern warfare when he moved Swedish troops across the field to create a second front in place of a Saxon line that had been broken by the imperial army under Graf von Tilly. A counter-attack personally led by Gustavus won the day for the Swedes.*

■ *After the battle of Lützen, the Swedish King's body was found under a pile of dead; he was naked, with a bullet hole through his head, a dagger thrust in his side, and another bullet in his back.*

HORATIO NELSON

Horatio Nelson (1758–1805) won naval victories that gave Britain dominance of the seas for a century. His charisma and the manner of his victories are such that he is known simply as 'The Hero', and every year, on Trafalgar Day, the Royal Navy toasts 'The Immortal Memory'.

HORATIO NELSON was the son of a Norfolk parson and went to sea aged twelve. His early years under sail saw him serve in the West Indies, the Arctic, Nicaragua, and the American War of Independence, suffering much ill health. He was appointed captain in 1779 and married in 1787, only to spend nearly six years unemployed in England before the outbreak of the French Revolutionary Wars.

Nelson shot to fame when serving under Admiral Sir John Jervis at the Battle of Cape St Vincent on St Valentine's Day 1797. This battle promised to be inconclusive (as so many of the battles of the period were), until Nelson broke away from the British line of battle – in normal circumstances an unforgivable breach of discipline – so as to cut off the enemy's retreat. He first captured one Spanish ship which he then used as a stepping-stone, his own ship being unmanageable, to capture a second, the enormous *San Josef*.

Six months later, Nelson lost his right arm in a failed attack in Tenerife. After a period of recuperation, he was given command of a squadron charged with hunting down the fleet with which Napoleon had sailed for Egypt. Nelson eventually tracked them down to the mouth of the Nile, at Aboukir Bay, on the evening of 1 August 1798. He launched an immediate attack, sailing both inside and outside the French moorings and obliterating their fleet. The climax of the night-time battle was marked by the gigantic explosion of the French flagship *L'Orient*. It has been said that 'a victory so decisive, so overwhelming, was unknown in the annals of modern war'.

Nelson was seriously wounded and spent the next few months at the Sicilian court, where he began his passionate romance with Emma Hamilton, wife of the British ambassador. To this period belongs the most controversial episode of his career, the suppression of the revolution led by Commodore Caracciolo and Caracciolo's execution, for which the King of Sicily conferred upon Nelson the dukedom of Bronte.

Nelson separated from his wife on his return to England in 1800. The following year he was sent under Admiral Hyde Parker to the Baltic and, facing formidable obstacles, defeated the Danes at Copenhagen on 1 April (turning the famous blind eye to a signal ordering him to break off action). The next few years were spent in arduous service, much of it blockading the French fleet at Toulon. After pursuing the French to the West Indies, he took command of the fleet that was keeping watch on the French and Spanish fleets sheltering in Cadiz. The combined fleet left harbour on 19 October, and on the 21st Nelson, hoisting his celebrated signal 'England Expects that Every Man Will Do his Duty', attacked in two columns (an extremely novel strategy for the time). He died from a sniper's bullet at half-past four in the afternoon, just as the complete and overwhelming victory for which he had striven was secured.

CHRONOLOGY

1758	Born at Burnham Thorpe, Norfolk, on 29 September
1771	Goes to sea as a midshipman
1787	Marries Frances Nisbet
1794	Wounded in his right eye at Calvi
1797	Promoted rear admiral
1797	Battle of Cape St Vincent, made a Knight of the Bath
1797	Loses right arm at Santa Cruz
1798	Battle of the Nile, created baron
1799	Begins love affair with Emma, Lady Hamilton
1799	Created Duke of Bronte by the King of Naples
1801	Battle of Copenhagen, created viscount
1805	Killed at the Battle of Trafalgar, 21 October

'England expects that every man will do his duty'

The Nelson Touch

Nelson's memorandum before the Battle of Trafalgar has been held as a model of management method. It sets out the revolutionary tactics that he wished to be followed – the famous 'Nelson touch' – while leaving initiative with individual officers, concluding that, if his signals could not be seen, 'no captain can do very wrong if he places his ship alongside that of the enemy'.

■ *As a leader Nelson did not shrink from the limelight, relishing public recognition and honours. But he was generous to his subordinates, and delegated a good deal of responsibility to his captains whom he called his 'band of brothers'. He was not just admired but loved by those who served under him.*

■ *Nelson is famous for having only one eye; but he lost only the sight of his right eye rather than the eye itself: what appears in some portraits to be an eye-patch is in fact a shade to protect his undamaged left eye from strain.*

NAPOLEON BONAPARTE

Napoleon Bonaparte (1769–1821) was among the greatest military leaders of all time. He rose from humble origins to become Emperor of France and, for a while, master of Europe.

BORN IN 1769 in Corsica, Napoleon was commissioned into the French artillery in 1785 and rose rapidly, distinguishing himself at the siege of Toulon (1793), and in dispersing a Royalist uprising in Paris (1795) and conquering North Italy for France (1796–97). On returning from the Egyptian campaign (1798–99), he engineered a coup d'état and became First Consul, and crowned himself Emperor in 1804. After a short-lived peace, Britain provoked a war that lasted from 1803 to 1812. Napoleon knocked out Britain's allies, Austria, Prussia and Russia, at Austerlitz (1805), Jena (1806), Friedland (1807) and Wagram (1809), but Britain fought on. Napoleon invaded Portugal (1807), Spain (1808) and Russia (1812), to undermine Britain economically, but this led to the turning of the tide; driven from Russia and Spain, Napoleon lost Leipzig (1813) and was forced to abdicate in 1814. Made sovereign of Elba, he escaped to France in 1815 and ruled for a 'Hundred Days' before being outnumbered and defeated at Waterloo and banished to St Helena. He was twice married, to Josephine Beauharnais, and Marie-Louise of Austria.

CHRONOLOGY

1769	Born in Ajaccio, Corsica, 15 August
1785	Commissioned into artillery
1793	Makes name for himself at siege of Toulon
1795	Suppresses Royalist uprising in Paris
1796–97	Victory over Austrians in North Italy
1798	Egyptian campaign
1799	Seizes power in coup and becomes First Consul
1800	Defeats Austrians at Marengo
1804	Crowns himself Emperor
1805	Defeats Austrians and Russians at Austerlitz
1806	Defeats Prussians at Jena
1807	Invades Portugal, begins Peninsular War
1812	Invades Russia
1813	Defeated by Allied force at Leipzig
1814	Abdicates, becomes sovereign of Elba
1815	Escapes to France, defeated at Waterloo, exiled
1821	Dies at Langwood House, St Helena, 5 May

Napoleon inherited from the early post-revolutionary years a French style of warfare – offensive, mobile, ruthless – that confounded opponents. He perfected it through his charismatic leadership and his tactical intelligence. Wellington valued Napoleon's presence on a battlefield at an extra 40,000 men.

Napoleon was adept at inspiring from all ranks the devotion and courage he prized. In choosing subordinates he looked for luck, unorthodoxy and aggression ('I only like officers who make war'); they led from the front and died for him in comparatively high numbers.

He never systematized his tactics. 'There are no precise or definite rules…everything is a matter of execution.' But his hallmarks, daring apart, were rapidity of movement and concentration, and subterfuge, seeking to divide adversaries, or throw them off balance, so as to achieve local superiority.

Austerlitz (1805) was his masterpiece. Feigning weakness on his right he provoked battle and split a larger Russo-Austrian force, then drove up the middle and rolled up the over-extended enemy left.

After 1807 victory came less easily. He resorted more often to frontal assaults, using massed artillery to blast holes in the enemy line. Some detect a decline in his powers. But his defensive campaign east of Paris in 1814 was as brilliant in its way as his first campaign in Italy.

In French eyes, Napoleon was also a great administrator. In the run-up to his Consulate it was said of him: 'Of all the soldiers, he is the nearest to being a civilian.' Possessing a lucid, penetrating

The Hundred Days

■ *After Napoleon's escape from his first period of exile on Elba, March 1815, he returned to France. He crossed the frontier into Belgium on 15 June, taking the Prussians by surprise and defeating them at Ligny on 16 June 1815. Defeat at Waterloo on 18 June, however, meant another period of exile for the Emperor, this time on St Helena, where he remained until his death on 5 May, 1821.*

'In the long run, the sword is always defeated by spirit'

brain, tremendous powers of concentration, and unflagging energy, imposing his will came naturally to him. His instincts included thrift, moderation, and social liberalism.

His achievements were many. He reformed the tax system, created the Bank of France and restored French finances. He drove through the drafting of a Civil Code which has stood the test of time. He reformed the criminal justice system and local administration (creation of the Prefecture). He strengthened higher education. He normalized relations between church and state. He invigorated French agriculture, and had roads, canals and ports built. He put France to work, generating a sense of stability and opportunity. Goethe described Napoleon's administrative work as a form of genius.

Napoleon set himself high standards, believing himself driven by noble ideals: love of France, honour, and the Rights of Man. He was courageous, magnanimous in victory, and generous. Metternich reported him as saying in 1813: 'A man such as I am cares little for the lives of a million men', but his treatment of wounded suggests otherwise.

Many (not all) English contemporaries saw him as an autocrat, a parvenu adventurer ('Sa majesté très Corse'), a monster of ambition, obsessed with his own glory. But, autocracy apart, this charge-sheet looks exaggerated by snobbery and fear.

His greatest failings – the cause of his downfall – were of judgement. He believed too readily in the loyalty of others; the list of those who let him down is long. He inclined to over-confidence and lacked a sense of his own limits, rendering his strategic vision at times defective.

Specifically, he miscalculated the consequences of invading Spain and compelling the Bourbons to renounce the Spanish throne. He failed to appreciate how much Germany Italy and Holland resented French occupation. He underestimated the risks before and during his Russian campaign. In the peace negotiations of 1813 and 1814 he showed little sense of reality.

It was also characteristic of Napoleon that, after the Battle of Waterloo, he misjudged the British view of him sufficiently to believe they would welcome him with open arms. They did not.

Duke of Wellington

Arthur Wellesley, 1st Duke of Wellington (1769–1852), was one of Britain's greatest military commanders, but he was also one of her worst prime ministers. At a time of peril, when his country most needed victories, this great soldier never lost a battle.

ARTHUR WELLESLEY WAS BORN in Dublin, the fourth son of an impoverished Anglo-Irish peer. He always denied being Irish, stating that being born in a barn does not make someone a horse. Unsuccessful at any of his schools, including Eton, he ended up in a French military academy in Angers, where he found his metier.

Following his mother's wishes he joined a Highland regiment. His initial rise was largely due to his family's influence, with his brother buying him command of the 33rd Foot Regiment, which, after a campaign in Flanders (1794), he took to India in 1797, where another brother Richard was governor general. Wellesley took part in several successful campaigns, the invasion of Mysore in 1799 and the Battle of Assaye in 1803, which he considered to be the finest of his sixty victories.

Promoted to major general and knighted, he returned home in 1805. The following year he married Lady Katherine Pakenham and was also elected Member of Parliament for Rye. In 1807, largely thanks to family patronage, he was made Chief Secretary of Ireland, and took time off to notch up a victory against the French in Denmark.

In 1808, by now lieutenant general, Wellesley was given command of the British expeditionary force sent to Portugal to aid in their insurrection against the French. The Iberian campaign started well with victories at Roliça and Vimiero. But Wellesley was summoned home to face a court martial (at which he was exonerated) and was therefore away from the Peninsula when Napoleon arrived to take personal command of the French forces, so the two men came face to face for the first and only time at Waterloo.

Wellesley spent six years driving the French from the Peninsula, rarely taking a day's leave. Frequently outnumbered by the huge French forces that were occupying Spain, he employed scorched-earth tactics to deny them territory, used speed and defensive positions to great advantage, and never lost a battle. Talavera (1809), Salamanca (1812) and Vitoria (1813) were among his famous victories. Wellesley showed exemplary leadership; he expected and exacted the best from his men, and he was a harsh disciplinarian when he did not get it. He described his men as 'the scum of the earth' but they admired him because he kept them well fed, never unduly risked their lives and showed personal bravery on the battlefield.

Wellesley crossed the Pyrenees into France to win a further victory at Toulouse before Napoleon abdicated in 1814. By now the Duke of Wellington, he was appointed British ambassador in Paris, and he was representing Britain at the Congress of Vienna when, in March 1815, Napoleon escaped from Elba to launch his final and doomed bid for European supremacy.

Wellington assumed command of the Anglo-Allied army in Brussels. This army was made up of a mix of British, Dutch, Belgian and German soldiers, many of whom were raw recruits. In June 1815 Napoleon marched on Belgium, making for

Chronology

1769 Born Dublin, 1 May
1787 Commissioned to 73rd Highlanders
1793 Promoted lieutenant colonel
1794 Campaigns in Holland
1797–1805 Commands army in India
1804 Knighted
1806 Elected MP for Rye
1807 Chief Secretary for Ireland
1808–14 Peninsular War
1814 Created Duke of Wellington
1815 Defeats Napoleon at Battle of Waterloo
1818 Enters Cabinet
1828–31 Prime Minister
1852 Dies at Walmer Castle, Kent, 14 September

Key Quotes

- 'I don't know what effect they will have upon the enemy, but by God they frighten me.' On seeing his raw recruits arriving in the Peninsula.
- 'By God! I don't think it would have been done if I had not been there.' After the Battle of Waterloo, 1815.
- 'An extraordinary affair. I gave them their orders and they wanted to stay and discuss them.' After his first Cabinet meeting as Prime Minister.

Wellesley spent six years driving the French from the Peninsula, taking only a few days' leave in the time

Brussels. On 16 June he simultaneously attacked the Anglo-Allied army at Quatre Bras and the Prussian army under Marshal Blücher at Ligny, routing the latter. Wellington was forced to retreat to the slopes of Mont St-Jean, south of his headquarters at Waterloo.

Only three miles wide, the battlefield was protected by woods and villages on the flanks, and two well-defended farms in the centre. The French attacked at midday on Sunday 18 June, but failed to break Wellington's line. The Duke was everywhere on the field encouraging his men. Blücher's Prussians arrived in the nick of time in late afternoon to surprise Napoleon and attack his left flank, and by 7 pm the French were routed. After Waterloo, Wellington remained in France for three years as head of the allied army of occupation.

Returning to England and politics, he entered the Cabinet in 1818 and in 1828 he became Prime Minister. In office he changed his opinion on the Irish question, and came to favour Catholic emancipation, saying that the only alternative was conflict. Wellington was less liberal on the question of extending the franchise. He defended rule by the elite and feared the mob – a fear strengthened by riots against unemployment. His opposition to reform caused his popularity to fall to such an extent that crowds gathered at Apsley House, his London home. Wellington's nickname the Iron Duke was acquired not from his rigid command of the army, but because of the iron shutters he had installed at his home after it was attacked by mobs. Wellington resigned in 1830. Two years later he joined Peel's administration as Foreign Secretary and later as Leader of the Lords and, on Peel's resignation in 1846, he retired himself.

Wellington died in 1852 and though his political career was distinctly less impressive than his military, nothing can detract from the untarnished glory he earned in England and throughout Europe as the vanquisher of Napoleon.

Douglas MacArthur

General Douglas MacArthur (1880–1964) was one of the US army's most decorated soldiers. Called out of retirement in World War II to command the forces that defeated the Japanese in the Pacific, he presided over the creation of a new post-war Japan and was commander in chief of Allied forces in the Far East until sacked for insubordination during the Korean War.

DOUGLAS MACARTHUR WAS BORN in 1880 in the US army arsenal barracks at Little Rock, Arkansas, the third son of Arthur MacArthur, later the US army's senior ranking officer. After an irregular education, MacArthur entered West Point in 1889. In 1903, he graduated with the highest honours in his class. As a 2nd lieutenant, he served in the Philippines, and in 1904 he was promoted 1st lieutenant.

In 1906, he was appointed aide to President Theodore Roosevelt. Later, he served as a junior engineering officer and from 1913 as an officer on the general staff. In 1914, he was promoted captain and fought with US troops who occupied Vera Cruz, Mexico, earning a recommendation for the Congressional Medal of Honor.

MacArthur joined the Western front as major in 1915 and by 1917 he had become the US army's youngest divisional commander. He showed conspicuous courage in the trenches. Disdaining both a gas mask and a steel helmet, he led his men over the top armed only with a riding crop. He was wounded twice and decorated nine times for bravery in 1918.

After the war he remained in Europe as part of the force occupying the Rhineland. Returning home, he became the youngest superintendent of West Point and, after two commands in the Philippines, was promoted chief of staff in 1930. He spent five tough years protecting the army's meagre resources during the depression. From 1935 to 1941, he served as the military adviser to the Philippines government. He retired from the US army in 1937, but stayed on in Manila as field marshal in the new Philippines army.

As war clouds gathered, he was recalled to active service in July 1941 and told to prepare the Philippines' defences for a Japanese attack. The Japanese landed on 22 December and pushed MacArthur's 130,000 men back into the Baatan Peninsula. On 11 March 1942, on the direct orders of President Roosevelt, MacArthur reluctantly fled the Philippines, vowing: 'I will return.'

From his base in Australia, MacArthur coordinated a series of amphibious invasions to 'island hop' US forces back across the Pacific, starting with the capture of New Guinea. He was appointed a five-star general in December 1944, and as Allied Commander of the Pacific he took the Japanese surrender in Yokohama Bay on the battleship Missouri on 2 September 1945.

Chronology

1880	Born Little Rock on 26 January
1903	Graduated West Point with highest honours
1914	Vera Cruz raid: recommended for Congressional Medal
1918	Fighting in France, decorated nine times; promoted general
1919	Superintendent West Point
1930–35	Army Chief of Staff
1937	Retires from US army
1941	Recalled to arms
1942	Flees to Australia; launches 'island hopping' offensive
1943–44	Seizes New Guinea; attacks the Philippines; appointed five-star general in command Pacific Theatre
1945	Accepts surrender of Japanese forces on 2 September
1945–51	Proconsul of Japan
1950	General in command UN forces in Korea
1951	Sacked by President Truman; retires into private life
1964	Publishes Reminiscences; dies in Washington, DC, 5 April

'Old Soldiers'

■ MacArthur was given a hero's welcome on his return to the US in 1951, his first trip home since 1937. On 19 April, he addressed a joint session of Congress to defend his policy of taking the war to China. He closed his address with the words from an old army ballad, '...old soldiers never die; they just fade away'.

■ MacArthur accepted the chairmanship of the Remington Rand Corporation in 1952. Thereafter, he lived a mostly private life in his suite in the Waldorf Astoria Hotel in New York. In 1964, he published his memoirs, Reminiscences.

'I will be back'

From 1945 to 1951, as proconsul in Japan, MacArthur directed the demobilization of the Japanese forces, the purging of militarists, the trial and execution of Homma and Yamashita, the restoration of the economy, public health and education and the introduction of land reform, women's rights and the drafting of a liberal constitution. He also astutely preserved the institution of emperor, minus his divine attributes.

When the Korean War started in 1950, MacArthur was given command of the United Nations forces. The North Koreans had pushed across the 38th parallel, the boundary between North and South Korea, captured Seoul and driven the South Korean forces to the Pusan perimeter on the southeastern tip of the Korean Peninsula. The seventy-year-old MacArthur outflanked the North Korean forces, by landing at Fuchon in September, recaptured Seoul and advanced into North Korea as the North Korean army disintegrated.

The Chinese had massed north of the Yalu River, the boundary between North Korea and China. MacArthur assured President Truman that the Chinese would not attack. Based on this assurance, Truman allowed MacArthur to drive on towards the Yalu River. But on 24 November the Chinese attacked and drove MacArthur's troops south of the 38th parallel. MacArthur's counter-attack in February 1951 was inconclusive. MacArthur blamed the restrictions placed upon him; he rejected a policy which aimed merely to restore the pre-war boundary along the 38th parallel.

In March 1951, just before Truman was to propose a ceasefire to the North Korean and Chinese leaders, MacArthur issued a public demand that Chinese forces surrender or risk attacks upon their homeland. In April 1951, Truman dismissed MacArthur for insubordination. A ceasefire was negotiated, and the boundary along the 38th parallel was restored.

William Slim

General William Slim (1891–1970) joined the British Army as a private and left as Chief of the Imperial General Staff. He commanded the Fourteenth Army during the Second World War and was the architect of the British victory over the Japanese in Burma in the face of overwhelming odds. He is widely recognized as one of Britain's finest generals.

Born the son of an iron merchant in Bristol in 1891, Slim volunteered as a private soldier in the Royal Warwickshire Regiment as the First World War broke out. He saw action during the abortive Gallipoli landings, where he was wounded so badly that he was invalided out of the army. After persuading the army that he was not so badly wounded after all, he saw action on the Western Front and in Mesopotamia, where he was wounded once again.

At the outbreak of the Second World War, Slim was in command of the 10th Infantry Brigade, 5th Indian Division, which threw back the Italian invasion of Eritrea and prevented them from entering the Sudan. Wounded again, he recovered to lead the 10th through Syria, Iraq and Persia, joining up with the Russian army at Tehran. The success of these operations won him the DSO.

Posted to India, Slim was given charge of the two British-Indian divisions retreating from the Japanese invasion in Burma. Outnumbered and outgunned, Slim led a superbly-organized retreat almost 1,000 miles to cross the Chindwin River into India, where he set about re-organizing the exhausted troops. In November 1943 he was given command of the Fourteenth Army, while Lord Louis Mountbatten took control of all Allied ground forces in India. Between them, the two commanders managed to transform a demoralized army into a keen fighting force. After the British XV Corps successfully took on the Japanese in the Arakan, close to the Indian-Burmese border, Allied troops realized that the Japanese army was far from invincible and morale quickly began to rise. When the Japanese Fifteenth Army launched a major offensive into India in May 1944, the British were waiting, at Imphal and Kohima. Aware of the crucial nature of these positions, Slim was determined to hold them at all costs, supplying the encircled 50,000 British troops by air, and massing the 33rd Corps to their rear. In some of the fiercest fighting of the war, Slim pushed the Japanese back out of India. The moment he had been waiting for had arrived; as 1945 opened, Slim and the Fourteenth Army recrossed the Chindwin river, and began the advance into Burma. Unconvinced that the Japanese were giving up, Slim advanced cautiously, realizing that the Japanese were hoping to entice the bulk of his forces into central Burma, where they could be cut off and destroyed by the far from finished Japanese army. In a monumental piece of trickery, using fake radio traffic and dummy headquarters, he fooled the Japanese into believing he was indeed advancing with all speed into the Burmese heartland. As the Japanese waited to spring their trap to the south of Mandalay, however, they found they themselves outflanked and outmanoeuvred by the Fourteenth. By 4 March, Mandalay had been recaptured, and British forces

Chronology

1891 Born Bristol, 6 August
1914 Joins Royal Warwickshire Regt. as private
1915 Wounded at Gallipoli
1916–1918 Service on the Western Front and Mesopotamia; awarded the Military Cross
1920 Receives his commission; transfers to 6th Gurkha Rifles of the Indian Army
1939 Commands troops in Middle East
1942 Commands British retreat from Burma
1944 March–September, holds off Japanese attacks on Imphal and Kohima
1945 January; leads British advance into Burma; March, captures Mandalay; 2 May, fall of Rangoon; victory in Burma.
1953–1960 Governor General of Australia
1970 Dies in London

'The finest general the Second World War has produced'

LORD LOUIS MOUNTBATTEN ON SLIM

had cut the main railway route south to Meiktila. Slim entered Rangoon on 2 May, prompting Lord Louis Mountbatten to remark that: 'Slim is the finest general the Second World War has produced'.

As the Fourteenth continued to mop up Japanese resistance in Burma, and to prepare itself for further fighting elsewhere, the atomic bombs on Hiroshima and Nagasaki brought the surrender of the Japanese. In the chaotic jubilation that followed the end of six years of war, Slim's superhuman efforts in the jungles of Burma slipped from the public awareness, overshadowed by events in Europe and the Pacific, and the Fourteenth became the 'Forgotten' once more. Slim went on to become Montgomery's successor as Chief of the Imperial General Staff in 1948, was promoted to Field Marshal, and decorated with the CBE and the KCB. He served as Governor General of Australia from 1953 to 1960, when he was created a viscount. General Slim died in London on 14 December, 1970.

'UNCLE BILL' IN BURMA

■ *On his arrival in Burma, Slim realized that the common image of the Japanese soldier as 'indestructible' was damaging in the extreme to Allied morale. He at once set about rebuilding morale amongst the troops, giving them proper jungle training and a constant succession of pep talks. The measure of success enjoyed by XV Corps in their incursion into the Arakan in December 1943, coupled with the activities of Orde Wingate's Chindits behind Japanese lines, brought home to the Allies the fact that Japanese soldiers were much like any others, and could be taken on and defeated.*

■ *Much of Slim's success in rebuilding his troops into the Fourteenth Army stems from his own character. A down-to-earth, approachable man, 'Uncle Bill', as he became known throughout the Fourteenth, inspired not only great respect but genuine affection from his subordinate commanders and men, in a way that perhaps no other commander since the days of Nelson and Wellington had achieved.*

DWIGHT D. EISENHOWER

Dwight D. ('Ike') Eisenhower (1890–1969) was a professional soldier who began World War II a major and ended it as commander of the greatest amphibious operation in history with four million men under his command. He was later US President for eight years from 1953 to 1961.

BORN DAVID DWIGHT EISENHOWER (he later reversed the names) in Denison, Texas, this most famous son of Kansas was always set for a career in the military. A Swiss-German Protestant by descent, Eisenhower would epitomize the unglamorous virtues of modesty and meticulousness. Of the 164 members of his 1915 class at West Point, 59 would become generals, a record never surpassed. Eisenhower graduated 61st and began an unspectacular career, training troops in World War I and then serving in the obscurity of the Panama Canal Zone.

In 1925–26, however, he graduated first in a class of 275 at the Command and General Staff School at Fort Leavenworth. Administrative ability then took Eisenhower via the War College, the Office of Assistant Secretary of War and the Army Industrial College to become aide to General Douglas MacArthur in creating an army for the Philippines. Within a year of Pearl Harbor, Eisenhower had been recalled to Washington and was commanding an Allied invasion of North Africa, followed by equally successful operations in Sicily, Italy and Normandy.

Eisenhower helped General Marshall to draft a strategy for victory, and it fell to him to implement it. He accepted the surrender of the German army at Rheims on VE Day, commanded the occupation of the defeated foe and presiding over the unification of the US armed forces, he then retired to become President of Columbia University.

Declining presidential nomination in 1948, Eisenhower returned to service as European commander of NATO forces (1950–52) before accepting the Republican ticket in 1952 to win decisively over Adlai Stevenson. Eisenhower's first presidency matched America's yearning for normality after the radicalism of the Roosevelt era, the strains of war and the uncertainties of an unexpectedly fragile peace. The nation and its leader enjoyed prosperity and golf. Eisenhower successfully disengaged US forces from Korea, side-stepped the anti-Communist antics of Senator McCarthy and dutifully enforced the desegregation of schools. Reactive rather than proactive in foreign policy, he committed the US to resist the spread of Communism into South Vietnam and pressured the UK into abandoning its military intervention in Egypt. Re-elected in 1956 by the largest popular vote in US electoral history, Eisenhower supported the Lebanese government against internal rebellion but failed to achieve any significant improvement in relations with the USSR.

A telling cartoon of the day depicted Eisenhower asking his Cabinet what the administration should refrain from doing that day. Subsequent historians were to castigate the thirty-fourth president's tenure of office as an era of drift, indecisiveness and lost opportunities. The bravura panache of the following Kennedy administration perhaps made such comparisons irresistible. Despite the image of bridge-playing insouciance, however, Eisenhower

CHRONOLOGY

1890 Born in Denison, Texas, 14 October
1909–15 West Point
1917–19 Commands tank training centre
1933–35 Aide to General Douglas MacArthur
1941 Assigned to prepare for Allied invasion of Europe
1942 Commands Allied invasion of North Africa
1943 Commands Allied invasions of Sicily and Italy
1944 Appointed Supreme Commander of Allied Expeditionary Force to invade France
1945 War ends in Europe
1953–61 US President
1969 Dies in Washington, DC, 28 March

'I hate war as only a soldier who has lived it can'

put in long hours and enjoyed the exercise of power without needing to parade it before the public. Just as he had successfully managed the egomania of wartime subordinates like Patton and Montgomery, Eisenhower worked effectively with a Congress under Democrat control to promote moderate social reform.

By his caution he used the prestige of a war-winning general to de-escalate tensions abroad. Emollience and patience are qualities not normally associated with the military but they served Eisenhower well. Far more subtle than his critics ever realized, he distrusted any show of brilliance because it created distrust in others. Eisenhower, who had never seen battlefield action in person, managed to wage eight years of peace at the height of the Cold War. A 1962 poll of presidential historians rated him twentieth, at the bottom end of the 'average' cohort. By 1995 he was rated ninth, his highest score being for – character.

The Quiet Man

■ *Eisenhower was appointed Supreme Commander of the Allied Expeditionary Forces for the invasion of France on 24 December 1943. Less than six months later, on 6 June 1944, he sent a million men in some 4,000 ships across the Channel to Normandy in the biggest amphibious landing in history.*

■ *By 25 August the Allies had liberated Paris, and, after reversing a fierce German counter-attack in the Ardennes in December, Allied troops crossed the Rhine on 7 March 1945. On 7 May Admiral Karl Doenitz surrendered all German forces to the Allies.*

■ *It was Harry S. Truman who observed that it was surprising how much could be achieved in politics if one was willing to let someone else take the credit. Few followed this maxim more successfully than Dwight D. Eisenhower.*

Erwin Rommel

Field Marshal Erwin Rommel (1891–1944) was a popular and able German commander, noted for his desert victories in North Africa. One of the most admired generals of World War II, he was forced to commit suicide after being implicated in the failed plot to assassinate Hitler.

THE SON OF A SCHOOLMASTER far removed from the traditional Prussian officer class, Rommel entered the army as an infantry officer cadet in 1910. He won the Iron Cross twice for bravery in the 1914–18 War. As a battalion commander in 1917, he led 200 men on an attack high in the Italian Alps to capture the mountain stronghold of Caporetto, taking 9,000 prisoners. The assault was a bold display of *Stosstruppen* (shock troop) tactics.

After the war, Rommel became an army instructor at the Infantry School in Dresden, where he further developed his theories on the supremacy of mobility and speed, which he later published as a textbook – *Infanterie Angriffe* (Infantry Attacks). The book was praised at home, notably by Adolf Hitler, and widely read in foreign armies. Promoted lieutenant colonel in 1935, Rommel took command of an Alpine battalion, and in 1938 he was in charge of the War Academy in Wiener Neustadt, near Vienna. As one of Germany's most decorated officers, he was selected by Hitler to command the battalion responsible for his safety during the march into the Sudetenland, one of Hitler's final land grabs before the outbreak of the 1939–45 War. Rommel was a major general on Hitler's staff during the blitzkrieg on Poland in 1939, and afterwards Hitler asked him to pick his command. He chose the 7th Panzer Division.

The panzer divisions spearheaded Germany's attack on France and Belgium in May and June 1940, with their tanks rapidly outflanking the Maginot line and punching holes in the French defences. Rommel was in the forefront of the push; his 7th became known as the 'Ghost Division' because it would appear out of nowhere. Rommel took more than 100,000 captives but he was chivalrous with his prisoners.

In February 1941, he was appointed to command German troops in Libya, the Afrika Korps. North Africa was essentially a sideshow to the conflict, but with continental Europe firmly in the hands of the Axis powers the desert became a major battlefield. For twenty-five months Rommel led a joint German–Italian campaign in the deserts of North Africa, and it was there that he gained his formidable reputation as the great 'Desert Fox'. The desert suited Rommel's appetite for speed, surprise and action. He immediately went on the offensive and pushed the British all the way back to the Egyptian border. For two years he had only three German divisions to fight everything that the British, and Americans in Tunisia, could throw at him. He saw off a succession of British commanders, all brought home in disgrace by Churchill. One of them, General Auckinleck, complained in a memo: 'There is a real danger that our friend Rommel is becoming some kind of a magician or bogeyman to our troops who are talking far too much about him.' Rommel added to his aura by pulling off victories against the odds. He was the master of surprise attacks. Whenever he appeared on the battlefield, wearing his trademark sun and sand goggles, he inspired. He was eventually overwhelmed by sheer numbers; Montgomery fielded 230,600 men at El Alamein to

Chronology

1891 Born at Heidenheim, Württemberg, 15 November

1910 Officer cadet in 124th Württemberg Infantry

1917 Leads raid on Caporetto, awarded *Pour Le Mérite*, Germany's highest decoration for valour

1937 Publishes *Infanterie Angriffe*

1940 Commands 7th Panzer Division in France

1941–43 Command of Afrika Korps

1944 Oversees the defences of Normandy

1944 Takes his own life at Herrlingen, near Ulm, 14 October

The Bomb Plot

- *Rommel, a professional soldier, was not directly involved in the plot to assassinate Hitler. But, as it looked increasingly likely that the war was lost, some of his friends had persuaded him that it was his duty to take over as head of state and sue for peace, after Hitler had been overthrown.*
- *Rommel was not informed that the plotters intended to kill Hitler, and he probably would not have agreed. He did not accept the idea of murder for political ends, and he had invariably ignored any execution orders given by Hitler.*
- *He agreed to suicide, avoiding a public trial, in exchange for an undertaking that his wife and son would be looked after.*

The North African desert ideally suited Rommel's taste for speed, surprise and action

Rommel's 80,000. The British also had air and armour superiority, and better supplies.

Promoted field marshal, Rommel returned to Europe, had a spell on Hitler's staff and was then given a command in France with a brief to shore up the coastal defences for an Allied invasion. He understood from the outset that the war would be lost if the enemy established bridgeheads beyond the beaches, and that it was therefore imperative to keep a strong mobile force in reserve for counter-attack. His advice was ignored and, a few days after he took over, the Allies landed in Normandy. On 17 July 1944, just five weeks into the job, his car was attacked and destroyed by an RAF fighter. Rommel suffered a fractured skull and a wound to the eye. Three days later, on 20 July, Hitler survived a bomb blast at his army bunker in Prussia. Rommel was implicated, and on 14 October two senior generals arrived at his house and confronted him with the evidence – and a capsule of poison. Rommel, a hero of the Third Reich, was given a state funeral with full military honours.

Moses

Moses, a Hebrew prophet who lived around the fourteenth and thirteenth centuries BC, comes down the ages through biblical story and tradition as lawgiver, liberator and leader of the Jewish people, and a great patriarch who is also venerated by Islam and Christianity.

THE BIBLE ACCOUNTS place Moses in Egypt at the time of the Pharaohs Seti (reigned 1318–1304 BC) and Ramesses II (1304–1237 BC). He belonged to a small Semitic tribe, known to the Egyptians as the Habiru, who were living in servitude or slavery. Just before the birth of Moses, the Pharaoh had ordered the murder of all Hebrew males; Moses escaped death because his mother placed him in a papyrus basket on the River Nile. He was found and brought up in court by Pharaoh's daughter. When he was an adult, he murdered an Egyptian slave master, and fled to live as a shepherd in Arabia, where he married.

Returning to Egypt at the command of Yahweh, the God of the Hebrews, who had appeared to him in a 'burning bush', Moses sought to persuade the Pharaoh to release the Hebrew people from their bondage. The Pharaoh eventually relented after a series of disasters afflicted Egypt; the Nile turned blood red, and many died in plagues and floods. Moses led several thousands of 'his people' out of Egypt over a stretch of water, which miraculously parted for them, only to close again to engulf the Pharaoh's pursuing army.

When the Hebrews reached the Sinai Peninsula, Moses ascended a mountain – identified today as Mount Sinai – where he spent forty days in prayer. He came down with two tablets of stone on which were inscribed the Ten Commandments, thereafter the fundamental laws of the Jewish people. Jews, and many others, hold that the Commandments were given directly to Moses by Yahweh.

Moses led his people and laid down their laws for another forty 'biblical' years – enduring many hardships on a long and arduous journey through the wilderness and desert, until at last they came to the borders of Canaan, the Promised Land, now modern Israel. Moses never got there, but he died within sight of it, on top of Mount Pisgah.

Chronology (Dates Unknown)

- Σ Born Goshen, ancient Egypt, late fourteenth century BC
- Σ Brought up by daughter of Pharaoh
- Σ Flees Egypt after murdering an Egyptian overlord
- Σ Lives as a shepherd in Arabia
- Σ Returns to Egypt to rescue the Hebrews
- Σ Leads the Hebrews out of Egypt through the Red Sea
- Σ Promulgates the Ten Commandments in Sinai
- Σ Leads Hebrews through the wilderness and desert
- Σ Dies on Mount Pisgah (now in Jordan) in sight of Canaan, the Promised Land

Written Records

- *Four books of the Bible – Exodus, Leviticus, Numbers and Deuteronomy – are practically the only sources for the life of Moses. Very few scholars today take the stories of the Bible as straightforward factual narrative, yet many would agree that there is some form of transcending truth in them.*
- *Archaeological evidence corroborates much of the Bible after the Jewish settlement of Canaan but does little to underpin the epic story of Moses. Although it was claimed that he kept written records, there is little evidence to support the tradition that he was the actual author of the Torah (Law), also called the Pentateuch, or the first five books of the Bible.*
- *Moses, however, was an Egyptian name and the events described in Exodus correspond with a period of upheaval and turmoil in Egypt in the early thirteenth century BC.*
- *Jews mark the night of the exodus from Egypt, in which their ancestors prepared to depart in advance of the threatened slaughter of all first-born, by their annual feast of Pasch or Passover.*

Many believers hold that the Ten Commandments were given to Moses directly by God

BUDDHA

In India in the sixth century BC Siddhartha Gautama gained enlightenment to become the Buddha ('Enlightened One'), founding the religion and philosophy of Buddhism that had a profound impact on Oriental civilization and subsequently spread to the rest of the world.

ALL THE SURVIVING ACCOUNTS of his life were written by his followers many years after his death, so it is sometimes difficult to unweave the myths and legends from the historical facts. Buddha was born Siddhartha Gautama in Lumbini in Nepal among the ruling class of a people called the Sakyas. He would become known as Sakyamuni, the sage of the Sakyas. At his birth it was predicted that he would grew up to be a world ruler but it was not clear whether this would be political or spiritual. Legend says that the birth was miraculous. His mother Mahamaya dreamed that the Buddha-to-be entered her womb as a white elephant. His father Suddhodana was a ruler, and the young Siddhartha grew up in luxury, was married and had a son. Struck by four sights – a very old man, a sick person, a corpse being taken to the burning-grounds, and a holy beggar who seemed to have found contentment – he changed his princely clothes for ragged garments and suddenly and secretly left his wife and baby to live an austere life with ascetics. This decision, known in Buddhism as the Great Renunciation, is regarded by Buddhists as a turning point in history.

For almost six years he strove to achieve enlightenment through the strictest austerities that virtually emaciated him, but he found neither peace of mind nor enlightenment and so went his own way, eventually sitting in meditation under a sacred fig tree or pipal at Bodh Gaya, which is now in the state of Bihar. Here he was tempted by Mara, the personification of carnal desire, but resisted. He then attained full insight into the nature of the world and of the way to overcome suffering and tribulation. He would now be called the Buddha, the Enlightened One.

CHRONOLOGY

Born in Lumbini, Nepal, probably in the fifth or sixth century BC, possibly 586 or 566 BC.
At the age of twenty-nine he made 'the Great Renunciation' of the world and its pleasures.
After practising and abandoning ascetic penances he meditated under the Bo tree, the 'tree of enlightenment', at Bodh Gaya, and at 35 became the Buddha – the Enlightened.
He preached his first sermon at the Deer Park at Sarnath outside Varanasi and devoted his life to teaching
He died at nearly eighty, at Kusinagara, the modern Kasia, in Gorakhpur district, India.

After attaining enlightenment, the Buddha returned to Benares (Varanasi), where he had left his companions at a deer park in Sarnath outside the city. Here he expounded his insight, the Sermon of the Turning of the Wheel, in which he set the wheel of dharma (the law of life) in motion. These companions became his first disciples and the core of the new order of the Sangha, the great monastic organization that would carry Buddhism around the world. A principal tenet of his doctrine was the Middle Way – a balance between the extremes of self-denial and self-indulgence. Yoga is the most important practice in the Buddha's teachings. Buddhism is above all a faith of meditation and self-training. It also encompasses complex psychological analysis and a profound philosophical system.

For the next forty-five years, the Buddha travelled and taught, establishing monastic communities that were open to all, regardless of their social status or caste. He visited the great new cities of North India, consorted with kings and princes, courtesans and

'Better than a thousand useless words is one word that gives peace'

Noble Truths

■ The doctrines of the Buddha gave a radical new interpretation to the religion of the time: everything is impermanent and interdependent. From this he enunciated the Four Noble Truths:
■ All life is permeated by suffering.
■ The cause of suffering is craving for existence.
■ This cause can be eliminated by following the Noble Eightfold Path, which is: Right Belief, Right Attitude, Right Speech, Right Bodily Action, Right Livelihood, Right Effort, Right Self-Awareness, Right Meditation.
■ The Path is a way between extremes.

artisans. Sri Lankan chronicles say he visited the island three times, including a journey to the peak of Sumanakata, later called Adam's Peak, where he left a huge footprint that became the focus of the most important pilgrimage on Sri Lanka.

The death of the Buddha at the age of eighty was accompanied by earthquakes, showers of flowers and other heavenly and earthly portents, according to Buddhist teaching.

Buddha is believed to have passed through a great number of existences to prepare for his final life. The legends of these lives are the famous Jataka tales which were the inspiration for many ancient sculptures, paintings and literary works in Buddhist countries. The three Dhyani Buddhas who preceded Gautama, and a future Buddha called Maitreya, have been the subject of many statues as far afield as in the caves at Dunhuang on the edge of the Gobi Desert. Buddha is commonly shown in one of three yogic attitudes: sitting cross-legged, either with both hands raised in the preaching posture or with his hands together in deep meditation, or with one hand pointing to the earth.

The life and teachings of Buddha laid the foundations for the first world religion to spread beyond the society in which it was born. Buddhism reached its peak in India in the fifth century AD, and filtered along the Silk Road to China and Japan, and by sea to Sri Lanka and Southeast Asia, to become the most widespread religion in Asia. Buddhist missionaries travelled to Egypt and Rome and may have inspired early Christian hermits who practised asceticism in the deserts. In modern times Buddhism has become popular in Europe and America, and it is the fastest-expanding religion in the world.

Jesus of Nazareth

Some 2,000 years after the birth of Jesus of Nazareth (died AD 30), a third of the world's population, two billion people, count themselves Christians and are thus his followers; yet Jesus achieved no visible worldly success, and said simply: 'Follow me.' Most Christians believe he was the incarnate son of God, born of a virgin, and that he rose from the dead – beliefs that have shaped two millennia of world history.

THE PRIMARY SOURCES for the historical life of Jesus are the Gospel accounts and letters of St Paul, written in the main by those who had known him or his disciples, and brief references by the Roman historians Tacitus, Suetonius and Josephus. The theological writings about Jesus, by contrast, are abundant.

Jesus was born near the end of the reign of Herod the Great (37–4 BC), in Bethlehem, near Jerusalem, and grew up in Nazareth, in Galilee. His parents were Mary and Joseph, a carpenter, and he had three named brothers and some sisters. There is an eighteen-year gap in all the narratives between his childhood and the time when, aged about thirty, Jesus began his ministry by being baptized in the River Jordan by a prophet named John, who drew large crowds before he was arrested and executed.

Jesus started his mission in Galilee with his headquarters at Capernaum. His public life may have lasted less than a year, and was certainly no more than three. He gathered around him twelve disciples and travelled as far north as Tyre and on one or two occasions south to Jerusalem. Drawing large crowds, Jesus preached the coming of God's Kingdom, stressing salvation and forgiveness, rather than judgement, and portrayed God as a loving father. He made use of parables, stories about everyday agricultural and village life, to illustrate spiritual and moral truths and frequently used paradox – such as, 'the last shall come first'. He also healed the sick in body and mind with apparently miraculous cures. Jesus seemed to prefer to associate with the poor, outcasts and prostitutes, even eating with them, and this made him ritually impure in terms of Jewish law. Jesus, as a Jew,

Chronology

6-4 BC	Born in Bethlehem
AD 24	Baptized in the River Jordan by John the Baptist
AD 24	Begins to gather disciples around him: becomes itinerant preacher and teacher
AD 30	Arrested by Jewish authorities and charged with blasphemy: condemned to death. Sentence confirmed by Pilate: Jesus is crucified, outside Jerusalem

The Growth of Christianity

■ *On Jesus' death, his followers were only a tiny Jewish sect, one of many, and yet within fifty years this had grown into a religion with a powerful following. A lot was due to Paul of Tarsus, a persecutor turned follower, who was perhaps the greatest influence on the early development of Christianity after Jesus himself.*

■ *A core of Jesus' teaching is the Sermon on the Mount, the Beatitudes, in which he blesses above all the poor and meek.*

■ *Of the four primary Gospel accounts of Jesus' life, those of Matthew, Mark and Luke are so similar that they can be read together in a work called a synopsis; hence they are known as the synoptic Gospels. John's account is markedly different.*

■ *The Universal Calendar is based on the birth of Jesus, although scholars today now believe he was in fact born between 6 and 4 BC.*

■ *The name Jesus comes from the Greek rendering of the Hebrew name Yehoshuah, or Joshua. Christ was not originally a name but a title that is derived from the Greek Christos, a translation of the Hebrew Mashiakh or Messiah, meaning the 'anointed one'.*

'Blessed are the meek, for they shall inherit the earth'

upheld the law, but he preferred to emphasize moral sincerity rather than the strict letter of the law, and he was defiant of petty observances.

Jesus thought he was close to God in a special way and appointed by Him to his mission; he sometimes referred to himself as the 'Son of Man'. Others saw him as a holy man, or reincarnation of a prophet such as Elijah, or a Davidic Messiah, either political or spiritual.

The Jewish authorities sought to get rid of Jesus. They resented his criticism and his claim to be directly validated by God. They feared that his talk of 'kingdom' might upset their Roman rulers, especially as Jesus came from Galilee, which was notorious for its rebels. So they decided on his death in the spring of AD 30.

Jesus spent his last evening with his disciples in Jerusalem at a supper, sharing bread and wine with them, the basis of the Christian Eucharist. After praying on the Mount of Olives he was captured, charged with blasphemy before a Jewish court and then condemned to death by the Roman governor, Pontius Pilate, as a false claimant to the Jewish throne. Jesus suffered the extreme penalty of crucifixion after scourging.

His body was removed from the cross and placed in the tomb of one of his wealthy and influential followers, Joseph of Arimathea. What happened next has challenged mankind ever since.

Jesus' disciples claimed he had risen from the dead; they had spent time with him and he had granted them miraculous powers. The resurrection, which implied hope for humanity of life after death, became the central compelling belief in a new religion that emerged in Jesus' name as Christianity and bore his teaching around the world.

Gregory the Great

Pope Gregory I (540–604), the first monk to sit on St Peter's throne, established papal power, sent missionaries to convert England to Christianity and had a profound influence on church teaching. One of the four original Doctors of the Church, he became known as Gregory the Great.

BORN INTO A PROSPEROUS and influential Roman family, Gregory was the son of a senator and the great-grandson of Pope Felix III. Rome was long past her glory, and the city was attacked twice in Gregory's childhood by Goths, disasters that left their mark on him. He entered state service and rose effortlessly to become Prefect of the City of Rome in 572, but a few years later he decided to abandon everything and become a monk. In 574, Gregory converted his family estate on the Caelian Hill in Rome into a Benedictine monastery, which he dedicated to St Andrew, gave away his Sicilian estates for similar foundations, and himself became a monk. Swapping his grand city robes for the cowl, he described the next few years as the happiest in his life.

But the simplicity and poverty he sought in the monastery soon eluded him; Gregory was ordained as one of the seven deacons of Rome and sent by Pope Pelagius II as his ambassador or nuncio to the Emperor Tiberius in Constantinople, ostensibly to obtain military aid against the Lombards who had invaded Italy. He maintained his monastic life as much as he could amid the splendours of the Byzantine court; he spent six years there and failed to elicit any help from the eastern empire. Rome, he concluded, would henceforth have to stand alone. He returned there in 585 and resumed his life at St Andrew's. Now a renowned teacher and writer, he attracted many followers. Following a year of great floods and plague in Rome, Pelagius II died in 590 and the Abbot of St Andrew's was elected Pope in his place. Again faced with the prospect of leaving his cloister, he accepted with deep reluctance. Gregory was consecrated at St Peter's on 3 September 590 and, battling ill health, he spent the remaining fourteen years of his life reforming the church and transforming the papacy.

On a temporal level, Gregory established the papacy as a leading power in Italy; he reorganized the vast papal estates and brought them under proper management, and used the profits and produce from them to finance charity for the citizens of Rome. He was revered for his charity and pastoral care. Pope Gregory also stepped into the vacuum left by weak government in Rome to negotiate peace with the Lombards, who had overrun much of Italy. His aim was to protect Rome at all costs, and to this end he was the first pope to exercise real temporal power.

With equal energy, Pope Gregory promoted the papacy as the supreme authority over the church – a primacy that it still exercises today. Gregory also introduced changes in the church liturgy and incorporated the Gregorian chant. He was a zealous missionary, sending his monks as far afield as Africa and England. From his reign forward, the papacy emerged as a significant force in church and European history.

Chronology

540	Born in Rome
572	Prefect of Rome
574	Converts his estate into monastery, becomes a monk
579	Papal ambassador to Constantinople
585	Returns to Rome
590	Becomes Pope
594	Prevents Lombard invasion
597	Sends Augustine to England
604	Dies in Rome, 12 March

Gregory's years spent as a simple monk were, he said, the happiest of his life

'Not Angles, But Angels'

■ *Gregory is said to have seen fair-headed English boys for sale in the slave market in Rome. When told they were English, he declared: 'Non Angli, sed angeli' (Not Angles, but angels). Soon afterwards, he dispatched forty of his monks, led by Augustine, to convert the English.*

■ *Gregory's letters and books, although not highly original, were hugely influential in the Middle Ages.*

■ *The plainsong of the Latin Church is called Gregorian chant in honour of Pope Gregory who fixed its eight component modes and collected some 3,000 melodies.*

■ *Gregory's* Moralia *(Morals on the Book of Job) discusses questions of church doctrine and discipline, the* Liber Pastoralis *(Pastoral Care) is a manual for bishops and preaching, and* Dialogues *is a collection of legends about saints.*

MUHAMMAD

Muhammad (570–632) was a holy prophet whose followers established Islam and the Islamic Empire on the basis of his teachings. He is the figurehead of one of the three great monotheistic religions, which today has millions of Muslim faithful all round the world.

MUHAMMAD WAS BORN around 570 in the oasis city of Mecca in western Arabia, and was soon orphaned. He belonged to an important Bedouin tribe, the Quraysh, one of the many nomadic peoples in the vast rocky mountainous desert of the Arabian Peninsula. In manhood, according to Muslim teaching, he was visited by the Angel Gabriel, while he was praying in a cave on Mount Hira outside Mecca. He was commanded to recite the first of many divine revelations that he would receive over the years. He then began preaching the message that there is but one Allah (God) and that He is just and will judge all men, for whom salvation is possible by following His will. Muhammad's simple but powerful message attracted followers, but incurred the hostility of the Meccan merchants whose business depended on their own indigenous pantheon of gods and goddesses, highest among them the black meteoric stone, the Ka'aba, which attracted many pilgrims. Muhammad's monotheism was seen as subversive, and Meccans persecuted his Islamic converts.

When Muhammad's position in Mecca became gravely endangered, he persuaded his followers to migrate to the desert oasis of Yathrib, a symbolic act of religious unity and intent. This marked the beginning of a new polity. For the first time in Arabia, members of a community were bound together not by the traditional ties of clan and tribe but by their shared belief of one true God, bestowed upon them by the Prophet. Here Muhammad started to organize a society, with practical statements about food, drink, marriage and war – in effect laying the foundations of Islamic civilization. Later Muslims recognized the event's seminal importance by designating it as the first year of their new era by the Hijra calendar. Yathrib was renamed Medina, coming to mean 'the city of the Prophet', in Muhammad's honour.

CHRONOLOGY

570	Born in Mecca
610	Muhammad visited by Angel Gabriel
622	Migration of Muslims to Medina
624	Victory at the battle of Badr
627	Defence of Medina
630	Surrender of Mecca to Islamic forces
632	Muhammad dies

Not content with the expulsion of Muslim compatriots, the Meccans sent a powerful army against the Prophet, who opposed them at Badr in 624. There, the Muslims under the leadership of Muhammad conquered an army three times the size of their own. In the following year, the Meccans launched an even greater attack upon Medina and were once again defeated in a bloody encounter at Uhud.

In 627, a final attack was launched by an alliance of Meccans and Jews from Medina under the leadership of Ka'b ibn Al-Ashraf. With astute diplomacy, the Prophet fractured the entente, and the different enemy groups retired one after the other. Once again, Muhammad defied all odds through political skill and the loyalty of his fellow Muslims, and ensured the survival of the nascent core of Islam. Once peace was secured, the Prophet launched an intensive programme to spread the word of Islam by addressing missionary letters to the foreign rulers of Byzantium, Persia and Abyssinia.

In 628, Muhammad finally negotiated a truce with the Meccans and in the following year returned there on a pilgrimage (Hajj). The murder of one of his followers provoked him to attack the city, which soon surrendered. Muhammad acted generously, demanding only that the pagan idols around the Ka'aba be destroyed. As a result, his prestige grew immediately as embassies from all over Arabia came to Medina to submit to him. In

Yathrib was renamed Medina, 'the coming of the Prophet', in Muhammad's honour

all of these 'wars' extending over a period of ten years, Islamic historians maintain that non-Muslims lost only 250 men on the battlefield and that the Muslim losses were even less. Muhammad created a well-disciplined state out of existent chaos and left a new constitution of law which dispensed impartial justice in which even non-Muslim inhabitants equally enjoyed complete juridical and cultural autonomy

The Prophet's extraordinary life and career were cut short by his sudden death on 8 June 632, aged about 60, less than a decade after he had set off to the oasis of Yithrab with his small band of dedicated followers.

A Mortal Man

- *Muslims revere Muhammad as the embodiment of the perfect believer and take his actions and sayings as an example of ideal conduct. Unlike Jesus, who Christians believe was the son of God, Muhammad was a mortal.*
- *Muhammad's earliest Arabic biographer, Ibn Ishaq, did not write about him until a century after his death. Some of the details of his early life are therefore conjectural.*
- *The Koran, also written after his death, is a collection of the Prophet's recitations, taken down by his entourage. Muhammad saw himself as a mouthpiece of God, and through him, he said, God spoke his final message to mankind. In addition to its universal religious significance, the Koran is also a crucial document of the Arabic language and of Arabic civilization.*
- *The migration (Hijra) to the oasis of Yathrib marks the birth of the Muslim calendar.*
- *The word Islam means submission or surrender.*

St Benedict

Benedict of Nursia (c480–c547) founded the Benedictine order and is regarded as the father of Western monasticism. His Rule book is an ordered routine of worship, prayer and labour, by which his followers still live today some 1,500 years later in many communities around the world.

BORN INTO A DISTINGUISHED FAMILY in Nursia, in central Italy, Benedict spent his youth studying in Rome during its final years as an imperial city. Little is known for certain about his life, except his achievement. Pope Gregory I wrote a biography, but it has no dates and is peppered with accounts of miraculous events.

Tradition says that Benedict and his twin sister, Scholastica, were the children of Entropius and Abundantia. Appalled by the degeneracy of Rome, Benedict went to live in a cave as a hermit at Subiaco, some forty miles east of the city, in the foothills of the Abruzzi Mountains. He spent three years there in solitude and, after a failed stint as abbot of a community in Vicovaro, he began to gather his own disciples, whom he organized into twelve communities of twelve monks, each led by a dean. In time, the Roman aristocracy brought their sons to him to be educated. Two of them, Maurus and Placid, became his best-known followers.

In 529, Benedict moved south to Monte Cassino, halfway between Rome and Naples, where he brought together the majority of his monks and established one of Europe's greatest monasteries. Here also he wrote his Rule. His sister Scholastica set up a community nearby. Monte Cassino grew up at a time of upheaval, famine, plague and war; Italy was invaded by Lombards, and by Byzantine armies trying to reclaim the West for Constantinople, and Benedict witnessed the extinction of the Roman Empire. A representative of the new order, the Gothic King Totila, came to visit him at Monte Cassino.

Chronology

c480	Born in Nursia
c494	Sent to study in Rome
c510	Elected Abbot of Vicovaro
c520	Founds the monastery of Subiaco
529	Establishes monastery at Monte Cassino
536	Benedict sends Placid to found a monastery at Messina
543	Gothic King Totila visits Benedict at Monte Cassino. Death of Scholastica
c547	Benedict dies at Monte Cassino

In his *Rule*, Benedict stressed communal living and physical labour. A short Latin text with a prologue and seventy-three chapters, the Rule was the first widely propagated codification of communal monastic living in the West. Benedict called it 'a little rule for beginners'. It brought about a great transformation – replacing the ascetic eremitical individualism of traditional monasticism with a powerful new communal endeavour. Its supreme achievement was to lay down clear instructions for the government of the community and the powers and duties of the abbot. The *Rule* was, moreover, simple and not too harsh; it was within reach of ordinary men. Very quickly Benedictine monasteries appeared everywhere in the West; they provided a well-spring of learning that would carry the church into the Middle Ages and produce the missionaries who would convert pagan England and Germany.

In 529 Benedict came to Monte Cassino, where he founded one of Europe's great monasteries

The Rule of St Benedict

■ The Rule of St Benedict *is a seminal document of Western Christianity and therefore of Western civilization. It borrowed from some lesser-known antecedents, particularly from John Cassian, and formed the basis of all the great monastic orders which sprang up in Europe over the ensuing centuries.*

■ *The* Rule *was not unduly austere. Even allowing for night offices, the monks had unbroken sleep of between seven and a half and eight hours, and the religious duties of the day would normally have taken four to five hours, except on Sundays when they would have been more. The rest of the monk's time was divided between work (six hours) and reading (four hours), probably of the Bible and the Church Fathers. The work at that time would usually have been in the fields, but in any case whatever was most useful to the community. All property was shared by the community, which in turn set out to be self-sufficient.*

■ *The Benedictine tradition of teaching was established from the outset, and continues in England with a number of Benedictine schools, such as Ampleforth, Downside and Worth.*

St Francis of Assisi

St Francis of Assisi (c1181–1226) was the son of a rich merchant who revolutionized the Christian Church in the early Middle Ages, starting a movement based on poverty. His charismatic personality attracted thousands of followers to the order he founded, the Franciscans.

BORN GIOVANNI Francesco Bernardone to a wealthy cloth merchant of Assisi in Umbria, Francis appears to have had little education, and as a young man he was well known among the youth of Assisi for sporting smart clothes, singing and partying. But his carefree youth came to an abrupt end. He was taken prisoner fighting in a battle against the nearby town of Perugia, and held captive for more than a year. In captivity, he fell seriously ill and began to rethink his life.

He returned to Assisi in 1205 a changed man. Soon afterwards he had a vision in the crumbling chapel of San Damiano, in the fields below Assisi, when Christ ordered him to repair the building – a call he later understood as a summons to rebuild the Christian Church. Francis instantly sold bales of cloth from his father's shop to raise funds to restore the building. His father was so angered by this impulsive act that he forced Francis to give up his inheritance, and took him to the local bishop. Francis reacted, in turn, by stripping naked and vowing to serve his 'heavenly' Father. He spent the next three years working among lepers and rebuilding ruined churches.

In 1208, words from St Matthew's gospel, 10:5–14, inspired Francis with a vocation to preach penance, love and peace, and to give up all possessions; he determined to go out into the world and to imitate as best he could the life of Christ. Francis gathered twelve companions, and he wrote a simple rule for them; they became the First Order of Friars Minor. The local Benedictines gave them the small oratory chapel of the Porziuncola in the valley near Assisi to use as their first friary. The friars, who went out in pairs, preaching, singing, working and begging, made a huge impact wherever they went. After some reluctance, Pope Innocent III sanctioned the order in 1210, and in 1212 Francis assisted a young woman from Assisi, Clare, who had followed him and given up her wealth and become a nun, to establish the Second Franciscan Order of the Poor Ladies (Poor Clares).

Chronology

c1181	Born in Assisi, Italy
1202	Taken prisoner in local war between Assisi and nearby town of Perugia
1205	Has a vision and begins repairing churches
1208	Starts preaching; gathers twelve friars around him – this was the First Order
1210	Franciscans recognized by Pope Innocent III
1212	'Poor Clares' – order for women – established
1212–20	Missionary work in Italy, Spain, Egypt, and possibly the Holy Land
1223	Begins the tradition of the Christmas crib
1224	Receives the stigmata – five wounds of Christ
1225	Composes the Canticle of the Creatures
1226	Dies in Assisi, 3 October
1228	Canonized by Pope Gregory IX, 16 July

Wherever Francis travelled, he attracted a popular following. Stories tell of him preaching to the sparrows, and ordering a fierce and hungry wolf in Gubbio to stop terrorizing the locals. In 1217, he divided the Friars Minor into provinces and world-wide missions. His missionary zeal took him to Spain, where he tried to convert Moors, and to Egypt, where he preached to the Sultan al-Kamil. There is no evidence that he reached the Holy Land, but his obsession with it led the Franciscans to obtain the right – which continues still – for their friars to be guardians of the 'holy places'. On his return to Italy in 1220 he attended the assembly at the Porziuncola called the Chapter of Mats with 5,000 friars. The movement had grown, and in his absence there had been disagreements among the friars. Francis stepped down from the day-to-day running of the order, and appointed a new head. But he remained spiritual leader, and in

'Where there is hatred, let me sow peace'

AN ASCETIC LIFE

■ *St Francis became known as Il Poverello (little pauper). He expressed his love of nature in the* Canticle of the Creatures *in which the sun, the stars, animals, birds and even death are referred to as brothers and sisters.*

■ *St Francis is one of the patron saints of Italy together with St Catherine of Siena.*

■ *Christmas was one of St Francis's favourite feasts. In 1223, he recreated the stable at Bethlehem, so introducing the popular concept of the Christmas crib.*

■ *'Lord, make me an instrument of your peace; where there is hatred let me sow peace, where there is injury, pardon, where there is doubt faith...' from a prayer attributed to St Francis.*

1221 he founded a Third Order (Tertiary) of lay Franciscans.

In 1224, he received the stigmata – the five wounds of the crucified Christ – after experiencing a vision when meditating at the end of a forty-day fast. He did his utmost to conceal the marks. Though now ill and increasingly blind, Francis continued preaching and writing, and in 1225 he composed the *Canticle of the Creatures*, in which the elements of nature are praised as brothers and sisters. He died aged forty-four in his little hut at the Porziuncola praising 'Sister Death', and was canonized less than two years later in 1228. His body was secretly reburied in the lower chapel of the great church dedicated to St Francis at Assisi in 1230.

MARTIN LUTHER

Martin Luther (1483–1546) was a German theologian and religious reformer, who initiated the Protestant Reformation which split the Western Christian Church and changed the course of European and world history.

MARTIN LUTHER, the son of a prosperous copper miner, studied at Erfurt University in 1501–05. Intending to become a lawyer, he changed his mind and entered the Augustinian monastery in Erfurt. He made his profession as a monk in 1505 and was ordained to the priesthood in 1507. A precocious scholar, he was sent to study theology and teach at the new University of Wittenberg, where, after a spell back at Erfurt, he took his doctorate and became Professor of Theology.

During a visit to Rome in 1510, Luther was shocked by what he saw as the depravity and worldliness of the clergy and papacy. He was particularly incensed by the sale of indulgences – paper certificates guaranteeing 'time off' from punishment after death – and he started fulminating against Rome. His fury came to the boil in 1517 when a friar, Johann Tetzel, began peddling indulgences in Germany. On 31 October, Luther 'nailed' a sheet of Ninety-Five Theses, or arguments against indulgences, to the door of Wittenberg Castle church. Written in Latin, they were hastily translated into German and, with the aid of the new technology of printing, they spread like an earthquake.

Challenged, condemned and formally excommunicated by the church authorities in January 1521, Luther fired back with his pen, producing the primary treatises of what would become known as Lutheranism – 'Address to the Christian Nobility of the German Nation', 'A Prelude Concerning the Babylonian Captivity of the Church', 'Of the Freedom of a Christian Man'. Fortunate in enjoying the protection of Frederick of Saxony, Luther also later translated the New Testament from the original Greek into German, as he did eventually the entire Old Testament.

The papal sanction against him, and his defiance, split Germany. In 1521, he was summoned under safe conduct by the Emperor Charles V before the Imperial Diet of Worms, where, unyielding, he articulated his belief in justification by faith, which struck at the very root of traditional church teaching.

'I am overcome by the Scriptures I have quoted; my conscience is captive to God's Word. I cannot and will not revoke anything, for to act against conscience is neither safe nor honest,' Luther declared. He is popularly supposed to have added: 'Here I stand. I can do no other.'

Luther was now outlawed, and Germany erupted in political revolt; the Imperial Knights rebelled in 1522–25, and an uprising in the Black Forest area in 1524 sparked a bloody two-year Peasants' War. Horrified at the excesses that were now committed in his name, Luther published an appeal 'Against the Murderous and Thieving Hordes of Peasants', and the peasant rebels were brutally crushed. But his defiance against the established church continued to gather pace. In 1526, Luther's supporters persuaded the First Diet of Speier to

CHRONOLOGY

1483 Born in Eisleben, Germany, 10 November
1501 Enrols at Erfurt University
1505 Enters Augustinian monastery in Erfurt
1508 Studies theology at Wittenberg University
1510 Visits Rome as an Augustinian monk
1512 Appointed Theology Professor at Wittenberg
1517 'Nails' Ninety-Five Theses to Wittenberg Castle church
1521 Diet of Worms
1524–25 Peasants' Revolt
1525 Luther leaves monastery and marries
1534 The first complete Bible translated by Luther is printed and distributed
1546 Dies in Eisleben, 18 February

'I am overcome by the Scriptures I have quoted; my conscience is captive to God's Word. Here I stand: I can do no other'

accept the revolutionary principle that the ruler has the right to determine religion and, at the Second Diet of Speier in 1529, they formally lodged the 'Protest' which gave them their name. In 1530, they condensed their beliefs into the Confession of Augsburg – in effect the Protestant manifesto, which revealed radical new interpretations of such core matters as the Eucharist.

Lutheranism caught on in Germany, appealing to its independent-minded princes, and was quickly adopted in several states and in most northern cities, from Bremen to Riga. The Protestants, however, also quickly splintered into different sects, and Luther's own followers were sorely tested when he condoned the bigamous marriage of Philip of Hesse, and also when he wrote a violent polemic against Jews.

Luther, a former monk, married an ex-nun, Katharina von Bora, who ran his household, managed his finances and bore him six children, and to whom he wrote loving letters whenever he was away. A sick man for much of his life, and ill tempered as well, Luther died unexpectedly while visiting his native Eisleben.

Luther and Music

■ *Luther was known throughout Germany as the Nightingale of Wittenberg. He sang well, played the lute and wrote hymns, among the most enduring his paraphrase of Psalm 49, 'God is our refuge'. Luther established a strong musical tradition in his churches, with cantors, organists and choirs, thus helping to transform Germany into the most musically educated country in Europe.*

■ *Among Luther's friends and colleagues were Philip Melanchthon, translator and scholar and Hans Lufft, who printed his first complete Bible, which sold 100,000 copies. Luther encouraged the vernacular, and the Luther Bible was crucial to the development of the German language, serving to bring many disparate dialects together. It also led to a new sense of unity among German-speaking people.*

St Ignatius of Loyola

St Ignatius of Loyola (1491–1556) was the Spanish founder of the Society of Jesus, known as the Jesuits, which dispatched missionaries around the world. His order opened schools, colleges and universities, setting new standards for education.

IGNATIUS WAS BORN in 1491, the youngest of thirteen children, to a noble and wealthy family in the northern Spanish Basque province of Guipúzcoa. As a page to the treasurer of Castile he was used to court life, ladies, gambling and swordplay, until he became a soldier in 1517. In 1521 when the French were laying siege to Pamplona, Ignatius's life was transformed. He was critically wounded in both legs by a cannon ball, undergoing painful surgery without anaesthetics. While convalescing he was given books on the life of Christ and the saints, rather than his preferred stories of knights and chivalry. He resolved to follow the saints, and in 1522 he confessed his sins at the monastery of Montserrat, and then spent some months in a cave living austerely, meditating and writing. These notes eventually evolved into the handbook of the Jesuits, *The Spiritual Exercises* (published with papal approval in 1548) – an instruction manual on how to achieve spirituality.

Ignatius then set out for the Holy Land on a journey full of dangers and deprivations. He intended to emigrate there, but the Franciscans who were (and still are) in charge of the Christian holy places ordered him to leave, and he returned to Spain in 1524. When young he had not had a formal education and knew no Latin, but now he decided to study, first at the universities of Alcala and Salamanca, where he was regarded as a troublemaker by the Inquisition, and then in Paris, where he went in 1528. Here he worked hard at theology, philosophy and Latin, and influenced a small group of fellow students, including his compatriot, the future Saint Francis Xavier.

In Paris, Ignatius and his followers loosely bound themselves together with vows of poverty, chastity and obedience, but they had no intention of founding a new order. Ignatius travelled during these years to England, Italy and the Netherlands. After completing his studies, and while living on alms, Ignatius decided to become a priest. By 1537, most of his followers were also ordained. Ignatius had a mystical experience the following year, and in 1539 he gathered his companions in Rome to discuss their future as a community. As well as undertaking vows of poverty, chastity and obedience they now placed themselves under a superior general at the Pope's service and founded a new order, which received papal approval in 1540. As a reflection of his military experiences Ignatius suggested the title of Company of Jesus, but it was officially called the Society of Jesus. For fifteen years until his death Ignatius was superior general, guiding the order, teaching children and adults, writing the constitutions of the society and advising Jesuits world-wide through letters.

The Jesuits, guided by detailed instructions from Ignatius himself, launched missions to Portugal, Ireland, Germany, India and even Ethiopia. Jesuit theologians participated actively at the Council of Trent. The order is best known, is indeed renowned, for its work in education. Colleges were originally founded for new recruits to the order, but demand from secular authorities soon led to the

Chronology

1491	Born in Loyola, 24 December
1521	Wounded by cannon ball in both legs at siege of Pamplona
1522	Vows to devote his life to service of church
1528	While studying in Paris forms initial group of six followers
1537	Ordained priest
1540	Pope Paul III approves foundation of Company of Jesus
1556	Around 1,000 Jesuits with 100 houses in ten provinces at his death on 31 July
1622	Canonized

Following a mystical experience, Ignatius founded a new order, the Society of Jesus

The Jesuits

- *Ignatius said: 'I have never left the army: I have only been seconded to the service of God.'*
- *He also said: 'Give me a boy at the age of seven, and he will be mine for ever.'*
- *He was fully aware of the importance and influence of education, and wrote in 1551: 'From among those who are now merely students, in time some will depart to play diverse roles – one to preach, another to government of the land and the administration of justice, and others to other callings.'*
- *The term Jesuit was first used in 1544 as a term of reproach.*
- *The Jesuit motto is Ad Majorem Dei Gloriam – 'To the Greater Glory of God'.*

rapid expansion world-wide of Jesuit schools.

Ignatius died from a fever in Rome in 1556 before receiving the last sacraments and a papal blessing. He was beatified in 1609 and canonized in 1622. His body lies under the high altar of the great Jesuit church, the Gesú, in Rome.

John Calvin

John Calvin (1509–64) was a French theologian and Protestant reformer, whose austere, hard-working ethics shaped the destinies of countries as diverse as Scotland, Switzerland and the USA. He was the founder of the most widely influential branch of Protestantism.

BORN IN NOYON, French Picardy, in 1509, Calvin studied for the priesthood at colleges in Paris, and then switched to law, attending universities at Orléans and Bourges. He was converted to the new Protestant thinking after hearing a homily on the sovereignty of the Scriptures by the Rector of the Sorbonne, Nicholas Cop. He resigned his benefice in his native Noyon and fled to the more tolerant city of Basle. There in 1536, he published his major work *Institutio Christianae Religionis* (Institutes of the Christian Religion). This thrust him into the forefront as a Protestant thinker and preacher, and Calvin became a popular figure in the new church communities. On his way through Geneva in 1536 he was asked to help establish the Protestant church there, and he stayed two years, until voted out of the city. In 1538–41, Calvin was in Strasbourg, where he married the widow Idelette de Bure, and here he published the first of many commentaries on the Bible.

Calvin's theology was radical and gloomy, above all his belief in predestination, which flew in the face of Roman Catholic teaching that all sinners are capable of salvation, if they repented. Calvin saw mankind divided in advance into the damned and the elect; most are depraved, and beyond redemption; only the elect few are predestined by God for salvation. He also departed sharply from the traditional church in one other key respect; Calvin insisted on the separation of church and state.

On ethical matters, Calvin was ultra-puritan. He urged his followers to abstain from all pleasures and frivolity – songs, dancing, gambling, drinking, dalliance and even colourful clothes. Their life was to be marked by hard work, self-restraint, sobriety, thrift and godliness. Their sole source of uplift and guidance would be from daily reading of the Bible, and their only music the hymns they sang. Here were the voices of the founding fathers of British North America, and the basic code of the low churches of western Europe and specifically of the religion of Scotland, a country which in turn would send engineers, teachers and missionaries around the world to forge the British Empire.

In 1541 Calvin was invited back to Geneva, where he spent the rest of his life. He helped draft a new constitution for a self-governing state – a remarkable advance, as most of Europe was still under the sway of autocratic kings, princes and dukes. He never had a formal government position but, as the de facto city leader, he worked hard to improve schools and hospitals and encouraged thrift and industry. But there was a bleaker side to his rule – the pastors ruled Geneva like a presbytery; there was virtually no entertainment. In 1552 the City Council proclaimed Calvin's *Institutes* 'holy doctrine, against which no man might speak'. The Bible had become a code of law. Heresy, as well as adultery, was punishable by death, and Calvin personally sanctioned the burning in 1553 of at least one such dissenter, a Spaniard Michael Servetus. Dozens more were put to death in the ensuing years.

Calvin's sect spread from Geneva, the training ground of its new pastors and now the Protestant Rome, to France, the Netherlands, England, Scotland, Hungary and also Germany, where it challenged the more worldly creeds of the Lutherans.

Chronology

1509 Born in Noyon, 10 July
1536 Publishes Institutes of the Christian Religion
1536–38 Geneva
1538–41 Strasbourg, where he marries
1541 Takes control of Protestant Church in Geneva
1564 Dies in Geneva, 27 May

Calvin believed mankind was divided in advance into the damned and the elect, with the former far more numerous than the latter

A Prolific Writer

■ *Calvin's writings were his lasting contribution to the Protestant Church. He wrote hymns, an influential catechism, and commentaries on almost every book of the Bible. He was also a prolific correspondent, and some 4,271 letters survive, most on theological matters. Manuscripts of 2,300 sermons also survive. Calvin's* Institutes *remain the standard of orthodox Protestant belief in all the 'Reformed' churches.*

■ *The* New Advent Catholic *encyclopaedia describes Calvin as 'undoubtedly the greatest of the Protestant divines, and perhaps, after Saint Augustine, the most perseveringly followed by his disciples of any Western writer on theology'.*

■ *Calvin's wife, Idelette de Bure, bore him a son, who died almost as soon as he was born. Idelette herself died in 1549, and Calvin did not remarry.*

John Wesley

John Wesley (1703–91) was an Anglican theologian and evangelist preacher who together with his brother Charles, founded the world-wide Methodist Movement within the Church of England, a movement with over 70 million followers worldwide.

THE FIFTEENTH CHILD of a Nonconformist vicar, Wesley grew up in rural Lincolnshire at his father Samuel's rectory in Epworth, before being sent away to complete his education, first to Charterhouse School in London and, from 1720, to Christ Church College, Oxford. Decided on a career in the Church, Wesley became a deacon in 1725 and, following election as a Fellow of Lincoln College and after spending time assisting his father in Lincolnshire, he was ordained a priest in 1728.

Back at Oxford, Wesley joined his brother Charles and fourteen others in a religious group that was known derisively as the 'Methodists' because they had devised a spiritual method for study and devotion. Also called the Holy Club, the group practised austerity to such extremes – fasting, sleep deprivation, even prostrating themselves for hours on winter frost – that one member died. Under Wesley's leadership, the group took on a wider mission, and began visiting prisons and workhouses, distributing food, clothes and medicine.

But he was looking for something beyond Oxford and in 1735 he set out, with his brother, to be a missionary in the American colonies. He spent two years in Georgia, failing to make much headway in converting the native Indians and falling out with the local community after he was spurned by Sophia Hopkey, the niece of the chief magistrate of Savannah.

However, on his way to America Wesley had met with a sect of German Moravians and had been deeply impressed by their intense, personal religion. On his return to London, he continued to attend their meetings and it was during one of these that he had the great mystical experience, or religious awakening, that was to change his life. It was on Aldersgate Street, by one of the ancient Roman gateways to the City of London, on 24 May 1738, and Wesley recalled: 'I felt my heart strangely warmed. I felt that I did trust in Christ, Christ alone for salvation; and an assurance was given me that he had taken my sins, even mine, and saved me from the law of sin and death.'

Chronology

1703	Born in Epworth, Lincolnshire, 17 June
1714	Admitted to Charterhouse School, London
1720	Undergraduate at Christ Church, Oxford
1725	Ordained deacon
1726	Elected Fellow of Lincoln College
1728	Ordained priest
1735–37	Missionary in Georgia
1738	Aldersgate: 'I felt my heart strangely warmed'
1739	First Methodist Society formed in London
1744	First Methodist Conference
1784	Wesley ordains his first Methodist priests
1791	Dies at City Road, London, 2 March

He was then aged thirty-five, and from that point on he viewed his life as a mission to proclaim the good news that salvation was possible for every person through faith in Jesus Christ alone. For the next fifty-three years he travelled an estimated 240,000 miles around Britain on horseback and carriage and preached over 40,000 sermons – an average of fifteen a week.

Wesley and a group of followers formed the first Methodist Society in a shop in West Street, London, on 1 May 1739 and the movement quickly spread. At first Wesley sought to work inside the established Anglican churches, but progressively doors were closed him, and he was forced to preach in the open. This is what really gave impetus to Methodism. Open-air preaching was the most effective way of reaching large audiences, and it enabled him to take his mission

Wesley's mission was to proclaim that salvation was possible for everyone through Jesus Christ alone

to remoter areas of Britain that were off the Anglican map, notably Wales. People in the harsh rough-and-tumble of eighteenth-century Britain were attracted to his message of personal faith and the importance of inner religion, and communities sprang up all over the country and, with them, new places of worship. Within thirty-five years of his Aldersgate experience, there were 356 new Methodist chapels around the country. Wesley published rules for the Methodist societies in 1743 but did not effectively break with the Church of England until 1784, when he started to ordain his own priests. He was forced to do so, when the Bishop of London refused to ordain some of his preachers who were now serving in the newly independent United States.

TRAVELS WITH A BIBLE

■ *John Wesley was an impassioned preacher, and he played pitilessly on the emotions of his congregations, particularly when warning of the perils that awaited unrepentant sinners. He was fiercely anti-intellectual, believed in the devil and witches, advocated primitive medicine, and would open the Bible at random and obey whatever command he found.*

■ *History is silent as to whether he found the command in the Bible, but in 1751, Wesley married a widow with four children, Mary Vazeille. The marriage was not a success, however, and she left him, possibly on the grounds that she saw practically nothing of him. In addition to his constant and wide-ranging travels, Wesley found time to write or edit some 400 publications. On his death in 1791, he left behind a movement of about 70,000 members, which has grown today to some 70 million with Methodist churches in nearly every country in the world.*

Sri Ramakrishna

Sri Ramakrishna (1836–86) was one of the three great leaders of the Hindu revival in the nineteenth century and a holy man who preached the harmony of all religions – 'as many faiths, so many paths'. His followers founded the Ramakrishna order.

Originally called Gadadhar Chatterji, Ramakrishna was born in Bengal, the son of a poor, orthodox Brahman. In 1852, poverty forced him and his brother, Ramkumar, to move to Calcutta where they became priests at a temple dedicated to Kali, the Hindu Goddess of creation and destruction. Ramakrishna developed a passionate devotion to Kali whom he worshipped as the mother of the world and, after much perseverance, he began to have ecstatic visions in which he was overwhelmed by blissful light.

When he was 23, Ramakrishna was forced to marry a five-year-old child bride, Sarada Devi. The marriage was never consummated because he believed in celibacy, but she became one of his pupils and followers. Soon after the marriage, Ramakrishna left the temple to wander the countryside. He learned Tantrism, Vedanta, Yoga, and other religious techniques and began to see and preach the fusion of all religions, including Islam and Roman Catholicism. In his trances, he had visions of Muhammad and Jesus, and he grew more and more convinced of the ultimate unity of the different religions.

The message that all religions were equally valid had powerful undertones in 19th century India where the British Colonial authorities and Christian missionaries had long disparaged Hinduism on social, religious and ethical grounds. It renewed self-confidence and fostered the climate that led to the Hindu revival, which was taken further by Ramkrishna's disciple Vivekananda and by Dayananda Sarasvati, founder of the Hindu reform movement Arya Samaj.

His fame spread as a guru, preacher and ecstatic mystic, and Ramakrishna gathered around him an increasing band of disciples from all religions, many of them Western-educated. He received them in a small room in the Dakshineswar temple garden on the outskirts of Calcutta. Local newspapers started to refer to him as 'the Hindu saint'.

His followers portray his whole life as uninterrupted contemplation of God. 'Ramakrishna was a living embodiment of godliness,' said Mahatma Gandhi. 'His sayings are not those of a mere learned man but they are the pages of the Book of Life.' The writer Christopher Isherwood saw him as God. 'I believe, or am at least strongly inclined to believe, that he was what his disciples declared that he was: an incarnation of God upon earth.'

After his death from cancer, his teachings were collated in Mahendranath Gupta's five-volume work, *The Nectar-Speech of the Twice-Blessed Ramakrishna*, known in English as Gospel of Ramakrishna.

Chronology

1836	Born Hooghly, Bengal State, India, 18 February
1852	Moves to Calcutta, becomes a priest
1859	Marries Sarada Devi
1886	Dies, Calcutta, 16 August

'His sayings are not those of a mere learned man but the pages of the Book of Life' Mahatma Gandhi on Ramakrishna

Ramakrishna's Teachings

■ *After his death from cancer, his teachings were collated in Mahendranath Gupta's five-volume work,* The Nectar-Speech of the Twice-Blessed Ramakrishna, *known in English as Gospel of Ramakrishna.*

Examples of Sri Ramakrishna's teachings:

■ *'I have now come to a stage of realization in which I see that God is walking in every human form and manifesting Himself alike through the sage and the sinner, the virtuous and the vicious.'*

■ *'Do you know what I see? I see him as all. Men and other creatures appear to me only as hollow forms, moving their heads and hands and feet, but within is the Lord Himself.'*

■ *'What are you to do when you are placed in the world? Give up everything to Him, resign yourself to Him, and there will be no more trouble for you. Then you will come to know that everything is done by His will.'*

■ *'Unalloyed love of God is the essential thing. All else is unreal.'*

Pope John Paul II

Pope John Paul II (1920–2005), leader of the Roman Catholic Church and the first non-Italian pope in more than four and a half centuries, bestrode the world like a colossus, triggering the chain of revolutions that swept away Communism, and preaching an unbending message of Christian morality to an increasingly secular age. Ever an actor, this great communicator lived out his final illness in public on the world stage.

KAROL WOJTYLA WAS BORN in the small southern Polish town of Wadowice, near Kraków, in a humble apartment house, the son of a Polish army officer. Drawn initially to the theatre and poetry, he began his studies at Kraków's Jagellonian University in 1938, the year before the Nazi Germans invaded Poland, and he spent much of the war studying clandestinely for the priesthood while working in a stone quarry and a chemical plant.

He was ordained in 1946 and went to Rome for two years, returning to Poland in 1948 to find his country in the grips of Stalinism. The Catholic Church remained one of the few independent organizations; it was a channel of Polish nationalism and of quiet opposition to the officially atheist Communist authorities. The future pope rose quickly through the church ranks, becoming a bishop at thirty-eight and Archbishop of Kraków in

Chronology

1920	Born Karol Wojtyla in Wadowice, 18 May
1938	Begins studies at Jagellonian University, Kraków
1939	Nazis invade Poland
1946	Ordained priest
1964	Archbishop of Kraków
1967	Becomes cardinal
1978	Elected Pope on 16 October
1979	Visits Communist Poland as Pope
1981	Survives assassination attempt
2000	Visits Holy Land

John Paul was the first Pope to preach in a Protestant church and a synagogue, the first to set foot in a mosque

1964. Three years later he was elevated to cardinal and, on 16 October 1978, he stunned the world by appearing on the balcony of St Peter's in Rome as the first non-Italian pope in 455 years.

The political shockwaves reverberated throughout Eastern Europe, and the following year the Pope made a triumphant nine-day journey through his homeland, setting off an unstoppable wave of opposition to the Communists, which triggered the Solidarity Revolution. Solidarity formed the East Bloc's first non-Communist government in 1989 and, soon after, Marxist regimes fell one by one across Europe.

'Behold the night is over; day has dawned anew,' the Pope said during a triumphant visit to Czechoslovakia in 1990.

Pope John Paul was a tireless traveller; he visited more than 130 countries, often drawing huge crowds that, as a one-time student actor, he would play to perfection. A decade after the fall of Communism, he fulfilled another of his dreams: he visited the Holy Land. Praying at Jerusalem's Western Wall, he asked for forgiveness for Catholic sins against Jews over the centuries. He worked his papacy from a global pulpit, speaking out for the poor and oppressed and against all forms of what he saw as injustice.

'I speak in the name of those who have no voice,' he said on a trip to Africa in 1980. He criticized left-wing and right-wing dictators alike, and warned that unbridled capitalism was not the answer to humanity's plight. A strong defender of human rights and religious freedom, he called for a 'new world economic order' and defence of workers' rights, leading him to be dubbed the 'socialist pope'.

He was the first pope to preach in a Protestant church and a synagogue, and the first pope to set foot inside a mosque (in Damascus). But although he was an advocate of Christian unity, he remained uncompromisingly conservative, thereby widening the gulf with the Anglican community. He waged an unflagging battle against abortion, contraception, pre-marital sex, divorce and homosexuality. Inside his own church, he ruled his one billion Catholics with an iron will, utterly rejecting liberal reforms that would, for example, have allowed married clergy and women priests.

'Church doctrine cannot be based on popular opinion,' he once said. On another occasion, he stated: 'God will always have the last word.'

Once known among the faithful as 'God's athlete' for his love of skiing and mountain hiking, the Pope was stricken with Parkinson's disease and arthritis in his later years, making it virtually impossible for him to stand or walk without intense pain. Speaking from a wheelchair, he said he had been reduced to 'human frailty'.

A Tireless Pope

- *Soviet leader Joseph Stalin once asked mockingly: how many divisions does the Pope have? None, but this did not prevent the 'divisionless' Pope John Paul from helping to bring down Stalin's successors.*
- *A tireless traveller, John Paul clocked up some 1.25 million kilometres (775,000 miles) on 102 foreign trips to 130 countries.*
- *He held more than 1,100 general audiences at the Vatican, attended by more than 18 million people.*
- *John Paul canonized more than 477 saints, more than all of his predecessors combined, and issued fourteen encyclicals on Catholic Church teaching.*
- *He also published books of theology, philosophy, poetry and drama.*
- *His pontificate was the third-longest in the history of the Roman Catholic Church.*

THE DALAI LAMA

The Dalai Lama Tenzin Gyatso (1935–) is the spiritual leader of the Tibetan people and the head of a government in exile. One of the world's leading advocates of non-violence, he fled Tibet in 1959, following a failed uprising against Chinese occupation. He is a thorn in China's side, but he has cult status and a huge following in the West.

THE 14TH DALAI LAMA was born Lhamo Thondub to a simple peasant family in the north of the mountain kingdom of Tibet, and in accordance with Tibetan tradition he was recognised as the reincarnation of his predecessor, the 13th Dalai Lama, and thus as an incarnation of Avalokiteshvara, the Buddha of Compassion.

He was taken away to be educated by Buddhist monks, and enthroned as the country's spiritual leader in the Potala Palace, in Lhasa, the capital of Tibet, on 22 February 1940. In 1950, he became head of state and government, at the same time as the Chinese Peoples' Army moved into Tibet at gunpoint, and he spent the next 10 years appealing for international help in an attempt to ward off a full-scale Chinese takeover. But events were precipitated by his people, who staged a mass uprising against Chinese occupation in 1959. The revolt was brutally crushed by the Chinese, and more than 44 years later the Red Army is still facing opposition in Tibet.

The Dalai Lama escaped to India where he established a Tibetan government in exile in Dharamsala, 'Little Lhasa'. Some 80,000 Tibetan refugees followed him into exile. The Dalai Lama appealed to the United Nations, resulting in three resolutions by the General Assembly – in 1959, 1961 and 1965 – calling on China to respect the human rights of Tibetans and their desire for self-determination. But China ignored them; Beijing has consistently argued that Tibet is a Chinese province, and has refused to allow the Dalai Lama to return home unless he bows to Chinese rule.

The Dalai Lama has devoted his life to a free Tibet, but he has had to make his home in the West, where he has acquired almost pop-star status. His smiling face, his shaven head and maroon robe and, above all, his Buddhist message of prayer, humility and non-violence, have made him a familiar and much loved figure around the world. He has been described as an 'ascetic Buddhist superstar'. The recipient of many awards, in 1989 the Dalai Lama was awarded the Nobel

CHRONOLOGY

1935	Born in village of Takster, northern Tibet, 6 July
1940	Enthroned as Dalai Lama, in Lhasa, Tibet
1950	Becomes head of state and government in Tibet
1959	Escapes to India after China crushes uprising
1965	United Nations passes third resolution on Tibet
1989	Dalai Lama awarded Nobel Peace Prize

TIBETAN AUTONOMY

■ *Will China ever grant Tibet its independence? Under the present regime, the answer is almost certainly no. But regimes change. Countries, such as Estonia and Kyrgyzstan, bounced back from the dead when the Soviet Union collapsed.*

■ *The Dalai Lama has over the years softened his stance on Tibet, calling only for 'genuine autonomy' within China, and suggesting the solution applied to Hong Kong when the former British colony was handed back to Beijing – 'one country, two systems'. The Chinese condemn the Dalai Lama as a 'splittist'.*

■ *Tibetans normally refer to the Dalai Lama as Yeshin Norbu, The Wish-fulfilling Gem, or simply Kundun, The Presence.'*

The Dalai Lama has devoted his life to a free Tibet, but has had to make his home in the West

Peace Prize for his constant opposition to the use of violence in the struggle for the liberation of Tibet.

'The prize reaffirms our conviction that with truth, courage and determination as our weapons, Tibet will be liberated. Our struggle must remain non-violent and free of hatred,' the Dalai Lama said. He added that he was accepting the prize on behalf of the oppressed everywhere and of all those who struggle for freedom and work for world peace and the people of Tibet.

The Dalai Lama has travelled extensively and met many world leaders. He has been to the United States at least 15 times and draws sell-out crowds from coast to coast. His writings and books about him are hugely popular. *The Art of Happiness* sold more than 1.2 million copies. There are more than 300 listings for Dalai Lama on amazon.com, although some are different editions of the same book. His image is no less popular in Tibet; pictures of him are carried on the dashboards in trucks, cars, buses and displayed in other public places in such numbers that there is not a great deal the Chinese can do about it.

WILLIAM WILBERFORCE

William Wilberforce (1759–1833). British statesman and reformer who displayed courage and persistence in leading the movement for the abolition of the slave trade. He presented a bill to Parliament to end the trade in humans no fewer than twelve times before it finally became law.

THE SON OF A WEALTHY merchant from the English east-coast port of Hull, Wilberforce lost his father when he was a young boy, and was brought up for a time by an aunt, who was a strict Methodist. Her influence left him a strong evangelical. He spent three years at Cambridge University, where he met William Pitt, who would become Britain's youngest ever Prime Minister, and at the age of twenty-one he entered Parliament as a member for his native city, Hull. He changed constituencies in 1784 and became a member for Yorkshire. That year he also converted to Evangelical Christianity, and he became interested in parliamentary and social reform, including issues such as Catholic emancipation (Catholics were still outlawed). A group of Quakers and Prime Minister Pitt persuaded him to take up the cause of the abolition of the slave trade, which had developed on both sides of the Atlantic into a highly profitable business.

Ports like Bristol and Liverpool had built their prosperity on the trade. Ships laden with goods, such as guns and cloth, would sail to West Africa, exchange their wares for slaves and then transport their human cargo to the West Indies, where they would barter them for sugar, tobacco, rum and molasses. Apart from this triangular maritime trade, which depended on slaves, people believed that the plantation economies of the Americas and the Caribbean would collapse without their labour. The slave owners would put up a determined fight.

Wilberforce and his religious-minded associates were first called the Saints, and later became known as the Clapham Sect, because they mostly lived and worshipped in the South London suburb of Clapham. Apart from the abolition of slavery, they supported Christian missions, and schools for the poor, and opposed blood sports and gambling.

CHRONOLOGY

1759 Born in Hull, England, 24 August
1776–79 Studies at Cambridge University
1780 Enters Parliament
1789 Makes first speech against the slave trade
1791 Presents first bill to abolish slave trade
1807 Parliament bans slave trade
1825 Retires from Parliament
1833 Dies, 29 July

Wilberforce made his first speech to Parliament against the slave trade on 12 May 1789, and he presented his first bill to abolish it in 1791, which was defeated by 163 votes to 88. He continued to campaign for it inside Parliament and, together with a group of friends, he helped form the countrywide Anti-Slavery Society. In 1792, he succeeded in getting a bill approved for the gradual abolition of the trade – but with no firm date agreed – and he battled on in vain throughout the 1790s. He tried again in 1804, and in 1805 he managed to get a bill passed in the lower House of Commons, but it was thrown out by the upper chamber, the House of Lords. A final attempt, in 1807, succeeded, and a bill to abolish the slave trade became law on 25 March 1807. Wilberforce was cheered by his supporters in Parliament.

A campaign to abolish slavery altogether continued, although Wilberforce, who switched constituencies again in 1812, becoming a member for Sussex, at first did not agree with this. He believed in gradual abolition, arguing that slaves were not ready to be granted their freedom. He eventually came round to accepting abolition, but had retired from Parliament by the time it was debated. Parliament passed the Slavery Abolition Act in August 1833, a month after his death.

'Thank God I have lived to see the day that England is willing to give £20 million for the abolition of slavery'

The Abolition of Slavery

- *Slaves were bought and sold down the ages in almost every so-called civilization. The trade was a major business in the eighteenth century, and was accepted on both sides of the Atlantic as normal and legitimate commerce. Slaves were mostly bought in Africa and sold in America.*
- *The abolition of the slave trade had some initially unforeseen consequences. Ship's masters caught flouting the law would sometimes have their human cargo thrown overboard, rather than pay the fines for carrying slaves.*
- *Wilberforce's strong puritan streak shows up in his description of arriving at St John's College, Cambridge: 'I was introduced on the very first night of my arrival to as licentious a set of men as can well be conceived. They drank hard, and their conversation was even worse than their lives.'*
- *When on his deathbed he heard that the bill for the total abolition of slavery would be passed, and that planters would be heavily compensated, Wilberforce said: 'Thank God that I have lived to witness a day in which England is willing to give £20 million for the abolition of slavery.'*

FREDERICK DOUGLASS

Frederick Douglass (1818–95) was an escaped slave who campaigned on both sides of the Atlantic with fine oratory for the abolition of slavery, and became the first black citizen to hold high office in the US government.

FREDERICK AUGUSTUS WASHINGTON Bailey was born of a white father and a black slave mother and brought up by his grandmother on a Maryland plantation. Aged eight, he became a house servant to the Auld family in Baltimore, where he received a rudimentary education and learned to read and write. He was put to work as a field hand at the age of sixteen, suffering beatings and deprivations, and in 1836 he made an abortive attempt to escape. After a brief spell in prison, he was hired out as a ship caulker in Baltimore. Two years later he fled to New York, and then to New Bedford, Mass., where he worked as a labourer, and, to elude slave hunters, changed his surname to Douglass, and married his Baltimore sweetheart, Anna Murray.

Douglass made his name, and got his first break, in 1841 when he was invited to speak at an anti-slavery convention in Nantucket, Massachusetts. His natural eloquence and his moving first-hand account of his experiences as a slave propelled him into a new career as agent for the local anti-slavery society. He went on a lecture tour, and became an instant hit as a platform speaker for the abolitionists. He addressed audiences from coast to coast, at times having to contend with rough treatment, particularly from pro-slavery activists.

In 1845, he published an autobiography, *Life and Times of Frederick Douglass*, and, still fearful of recapture, he left the US for two years on a speaking tour of Britain and Ireland. He returned with enough money to buy his freedom and start his own anti-slavery newspaper, the *North Star*, a weekly which he published out of Rochester, New York, from 1847 to 1860. He also became station master and conductor of the underground railway at Rochester.

Douglass went back to Britain on a second speaking tour in 1859, returning to the US the following year in time to campaign for Abraham Lincoln. During the Civil War, he sought to promote abolition of slavery as one of the North's primary objectives, and he helped raise two black regiments, the Massachusetts 54th and 55th. He complained personally to President Lincoln over the inferior conditions of black soldiers; they were only on half-pay. In the reconstruction following the war, Douglass was a prominent spokesman for former black slaves, and campaigned resolutely for amendments to the US Constitution to give freedmen full civil rights. 'Slavery is not abolished until the black man has the ballot,' he said.

In 1872, Douglass moved to Washington, and two years later he became President of the Freedman's Savings and Trust Bank – a disastrous move, as it quickly went bankrupt. He subsequently took on political and government posts, US marshal for the District of Columbia, recorder of deeds and, from 1889 to 1891, US minister and consul general in Haiti. He died in Washington in 1895.

CHRONOLOGY

1818	Born in Tuckahoe, Maryland, 7 February
1836	First escape plan fails; imprisoned
1837	Meets Anna Murray
1838	Escapes to New York; marries Anna Murray; changes name to Frederick Douglass
1841	Speaks at American Anti-Slavery Society meeting; invited to go on lecture tour
1845	Autobiography published; tours Britain
1847	Returns to the United States
1847	Starts the *North Star*
1859	Second lecture tour to Britain
1874	President of the Freedman's Savings and Trust Company
1877	US marshal for District of Columbia
1880	Recorder of deeds for Washington, DC
1889	American consul general to Haiti
1891	Resigns post and returns home
1895	Dies in Washington, DC, 20 February

'Slavery is not abolished until the black man has the vote'

TRUTH IS OF NO COLOUR

- *The masthead of the* North Star *proclaimed: 'Right is of no sex – Truth is of no color – God is the Father of us all, and we are all Brethren.'*
- *At public meetings, Douglass was presented as 'a recent graduate from the institution of slavery with his diploma on his back'.*
- *Douglass was impelled to write his autobiography largely because his natural intelligence and eloquence led some people to disbelieve his story as he told it to the assembled meetings up and down the country. His account became a classic in American literature and a major source about life as a slave. Published in 1845 as* Narrative of the Life of Frederick Douglass, an American Slave, *it was a runaway success.*

EMMELINE PANKHURST

Emmeline Pankhurst (1858–1928) was a militant leader of the British women's suffrage movement which campaigned for women's right to vote. She believed in direct action – something shocking for the age – and fought passionately for women's rights throughout her life. Imprisoned many times, and enduring numerous hunger strikes, she died just two weeks before the British Parliament gave equal voting rights to women.

EMMELINE PANKHURST was born in Manchester, the daughter of a successful businessman. In an age before universal suffrage, her parents, the Gouldens, were supporters of the vote reform movement, and Emmeline was taken to a women's suffrage meeting by her mother when she was only thirteen. After early schooling in Manchester she was sent aged fifteen to Paris for four years. Her French headmistress believed that girls should have a similar education to boys, including science and bookkeeping as well as embroidery.

When she returned to Manchester in 1878 she met Richard Pankhurst, a lawyer and keen supporter of women's suffrage. Pankhurst had helped to draft a bill that later became the Married Women's Property Act (1882), which for the first time enabled married women to control their property and earnings. In spite of an age difference of twenty-four years, Richard and Emmeline married in 1879, and had four children. Together they helped form the Women's Franchise League in 1889, and switched their allegiance to the new Labour Party in the hopes that it would further their cause.

In 1895 Mrs Pankhurst became a Poor Law Guardian. She was shocked by how inmates in workhouses – the elderly, the very young, but particularly women – were treated, and felt more strongly than ever that women's suffrage was the only way by which injustices like these could be eradicated.

Disillusioned by existing women's political organizations, Mrs Pankhurst founded the Women's Social and Political Union (WSPU) in 1903 and encouraged working-class women to join. A lack of interest by the media forced the WSPU to use radical methods – direct action – to attract attention. In 1905 Mrs Pankhurst's daughter, Cristabel, and Annie Kenney heckled a government minister. They were charged with assault, and on refusing to pay a fine were imprisoned. This defiance by two respectable women shocked Edwardian England. By 1907 Mrs Pankhurst had joined her daughters in London. She was jailed repeatedly for her violent demonstrations, but her example, and her captivating public speaking, inspired other women to press for the vote.

During World War I the WSPU suspended their militancy, but Mrs Pankhurst, reflecting the new realities of women working in munitions factories, turned her energies to campaigning for trade unions to allow women into male-dominated industries. Then in 1917 she and her daughter Cristabel formed the Women's Party. They advocated 'equal

CHRONOLOGY

1858 Born Emmeline Goulden, in Manchester, 14 July
1872 Aged thirteen, goes with mother to women's suffrage meeting
1872–76 Schooled in Paris
1876 Works for women's suffrage movement and meets future husband, a radical barrister
1889 Helps found Women's Franchise League
1892 Leaves Liberals; joins Labour Party
1903 With daughter Cristabel forms Women's Social and Political Union (WSPU)
1905 Demonstrations by Mrs Pankhurst and members of WSPU at House of Commons
1907–09 Arrested and imprisoned
1917 Women's Party formed
1917 Visits Russia, lives in USA, Canada
1925 Returns to England; joins Conservatives
1928 Dies 14 June

Emmeline Pankhurst died just two weeks before the British Parliament gave women the vote

pay for equal work, equal marriage and divorce laws, the same rights over children for both parents, equality of rights and opportunities in public service, and a system of maternity benefits'. Mrs Pankhurst visited revolutionary Russia after the war, and lectured in the USA and Canada. On her return to England in 1925 she again switched party, and became a Conservative parliamentary candidate for the East End of London, shocking another daughter, Sylvia, who was staunchly socialist. A bill giving women equal voting rights with men became law thanks to Mrs Pankhurst's single-minded inspiration and courage just two weeks after she died on 14 June 1928.

'Deeds Not Words'

- *'Deeds, not words' was the motto of the Women's Social and Political Union (WSPU) founded by Mrs Pankhurst in 1903. It was no idle boast: Emmeline Pankhurst endured ten hunger-strikes during an eighteen-month period, when she was in her fifties.*
- *She also recalled hearing her father say when she was a child, 'What a pity she wasn't born a lad.'*
- *'There can be no doubt about the singleness of her aim and the remarkable strength and nobility of her character... The end she had in view was the emancipation of women from what she believed, with passionate sincerity, to be a condition of harmful subjection.'*

Obituary of Mrs Pankhurst in The Times.

MARTIN LUTHER KING JR.

Martin Luther King Jr. (1929–68). Baptist Church minister who gave voice to America's blacks in the 1950s and 1960s and led a non-violent civil rights movement with magnetic eloquence immortalized in four words of a speech: 'I have a dream.' He was assassinated by a white man.

BORN IN ATLANTA, Georgia, the son and grandson of Baptist Church ministers, King was a precocious student and had a BA in sociology aged nineteen, a Bachelor of Divinity at twenty-two and a PhD from Boston University in philosophy and theology at twenty-six. He was ordained a Baptist Church minister in 1948 while still at college.

His first full-time ministry was as pastor from 1954 to 1959 at Dexter Avenue Baptist Church in Montgomery, Alabama, America's 'deep South' where discrimination against blacks was still institutionalized. It was the arrest in 1955 of a black seamstress, Rosa Parks, for refusing to give up a 'whites only' seat in a bus in Montgomery that transformed King's life.

He took up the struggle, determined to emulate his hero, Mahatma Gandhi, who had humbled the British Empire and gained Indian independence through non-violent protest. King was elected president of the Montgomery Improvement Association, which organized a boycott of the Montgomery buses for 381 days. Protesters were arrested and beaten and King's home was dynamited, but they offered no resistance and the boycott ended in total victory when the Supreme Court outlawed all segregated public transport.

King emerged from the protest as a pivotal figure in the civil rights movement, and was elected president of the Southern Christian Leadership Conference, which gave him a national platform from which to speak out against the continued and widespread discrimination against blacks. He became a prominent campaigner both at home and abroad, and his speeches and sermons stirred the nation's conscience and gave blacks a new sense of identity and self-worth. In 1963, he organized a massive civil rights campaign in Birmingham, Alabama, in which 3,300 protesters, including King, were arrested, and he led the historic march in Washington on 28 August 1963 when he delivered his 'I have a dream' speech. He also campaigned vigorously against the Vietnam War. Despite critics who demanded more radical action, King never tired of turning the other check, and he stuck to non-violent protest, such as sit-ins and protest marches. He was arrested no fewer than thirty times, and he was freed on one occasion in 1960 at the behest of John F. Kennedy on the eve of the presidential election. The gesture swung black votes behind Kennedy.

The pressures of leading the civil rights movement forced King to give up his full-time pastorate in 1959, and he took on instead the less demanding role of co-pastor to his father at Ebenezer Baptist Church in Atlanta. He was awarded the Nobel Peace Prize in 1964.

In the last sermon he delivered, on the eve of his assassination, he seemed to foreshadow his death. He said he had 'been to the mountain top and seen the Promised Land'.

King was shot dead the following day while standing on the balcony of a motel in Memphis, Tennessee. He and the ideals he stood for are commemorated each year in the US by a national public holiday, on the third Monday of January.

CHRONOLOGY

1929	Born in Atlanta, Georgia, 15 January
1948	Graduates with BA in sociology
1948	Ordained Baptist Church minister
1951	Bachelor of Divinity
1953	Marries Coretta Scott (four children)
1955	Doctorate from Boston University
1954–59	Pastor in Montgomery, Alabama
1955–56	Montgomery bus boycott
1956	Southern Christian Leadership Conference
1960–68	Co-pastor at Ebenezer Baptist Church
1968	Assassinated in Memphis, 4 April

'I have been to the mountain top and I have seen the Promised Land'

Birmingham Jail

■ *Among King's speeches and articles, his Letter from Birmingham Jail ranks as one of the most compelling. He wrote it in May 1963 after being arrested, along with 3,300 other peaceful protesters, by white police, who had set upon them with dogs, fire hoses and batons. 'We know through painful experience that freedom is never voluntarily given by the oppressor,' he wrote. 'It must be demanded by the oppressed.'*

■ *Despite the image projected, the Revd King was not an unalloyed saint. According to FBI tapes he spent the night before he was assassinated cavorting with prostitutes in his hotel room. The FBI tapes contain some graphic language.*

■ *Some 100,000 attended his funeral in Atlanta. His killer, escaped convict James Earl Ray, was sentenced to ninety-nine years in jail.*

THOMAS JEFFERSON

In the epitaph he wrote for himself, Thomas Jefferson (1743–1826) recorded that he had drafted America's Declaration of Independence and the Virginia Statute for Religious Freedom and had founded the University of Virginia – but omitted to mention that he had served two terms as President of the United States. An aristocratic revolutionary, cultured and learned, Jefferson was a brilliant American standard bearer of the Enlightenment.

THE SON OF A PROSPEROUS Virginian plantation owner and educated in law, Jefferson entered politics at twenty-six to become an early activist in the struggle against British rule over the American colonies. His assertive pamphlet A Summary View of the Rights of British America (1774) made him an obvious choice to lead the drafting of the rebellious colonists' Declaration of Independence in 1776. Jefferson's tenure of office as governor of his native state at the height of the revolutionary war was overshadowed by charges of incompetence and cowardice in the conduct of its defence. Although he was subsequently exonerated, the experience left him embittered. Coupled with the death of his wife in 1782, this may explain his willingness to serve the newly independent nation next in an overseas posting.

Jefferson's legislative legacy to Virginia included a commitment to complete religious freedom, which critics took as a deist's swipe at Christianity, and the abolition of entail and primogeniture to prevent the emergence of a 'pseudoaristocracy'. Jefferson's eloquent and much-quoted condemnations of slavery (the existence of which in America he blamed on the British monarchy) did not, however, cut any ice with fellow-members of Virginia's 'plantocracy' nor prevent him from remaining a substantial slave owner to the end of his life. Although he was instrumental in preventing the extension of slavery to the west and foresaw its inevitable abolition, as it was inconsistent with a constitution founded in liberty, Jefferson believed that abolition should be accompanied by the deportation of former slaves.

Ambassadorial duties in Paris precluded Jefferson from participating in the making of the new nation's constitution, and he deplored its failure to include a bill of rights or limitation on the number of terms a president could hold office. While abroad, Jefferson had only limited success in promoting American trade, finding Europeans largely ignorant of its potential, and managing to sign a commercial treaty only with Prussia. As a first-hand observer of the French Revolution he was, and remained, unmoved by its arbitrary cruelty and excessive violence but paradoxically he thought the French incapable of republican government and believed that they should adopt a constitutional monarchy like Britain.

Serving as the first Secretary of State under Washington and then as Vice President under John Adams, Jefferson came to head the emerging agrarianist Republican Party which opposed the Federalists and Alexander Hamilton's favour for

CHRONOLOGY

1743	Born at Shadwell, Albemarle Co., Virginia, 13 April
1769	Elected to Virginia House of Burgesses
1770	Starts building his mansion, Monticello, in Charlottesville
1779–81	Governor of Virginia
1790–93	Secretary of State
1785–89	Serves as American Minister to France
1796–1800	Vice President
1797–1815	President of the American Philosophical Society
1801–09	President of the United States
1803	Louisiana Purchase
1825	University of Virginia inaugurated
1826	Dies on 4 July
1943	Jefferson Monument inaugurated by Franklin D. Roosevelt in Washington, DC

'We are resolved with one mind to die as free men rather than live as slaves'

An Autodidact

- *Jefferson was a life-long learner. He grew up intensely interested in botany, geology, cartography and exploration, and with a love of Latin and Greek. He was widely read in history, philosophy and literature and was a keen scientist. He designed his own home, Monticello.*
- *A technophile in the tradition of Benjamin Franklin, Jefferson also invented the dumbwaiter, a swivel chair and America's decimal system of coinage.*
- *His 1775* Declaration on Taking Up Arms *sought to justify armed resistance by the colonists against Great Britain. 'Our cause is just. Our union is perfect,' Jefferson wrote. 'The arms we have been compelled by our enemies to assume, we will, in defiance of every hazard, with unabating firmness and perseverance of our liberties, employ for the preservation of our liberties; being with one mind resolved to die free men rather than to live slaves.'*
- *The purchase of Louisiana from France in 1803 gave America all the western land drained by the Missouri and Mississippi rivers.*

commercial and urban interests. As the nation's 3rd President, Jefferson lived in self-conscious austerity, reflected in his reduction of taxes and military spending. This was offset by a vision of America as a continental power, which led him to dispatch Lewis and Clark on a transcontinental odyssey of exploration and to undertake the Louisiana Purchase which doubled the nation's territory in size.

During his second term of office Jefferson ordered a ban on foreign trade to extricate his country from potential involvement in the war between Britain and France. Deeply unpopular with mercantile and maritime interests, his Embargo Act was repealed in 1809 as he withdrew from office.

Unlike Washington, Jefferson enjoyed a lengthy retirement, devoted to the indulgence of his many cultural interests but chiefly to the creation of the University of Virginia, whose buildings and curriculum were both designed by him. The 'Sage of Monticello' died on the fiftieth anniversary of the Declaration of Independence.

Toussaint L'Ouverture

François Dominique Toussaint L'Ouverture (1743–1803) was a black slave who led a rebellion that gave birth to Haiti, which in 1804 became the first independent nation in the Caribbean. Although he died in prison before independence was finally achieved, this self-educated slave had effectively outwitted Britain, Spain and the France of Napoleon Bonaparte.

IN 1789 THE FRENCH colony of Saint-Domingue, the western half of the island of Hispaniola that became Haiti, was one of the most profitable real estates in the world. Its sugar plantations supplied two-thirds of France's overseas trade – all produced by slaves. The French Revolution that year sent shockwaves across the Atlantic, even dividing the whites, and two years later the slaves rebelled en masse.

Toussaint was one of those fortunate slaves who worked for a humane master, as a livestock handler, coachman and house servant. He was self-educated, intelligent and energetic, and a devout Catholic. At the outbreak of the uprising in August 1781, Toussaint first ensured the safety of his master's family. He then joined the rebel forces and quickly made his mark with strategic and tactical planning, skills derived from his reading of history. He became a master of guerrilla warfare, and under his leadership the rebels achieved a string of military successes, initially in alliance with France's enemies – Britain and Spain. The Spanish of Santo Domingo controlled the eastern two-thirds of the island of Hispaniola.

But on 6 May 1794, and by now virtually in sole command of the rebels, Toussaint made a momentous decision and switched his allegiance back to France. He appears to have been prompted by the decision of the French National Assembly to abolish slavery – emancipation was his primary goal at that stage – and by fears that Spain and Britain would go back on their word and reinstate slavery. Winning seven battles in seven days, Toussaint's soldiers gained control of almost all the island.

Chronology

1743	Born in Saint-Domingue (Haiti)
1789	French Revolution
1791	Haitian slave revolt
1794	Toussaint switches allegiance back to France
1800	Toussaint controls Saint-Domingue
1801	Toussaint overruns Santo Domingo
1802	Toussaint surrenders to General Leclerc
1803	Dies in Fort de Joux, Jura Mountains, 7 April
1804	Haiti becomes an independent republic

Back under French protection, Toussaint was promoted general in 1797. He became lieutenant governor of Saint-Domingue in 1796, and he was later made commander in chief of all French forces on the island. But he was now habouring greater ambitions – to establish an autonomous state under black rule. US President John Adams, leading an independent but still fledgling nation, sent help, and the last vestiges of French mulatto forces were driven out of Saint-Domingue in late 1800. The following year, Toussaint liberated Spanish Santo Domingo and freed the slaves there.

He now held sway over the whole of Hispaniola, and he had a constitution drawn up that made him governor general for life. He applied his dictatorial powers to restoring order and getting the plantations back to full production.

Trouble, however, was brewing for him back in Paris where Napoleon still regarded Saint-Domingue as essential to the exploitation of his North American territory of Louisiana. Napoleon dispatched his brother-in-law, General Charles

Winning seven battles in seven days, Toussaint's soldiers gained control of almost all Hispaniola

BLACK NAPOLEON

■ *Toussaint, sometimes known as the 'Black Napoleon' or the 'Precursor', was given the name L'Ouverture – The Opening – in 1793 after his lightning military successes against the French.*

■ *Napoleon remained unrepentant about his treatment of Toussaint. 'What could the death of one wretched negro mean to me?' he said many years later, when he himself was in exile in Saint Helena.*

Leclerc, to retake the island at the head of a 20,000-strong force. Toussaint was defeated and surrendered to Leclerc on 5 May 1802. He was at first well looked after and assured of his freedom. But, under orders from Napoleon, he was seized a few weeks later and transported back to France, where he died of starvation and neglect in the freezing dungeons of Fort de Joux in the Jura Mountains.

Six months later Napoleon, by now back at war in Europe, signed away Louisiana, bringing French ambitions in the western hemisphere to an end. He abandoned Haiti, and the era of French colonial rule was over.

José de San Martín

José de San Martín (1778–1850) was one of the principal military leaders in the South American wars of independence against Spain, and is hailed as the liberator of his native Argentina, and of Chile and Peru.

BORN OF SPANISH PARENTS in Yapeyú, on the banks of the mighty Uruguay River in northern Argentina, San Martín moved to Spain as a six-year-old boy to complete his education. He enlisted in the Murcia infantry regiment in 1789 – the year of the French Revolution – and spent the next twenty years serving under Spanish colours, fighting against the Moors, the British, the Portuguese and finally the French. He resigned his commission in 1811, and the following year, after spending time in London, he returned to Buenos Aires, where he married a local girl, Maria Escalada. He found the continent in ferment; Napoleon's invasion of Spain had unsettled her South American colonies and set off a chain reaction of independence movements. San Martín, possibly also influenced by the Latin American revolutionaries he had met in London, was soon involved in one – the Lautaro Lodge.

The fledgling government in Buenos Aires welcomed San Martín, commissioned him as a lieutenant colonel, and put him in charge of a new regiment of mounted grenadiers. The regiment beat a loyalist force near the ravines of San Lorenzo on the River Paraná in its first engagement in 1813.

San Martín took control of the northern army in 1814. By now he was committed to a total break with Spain, but he realized that the only way to make Argentina secure was to drive the Spanish out of neighbouring Chile and then conquer Peru. In a masterstroke, he led an army of 4,000 men and horse across the Andes and, on 12 February 1817, surprised and crushed the Spanish at the Battle of Chacabuco. Some days later his army entered Santiago where he was offered the presidency of the new nation of Chile, an offer he declined in favour of his lieutenant, the Chilean general Bernardo O'Higgins.

Early in 1818, the Spanish launched a counter-attack, but San Martín inflicted a decisive defeat on them at the Battle of Maipú – his most celebrated victory.

San Martín now turned his attention to attacking Peru, and, in his next stroke of genius, he organized the rebels to put together a navy with which to launch a sea-borne assault. With British admiral Lord Cochrane in command, the motley naval force sailed from Valparaiso in August 1820; less than a year later San Martín had taken the capital Lima. He proclaimed the independence of Peru and was appointed protector of the country. The Spanish, meanwhile, had retreated to the Andean foothills.

What happened next has never been clear. But San Martín had a meeting with his fellow Latin American revolutionary, Simón Bolívar, whose armies had been fighting the Spanish to liberate the northern provinces of South America. The meeting between the two 'liberators' took place at Guayaquil on 26 July 1822, and after it San Martín resigned his position and withdrew from public life. He left Bolívar to complete the conquest of Peru and, following the death of his wife in 1824, left Latin America to spend the remainder of his life in retirement in Europe.

Chronology

1778	Born in Yapeyú, Argentina, 25 February
1786	Moved to Spain
1789	Joined Murcia regiment in Spanish army
1812	Returned to Buenos Aires
1817	Crossed Andes, victory at Chacabuco, Chile
1818	Battle of Maipú, 5 April
1821	Entered Lima, proclaimed Peru's independence
1822	Meeting with Simon Bolívar in Guayaquil
1850	Died in Boulogne-sur-Mer, 17 August

San Martín would display a distinct lack of political ambition when he declined the Chilean presidency

Crossing the Andes

■ *San Martín's crossing of the Andes has been compared to Hannibal's feat in leading an army over the Alps. His skill and leadership enabled his men to negotiate several passes more than 4,000 metres above sea level.*

■ *What happened at Guayaquil? The most likely answer is that Bolívar persuaded San Martín that his army alone was powerful enough to finish off the job. Bolívar was politically far more ambitious; he became president of two countries and had a third named after him, while San Martín displayed a distinct lack of political ambition when he declined the Chilean presidency. Did he sacrifice his career for the sake of South American independence?*

■ *San Martín left Buenos Aires for the last time in 1824 following the death of his wife. He died more than a quarter of a century later in 1850 in the French Channel port of Boulogne-sur-Mer.*

Simón Bolívar

Simón Bolívar (1783–1830) was one of South America's greatest generals, and his victories over the Spanish won independence for Bolivia, Colombia, Ecuador, Peru and Venezuela. Bolívar is called El Liberator (The Liberator) and the 'George Washington of South America'.

BOLÍVAR WAS BORN into a prosperous and powerful colonial family in 1783, in Caracas, Venezuela. His parents died when he was a child, and he was educated at home by tutors and guardians, and inherited a fortune. As a young man, he travelled in Europe, where he married a Spanish aristocrat, and came into direct contact with the new ideas of the Age of Enlightenment and watched enthralled and amazed as Napoleon consolidated his hold over the old order in Europe.

Shortly after returning to Venezuela, Bolívar's new wife died, and her death seems to have had a dramatic effect. This impulsive, passionate man now threw himself into political and military action. He returned to Europe for a few years and came back to Venezuela, via the newly freed United States, to find his country about to be torn apart by Napoleon's invasion of Spain. To whom would the Venezuelans now owe their allegiance – the usurper Joseph Bonaparte or the deposed King Ferdinand VII of Spain?

Bolívar joined a group of patriots and they dispatched him to Britain to seek help. On 5 July Venezuela became the first of Spain's American colonies to declare independence. Bolívar was given command of the strategic coastal town of Puerto Cabello, but he bungled its defence and the First Venezuelan Republic collapsed, and he fled the country to Colombia. Here he issued his Cartagena Manifesto, a call to arms against the Spanish occupation.

He returned to Venezuela the following year at the head of a larger patriot army, and, by now a seasoned campaigner and expert in guerrilla-style surprise attacks, he swept all before him to recapture Caracas in August 1813 and establish the Second Republic, with himself as dictator. But it did not last long; the Spaniards launched a ferocious counter-offensive to retake the city, and the following year Bolívar suffered a similar setback, first capturing and then losing Bogotá.

Bolívar was however beginning to learn the most important lesson of his struggle against Spanish rule; with barely a few thousand men under his command, he needed the support of local landlords and their horsemen. He turned the tide when he began to rally them to the cause of independence. From Jamaica he wrote a second manifesto and, meanwhile, with the backing of newly independent Haiti, he gathered a new force that included English and Irish mercenary veterans from the Napoleonic wars. He changed tactics, and secured a base in the Orinoco region, at Angostura (now Ciudad Bolívar). From here, on 17 December 1819, he proclaimed the Republic of Colombia (now Ecuador, Colombia, Panama and Venezuela), and became its first president. He now led his army of fewer than 2,500 men on one of the most daring attacks in military history – over flood-swept plains and the ice-covered Andes – and surprised the Spanish at Boyacá on 7 August 1819. Three days later he entered Bogotá.

Venezuela was finally freed from Spanish rule two years later at the Battle of Carabobo, and Bolívar then set about liberating Ecuador, and completing the conquest of Peru together with his trusted

Chronology

1783	Born in Caracas, 24 July
1799	Travelled to Europe for first time
1811	Revolt in Venezuela
1813	Captured and lost Caracas
1814	Captured and lost Bogotá
1819	Captured Angostura
1819	Battle of Boyacá, elected President of Colombia
1824	Elected President of Bolivia
1825	Elected President of Peru
1830	Abandons power; dies near Santa Marta, Colombia, 17 December

Bolívar began to turn the tide of war when he rallied local landlords to the cause of independence

Destiny Calls

- *It was on a trip to Rome that Bolívar first determined his destiny; standing on the Monte Sacro he made a vow to liberate his country from Spanish rule.*
- *Bolívar's dream of a united Latin America never became a reality. He called a congress in Panama in 1826 to discuss a confederation of Spanish American countries, but only Colombia, Peru, Mexico and the Central American states turned up.*
- *Bolívar married for a second time to Manuela Sáenz, an ardent revolutionary, whom he met in Quito. She saved him from an assassin's dagger in 1828.*

General Antonio José de Sucre at the Battle of Ayacucho on 9 December 1824. The new state of Bolivia, named in his honour, was established the following year. He now controlled more than half the continent.

But Bolívar was not successful as a government leader, and his vision of Grand Colombia gradually fell apart, as one by one the countries he had freed declared their independence from his increasingly autocratic rule. By 1828 Bolívar was left with only Colombia and, with failing health, he resigned in 1830, and died of tuberculosis, a broken man.

Chief Joseph

Chief Joseph (1840–1904) of the Nez Percé tribe was one of the leaders of the Native American resistance to white encroachment in the western United States, and led his people on an epic but ultimately doomed march to seek sanctuary in British-ruled Canada.

BORN WITH THE INDIAN NAME In-Mut-Too-Yah-Lat-Lat (Thunder Coming Up over the Land from the Water), Chief Joseph was the son of a Christian convert. Educated in a mission school, he succeeded his father as chief of the Nez Percé in 1873. Although the powerful tribe had been initially on friendly terms with the new settlers, the increasing white encroachments into the Pacific Northwest region led some native leaders to query the validity of land treaties made with the US government, on the grounds that the chiefs responsible for the agreements did not faithfully represent tribal interests. The Stevens Treaty negotiated in 1855 had provided for a large reservation in Oregon and Idaho but, when gold was discovered in Oregon in 1863, nine-tenths of the relevant territory was demanded back. Neither Chief Joseph nor his father had been a party to the latter negotiation. Hostilities broke out in 1877 after the US government forced the reluctant Nez Percé to leave their Wallowa Valley homeland in Oregon and move to Idaho.

Chief Joseph had initially assented but he reassessed his options when a band of his braves killed a party of whites. Fearing army retaliation he determined to lead some 300 warriors and their families to safety across the Canadian border. Between 17 June and 30 September the refugees fled over 1,400 miles from Oregon through Washington and Idaho into Montana, outmanoeuvring a pursuing force of regular soldiers and Indian auxiliaries at least ten times their number, and frustrating it in four major rearguard actions and numerous smaller skirmishes. Chief Joseph's role was primarily one of leadership, rather than of direct military command. Although American journalists were swift to dub him 'the Red Napoleon', his own immediate followers were led by his younger brother Olikut, and strategic direction was given by a chief called Looking-Glass (1832–77), who had fled the Idaho reservation to place himself at Chief Joseph's service. The dramatic tribal odyssey won widespread admiration not only for its leader's skill and inspirational example, but also for his evident concern for his most vulnerable followers, his humanity towards captured enemies and his integrity in purchasing rather than plundering supplies en route.

Chronology

1840	Born in the Wallowa Valley, eastern Oregon Territory
1877	Leads 1,400-mile fighting flight to the Canadian border
1879	Pleads unsuccessfully with President Rutherford B. Hayes
1903	Pleads unsuccessfully with President Theodore Roosevelt
1904	Dies 21 September on the Colville Reservation, Washington

Finally surrounded in the Bear Paw Mountains, less than forty miles from the border and deliverance, after a five-day siege Chief Joseph surrendered his people to the custody of the pursuit force commander General Nelson Miles with words of haunting melancholy – 'I am tired of fighting. Our chiefs are killed.'

Several of his war chiefs who had not been killed in combat did succeed in escaping to Canada. Dispatched initially to a barren tract of Oklahoma, where many sickened and died, the rest of Chief Joseph's surviving followers were in 1885 allowed to relocate to a reservation in the state of Washington. Chief Joseph himself made two journeys to Washington, DC to plead in person with presidents that his people might return to their native homeland valley. He received fair words but no restitution.

'Hear me, my chiefs. My heart is sick and sad. From where the sun now stands, I will fight no more forever'

A Dignified Surrender

After a five-day battle in the Bear Paw Mountains, Chief Joseph surrendered on 5 October 1877 with these words

■ *'I am tired of fighting. Our chiefs are killed; Looking-Glass is dead, Ta-Hool-Hool-Shute is dead. The old men are all dead. It is the young men who say yes or no. He who led on the young men is dead. It is cold, and we have no blankets; the little children are freezing to death. My people, some of them, have run away to the hills, and have no blankets, no food. No one knows where they are – perhaps freezing to death. I want to have time to look for my children, and see how many of them I can find. Maybe I shall find them among the dead. Hear me, my chiefs, I am tired; my heart is sick and sad. From where the sun now stands I will fight no more forever.'*

THEODOR HERZL

Theodor Herzl (1860–1904). Founder of Zionism, the movement to establish a Jewish homeland in Palestine. After a congress of Zionists in Basle in 1897 he became first president of the World Zionist Organization. Within fifty years of his death, the state of Israel was founded.

THEODORE HERZL was born in Budapest, Hungary, and brought up in the liberal spirit of the German Jewish middle class, appreciating secular culture. He left his secondary school because of its anti-Semitic atmosphere, switching in 1875 to a school where the majority of pupils were Jewish. His family moved to Vienna in 1882, and although Herzl was awarded a doctorate of law by the University of Vienna in 1884, he decided to concentrate on writing plays and journalism. He married the daughter of a wealthy Viennese Jewish businessman in 1889, and in 1891 was sent to Paris as correspondent for the leading Viennese newspaper *Neue Freie Presse*. He was shocked by anti-Semitism in France, and his experiences as a journalist there convinced him that the answer for Jews was not to assimilate into the countries where they were living, but to organise themselves on an international level and emigrate to their own state.

The wave of anti-Semitism that swept France during the Dreyfus Affair in 1894, in which a Jewish officer was unjustly accused of spying for the Germans, only reinforced his views. Herzl concluded that anti-Semitism was so deeply rooted in society that it would not be overcome by assimilation. He wrote a pamphlet *Der Judenstaat* (The Jewish State) in 1896 stating that the Jewish problem was a national, not just an individual one, and that the solution was for the international powers to agree to a Jewish state. He was not the first to have these ideas: Judah Alkalai (1798-1878) a Sephardic rabbi from Croatia who had travelled all over Europe founding organisations persuading Jews to return to Israel, had helped to pave the way.

Herzl's ideal Jewish state was planned as a pluralist, neutral, peace-seeking, secular one, where socialist co-operative schemes would help to develop the land.

CHRONOLOGY

1860	Born Budapest on 2 May
1878	Family moves to Vienna
1882	Studies law at the University of Vienna
1884	Awarded a doctorate of law; starts writing
1894	In Paris during Dreyfus Affair
1897	First Zionist Congress in Basle, Switzerland
1898	Travels to Ottoman Empire and Palestine
1903	Visits Russia and England
1904	Dies of pneumonia in Edlach, Austria, 3 July

Influential Jews such as Baron Hirsch and Baron Rothschild, were sceptical, but ordinary East European Jews were enthusiastic, and as a result the First Zionist Congress met in Basle with some 200 delegates in August 1897. This first meeting of Jews on a secular and national level adopted the Basle Program recognising the Zionist movement, passed the motion 'Zionism seeks to establish a home for the Jewish people in Palestine secured under public law'.

The international Zionist movement then met every year, moving its centre in 1936 to Jerusalem.

Herzl was indefatigable in his efforts to persuade the great powers to his point of view, travelling to the then Ottoman-ruled Palestine, Turkey, England and Russia. The ultimate aim of Zionism was the establishment of a Jewish state in Palestine, but when Britain proposed Uganda in east Africa as a home for the Jews, Herzl felt it could be a temporary alternative for Russian Jews who were suffering persecution. This led to uproar in the Zionist Congress of 1903, and the rejection of Uganda as a Jewish homeland by the 1905 Congress.

By the time Herzl died aged 44 in Vienna in 1904, Zionism was a budding force in world politics, and less than 50 years later the State of Israel was an established fact.

Herzl's ideal Jewish state was planned as a pluralist, neutral, peace-seeking, secular one

A Life for Zionism

■ *Herzl wrote in his diary after the First Zionist Congress of 1897: 'At Basle, I founded the Jewish state. If I were to say this today, I would be greeted by universal laughter. In five years, perhaps, and certainly in fifty, everyone will see it.'*

■ *Herzl's phrase 'If you will, it is no fairytale' became the motto of the Zionist movement.*

■ *His name lives on in the first Hebrew grammar school – Herzlia – to be founded in Tel Aviv, and in the town of Herzliya, north of Tel Aviv, as well as in forests, and streets throughout Israel. He was reburied on a hill known as Mount Herzl near Jerusalem in 1949, shortly after the foundation of the state of Israel.*

Kemal Atatürk

Mustafa Kemal Atatürk (1881–1938). War hero who created the secular republic of Turkey from the rump of the former Islamic Ottoman Empire. He became its first president and was a great modernizer, but his country sits uneasily with its secular–Islamic divide.

BORN MUSTAFA RIZI in Salonika, then a thriving port of the Ottoman Empire, the son of a customs official, he grew up to be a soldier. Nicknamed Kemal – 'the perfect one' – by his mathematics teacher, he attended army cadet schools and in 1899 entered the War College in Istanbul. He graduated as a lieutenant in 1902 and was promoted captain after completing Staff College in 1905. As a young officer, he became involved in the secret Young Turk movement, which opposed the autocratic Ottoman government, and his associations with the nationalists clouded his army career.

Kemal had already seen action before the First World War, in which the Ottomans sided with the Germans, but his great feat was the defence of Gallipoli in 1915, when he played a crucial role in repelling an Allied landing by British, Australian, New Zealand and Senegalese troops. He was hailed as the 'Saviour of Istanbul', and the following year, after winning a battle against the Russians, he was promoted to general and given the title Pasha.

The Allied victors of the First World War imposed humiliating terms on the old Ottoman Empire. Under the 1920 Treaty of Sèvres, it was broken up and occupied. Turks were not even allowed to run their own banks. The treaty gave Greece big slices of Anatolia and Thrace and set up an independent Armenian state. After the Sultan had signed it, the Supreme Allied Council in Paris invited Greece to move in 'to restore order in Anatolia'. They had not reckoned on Kemal, who had been appointed head of a small force to suppress protest during the occupation.

Kemal, instead, had turned against the occupation, and on 19 May 1919 had called on Turks to rise up and fight for their independence. He had set up a headquarters in Ankara, the Turkish heartland, where he established a provisional government. Invasion by a foreign army to uphold an unequal treaty was just what Kemal needed. Within two years, he had driven the Greeks back into the sea, deposed the Sultan, and dealt with the Italians and French, and, with Russian assistance, crushed the Armenians and Kurds in the east. The British decided to negotiate, and Kemal secured a new deal – the 1923 Treaty of Lausanne. This time it was on equal terms, and Turkey emerged from the ashes of six centuries of Ottoman rule, a free country with Kemal as its leader. The new Turkish Republic was proclaimed on 29 October 1923.

Kemal built the modern Turkish state. The cornerstone was secularization. Islam, long dominant in all walks of life, was confined to the mosque and the privacy of the home. The caliphate was abolished in 1924, and the law secularized. The new constitution of 1928 removed the statement that Turkey was an Islamic state. Religion was banned from public life, and the wearing of the veil was outlawed. Even the fez, a flat-topped coned cap that had originally been imported from Europe, went. The Western calendar was introduced, and Saturday replaced the Muslim Friday as the 'weekend'. The Turkish Arabic script was latinized.

Chronology

1881	Born in Salonika, 12 March
1899	Enters War College in Istanbul
1905	Graduates from Staff College as captain
1911–12	Fights Italians in Libya
1915	Repulses Allied force at Gallipoli
1916	Defeats Russians on the Eastern front
1918	Overseas Ottoman withdrawal from Syria
1919	Calls on Turks to fight for independence
1920	Establishes provisional government in Ankara
1921	Defeats Greeks at Battle of Sakarya
1923	Becomes President of new Turkish state
1934	Given title Atatürk
1938	Dies in Istanbul, 10 November

Hailed as the Saviour of Istanbul after Gallipoli, Atatürk was promoted and given the title Pasha

FATHER OF TURKEY

- *During the defence of Gallipoli, Kemal was hit by a piece of shrapnel, but the watch he kept in his breast pocket saved his life.*
- *Kemal Atatürk is still omnipresent in Turkey, with statues of him in many places and his portrait in public buildings, and on bank notes and postage stamps.*
- *But more than two generations after his death, Turkey is still seeking membership of the European Union, and militants inside Turkey are determined on returning the country to Islam.*

Polygamy was outlawed and women were given the vote. Kemal's secular revolution was in fact so sweeping that he had transformed Turkey by the 1930s into one of the most advanced liberal states in the world.

The National Assembly conferred the title Atatürk – 'Father of the Turks' – on Kemal in 1934, confirming his place in Turkish history. A lifelong heavy drinker, he died of cirrhosis of the liver in Istanbul on 10 November 1933.

Mahatma Gandhi

Mahatma Gandhi (1869–1948), nationalist leader, holy man and great proponent of non-violent protest, led India peacefully out of the British Empire, and shortly after died at the hands of a Hindu assassin.

BORN MOHANDAS KARAMCHAND Gandhi in the town of Porbandar in British-ruled India in what is now the state of Gujarāt, Gandhi was schooled in nearby Rājkot, where his father was prime minister to a local ruler. Married in accordance with custom at the age of thirteen, he sailed for London aged eighteen to study law, leaving behind his wife and infant son. Victorian England opened Gandhi's eyes to the realities of the industrial world, and also to philosophy and the major religions. He became a barrister in 1891 and, after trying to set up on his own in Bombay, he accepted an offer from an Indian businessman to work in South Africa.

Gandhi spent twenty-one years in South Africa, and it was there, faced with racial humiliation, that he became a political activist. A catalyst was being thrown out of a first-class railway compartment because he was a half-caste Indian, even though he had a first-class ticket. Gandhi soon emerged as the leader of the South African Indian community and secured some measure of racial and political justice for his fellow Indians. In 1894, he founded the Natal Indian Congress. In South Africa, he also developed a method of non-violent resistance, which he termed satyāgraha, and at the same time he nurtured his own distinct spiritual view of life.

In 1909, on a trip back in India, Gandhi wrote a small treatise on Indian home rule. He returned to India for good in 1915 and travelled extensively,

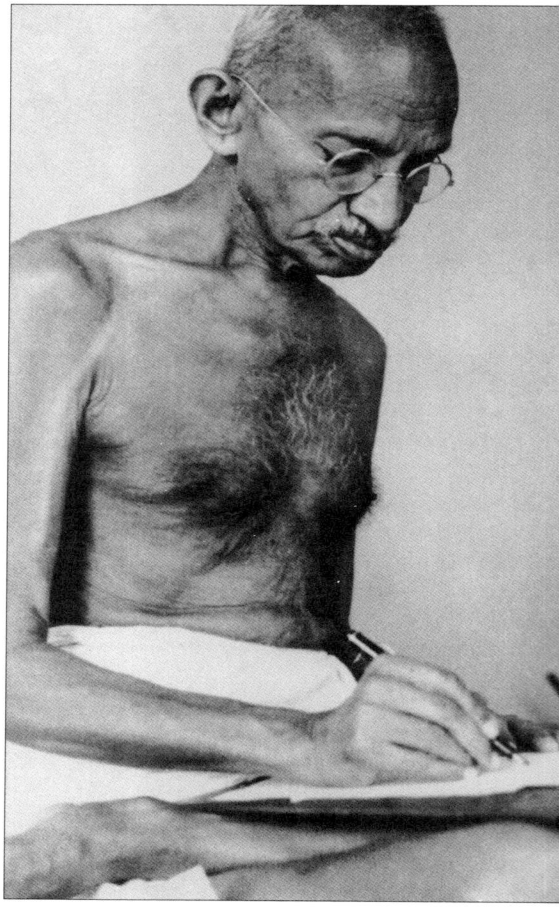

Chronology

1869	Born at Porbandar, Gujarāt, 2 October
1882	Marries a teenage bride
1888	Leaves for London to study law
1891	Becomes a barrister; sails for home
1892	Barrister in Bombay
1893	Moves to South Africa
1894	Founds Natal Indian Congress
1906	Starts Passive Resistance Movement
1915	Returns to India
1919	Amritsar Massacre; non-cooperation movement spreads nation-wide
1922–24	Two years in jail
1930	Anti-salt tax Dandi March
1931	Represents National Congress in London talks
1934	Resigns leadership of National Congress
1942	Interned for two years
1947	India granted independence
1948	Assassinated in New Delhi, 30 January

An Ascetic Life

- *'Non-violence is the greatest force at the disposal of mankind. It is mightier than the mightiest weapon of destruction devised by the ingenuity of man,' Gandhi said.*
- *'What do I think of Western civilization? I think it would be a very good idea.'*
- *Gandhi was attracted to a life of simplicity, manual labour and austerity. He cared nothing for money, power or sensual pleasure – only for the inner being.*
- *Religion, not politics, was his primary driver. 'What I have been striving and pining to achieve these thirty years', he wrote in his autobiography, 'is to see God face to face.'*

involving himself, as he had in South Africa, in numerous local struggles. He finally turned against the British after the First World War and plunged into politics. Following the Amritsar Massacre in 1919, when a British army general ordered his troops to shoot several hundred unarmed demonstrators, Gandhi initiated a nation-wide campaign of passive non-cooperation, including a boycott of British goods. He turned the inactive Indian National Congress into an effective movement, and assumed the mantle of India's nationalist movement. Gandhi was jailed for the first of many times in India in 1922, after delivering an impassioned indictment of British rule at his trial.

Released after two years, Gandhi set about preparing India psychologically and sociologically for independence; he spoke out against the caste system, called for inter-faith tolerance and worked to revive a sense of national self-confidence. He preached what he called 'the new science of non-violence' based on a belief in universal love, and earned himself the title of Mahatma, or 'Great Soul'.

To a growing audience, he propounded his ideas, on everything from hygiene and vegetarianism to education, and, to anyone who would listen, he promoted his ideals of a utopian, socialist society.

In 1928 Gandhi called on Britain to give India dominion status and he backed up his demands in 1930 by urging Indians to refuse to pay taxes, above all the tax on salt, against which he led a spectacular national march. The British wavered and he was sent to London for negotiations in 1931, but they came to nothing and he was rearrested on his return to India. While still in prison he started another hunger strike to protest against the government's decision to segregate India's 'untouchables'. On his release he vowed not to go back to his ashram until India was independent, and, after resigning the leadership of the National Congress in 1934, he set up home in a remote village in the very heart of the continent, Sevagram. He was by now a leader of unquestioned authority, and he had no need of political office; politicians instead beat a path to him.

Gandhi and the Congress leadership remained neutral during the Second World War, but most of its members were interned in 1942 after he made a speech in which he bluntly asked the British to 'quit India'. With Labour in power in London after the war, negotiations for independence intensified, and with them the tensions between Muslims and Hindus. Gandhi bravely walked from village to village trying to staunch the sectarian violence as up to one million people died in the run-up to independence and partition of the subcontinent in 1947, and he embarked on his final fast unto death. The fast halted rioting in Calcutta in September 1947, and persuaded both communities in Delhi to agree in January 1948 to live in 'perfect amity'. But a few days later Gandhi was shot dead on his way to evening prayers by Nathuram Godse, a Hindu angered at his pragmatic acceptance of the division of the subcontinent into Hindu India and Muslim Pakistan. His hands still folded in his final prayer, the dying Gandhi blessed his assassin: 'Hey, Rama' (Oh, God).

'What do I think of western civilization? I think it would be a very good idea.'

Ho Chi Minh

Ho Chi Minh (1890–1969). Vietnamese Communist leader who led his country in wars of independence against France and the United States. He died before the US was defeated, but his revolutionary zeal and determination shaped the post-colonial map of Southeast Asia.

BORN NGUYEN TAT THANH, the son of a minor official in French-ruled Vietnam, he was educated at French schools and became a school teacher. He went to sea as a steward on a French liner in 1911, worked his way round the world and then took a variety of jobs in London and Paris – bottle washer, gardener, sweeper, waiter and photo retoucher. During the Versailles Peace Conference following the First World War, he attempted to meet US President Wilson to press his case for Vietnamese independence. But he was fobbed off; the victors were not ready to apply the principles of self-determination to their colonies. He was active with the French Socialists, contributing articles to their newspaper, and in 1920, inspired by the Russian Revolution, he became a founder member of the French Communist Party.

He joined the ranks, and the payroll, of the Communist International and moved to Moscow in 1923. He spent two years at university in Moscow, and from then on he was a professional revolutionary. One of his first tasks was to organize a revolutionary movement among Vietnamese exiles in Canton. He founded the Vietnamese (later Indo-Chinese) Communist Party in 1930 in Hong Kong, where he was arrested at the behest of the French, who had condemned him to death in absentia. But he was released, much to French annoyance, in 1933. He lived as an exile in Moscow and China for the next few years, spending time with China's future Communist leader Mao Zedong in 1938 – an experience he disliked. In 1941 he set up the Communist-dominated independence movement, the Viet Minh, to fight the Japanese, who had taken over Vietnam. It was after them that he adopted the nom de guerre Ho Chi Minh, which means the 'Enlightener', and by which he would be known for the rest of his life. He fell out with the government of the anti-Communist Chiang Kai-shek and was imprisoned by him for eighteen months. Released with American assistance, he took up again with the Viet Minh and embarked on the long armed struggle for Vietnam's independence.

Following the fall of Japan at the end of World War II, Ho Chi Minh outfoxed the Chinese and the returning French, and deftly established his Viet Minh in Hanoi. There, on 2 September 1945, he proclaimed the Democratic Republic of Vietnam, becoming its first president. France, itself newly liberated from Germany and under the leadership of Charles de Gaulle, was not ready to let Vietnam go, and the stage was now set for Ho Chi Minh's great feat; talks broke down, and in 1946 he led his new country into a war against the French. Nobody believed this frail man with his thin goatee beard could win, least of all the French. But Ho Chi Minh

Chronology

1890	Born in Kim-lien, Central Vietnam, 19 May
1907	School teacher
1911	Joins French liner as steward
1912–23	Works abroad, mainly England and France
1920	Founding member of French Communist Party
1923	Moves to Moscow
1930	Founds Vietnamese Communist Party
1941	Founds the Viet Minh
1945	Founds Democratic Republic of Vietnam
1954	French defeated at Dien Bien Phu, 7 May
1969	Dies in Hanoi, 2 September

'We will never agree to negotiate under the threat of bombing'

MASTER OF DISGUISE

■ Ho Chi Minh had many pseudonyms and disguises. He had about ten aliases; one was a Buddhist monk. He wrote articles for the French socialist press under the name Nguyen Ai Quoc (Nguyen the Patriot), and travelled to China as Ly Thuy. Ho also wrote Notebook from Prison, perhaps unsurprsingly while in prison, in China, a book of poetry and a manual of revolution.

■ Saigon was renamed Ho Chi Minh City in his honour after the Communist conquest in 1975. He is buried there in a granite mausoleum, against his wishes. He had wanted his ashes buried on hilltops.

had a brilliant military commander, Vo Nguyen Giap, and eight years of bitter fighting culminated with the defeat of the French at Dien Bien Phu in 1954, and North Vietnam became an internationally recognized country. But the country was divided. South Vietnam remained under French and then American protection, while North Vietnam, cut off from the rest of the world, sank under 'Uncle Ho's' leadership into poverty and ugly, collectivized Communist totalitarianism.

Ho Chi Minh, however, wasn't finished. He continued to play the nationalist card and skilfully kept both Russia and China onside. He was still determined to reunite the country and, from 1959 onwards, the North began to arm insurgents in the South – the Viet Cong, led by Viet Minh veterans. But by now Ho Chi Minh's health was failing. He resigned the party leadership in 1959, although he remained head of state. He was still symbolically in charge when American bombs started dropping on Hanoi in 1965, and his name was on the North Vietnamese response to a personal message from US President Lyndon Johnson 'We will never agree to negotiate under the threat of bombing.'

Ho Chi Minh died of heart failure in 1969, six years before his victorious troops swept into Saigon, but he remains one of the principal architects of the first and (to date) only military defeat of the mighty United States. Ho Chi Minh is the undisputed father of modern Vietnam.

MAO ZEDONG

Mao Zedong (1893–1976) was a Chinese guerrilla leader who fought a civil war for twenty-two years to take over the world's most populous country, and then ruled it for another twenty-six years with his own brand of revolutionary Communism.

BORN TO A MODERATELY prosperous peasant family in the village of Shaoshan in Hunan Province, Mao was well educated in the Chinese classics. As a young man, he served as a soldier in the revolutionary army that overthrew the last imperial dynasty and established the Chinese Republic.

Mao later moved to Beijing where he first came into contact with revolutionary ideology. He studied Marx and Engels while working as a library assistant at Beijing University in 1918–19, and became a committed political activist. On 1 July 1921 Mao attended the founding meeting of the Chinese Communist Party in Shanghai. The party forged close relations with the Kuomintang, or Nationalists, until Chiang Kai-shek took over and dramatically broke with the Communists in 1927. Chiang's decision triggered a civil war that would last, on and off, for twenty-two years, and would end in his defeat and Mao's triumph.

Mao had by now returned to his peasant roots and started fomenting unrest, and building Communist support in the countryside; Chiang's Kuomintang remained the party of the cities and towns. Mao launched a series of uprisings, the most notable the disastrous 'Autumn Harvest Uprising' in Hunan, but they were brutally suppressed, so he retreated to the Jinggang Mountains where he set up a guerrilla army. In 1931, he overran part of Jiangxi and founded the Chinese Soviet Republic. His peasant guerrillas were now the Red Army and he had become de facto head of a rebel state.

Chiang, who had fought hard to destroy the warlords and unify the country, was determined to snuff out this last pocket of resistance. He encircled the breakaway republic with 700,000 men, and Mao lost half of his army. The remaining 100,000 broke out through the Nationalist lines and escaped to the northwest. Over the next two years, on the 'Long March', they travelled 6,000 miles to the safety of Yan'an, on the Soviet border, and Mao consolidated his grip over the party.

Mao's Communists held an uneasy peace with the Nationalists during World War II – both opposed to the Japanese invaders, Mao, more actively, from his base in Yan'an. But they fell apart after the defeat of Japan, and the civil war resumed. During the war years, the Communists had grown stronger and it took them just four years to drive Chiang over the Formosa Strait to Taiwan. Mainland China was now in Mao's hands and in 1949 he proclaimed it a People's Republic.

China was once more free from foreign domination and once more truly united – yet it was subservient to a hotchpotch of mainly imported Marxist ideology, which became known as Maoism. Mao's 'Great Leap Forward' – a massive reorganization of rural China into communes – resulted in widespread famine, and the deaths of up to twenty million people. Rivalry with Moscow over leadership of world Communism led to the Sino-Soviet split in the 1960s. The Chinese Communist hierarchy attempted to marginalize

CHRONOLOGY

1893 Born in Hunan Province, 26 December
1911–12 Soldier in Nationalist army
1921 Co-founder of Chinese Communist Party
1931 Founds Red Army; Chairman of the Chinese Soviet Republic
1934 Embarks on 'Long March' to escape Nationalist forces
1937 Alliance with Nationalists to fight Japanese
1945 Civil war resumes
1949 Proclaims People's Republic of China; elected Chairman
1958–61 'Great Leap Forward'
1966–69 Cultural Revolution
1976 Dies in Beijing, 9 September

'Political power grows out of the barrel of a gun'

Mao, and he responded in the late 1960s by launching the Cultural Revolution in which Red Guards ran amok. The revolution tore society apart and millions more suffered or perished. Mao, in his old age and stricken with Parkinson's disease, encouraged a cult of personality; his image in his trademark peasant tunic, and quotes from his writings were displayed ubiquitously.

The Little Red Book

- *His Little Red Book* – The Thoughts of Chairman Mao – *made him one of the richest men in China, where it was compulsory reading. He was a prolific writer.*
- *Mao's ideas on revolutionary struggle and guerrilla warfare influenced revolutionary movements around the world. 'Political power grows out of the barrel of a gun,' he said.*
- *Mao also had many critics. The official view of the People's Republic of China today is that he was a great revolutionary leader who made serious mistakes in his later life, particularly in creating a cult of personality.*
- *Mao loved swimming. He married three times and had four children. His first wife was shot by the Nationalists; his third wife, Lan P'ing, was a film actress.*

Fidel Castro

Fidel Castro (1926–) led a band of left-wing guerrillas to power in Cuba in 1959 in an armed uprising against the dictatorship of Fulgencio Batista, and has ruled his Caribbean island ever since as a one-party Communist state in the shadow of capitalist America.

FIDEL ALEJANDRO CASTRO RUZ grew up on his family's sugar plantation, a 23,000-acre estate near Birán, in Cuba's Oriente province. His father had originally been an immigrant labourer from Galicia in Spain. As a young boy, Castro worked in the sugar cane fields, but from the age of six he attended Jesuit schools, first in Santiago and later in Havana's Colegio Belén, where he was the top athlete.

In 1945, he began law studies at the University of Havana and graduated in 1950 with a PhD, but he spent a lot of his student days as a political activist, and developed a taste for direct action; he took part in a plot against the dictator of the Dominican Republic, General Trujillo, and joined in student street riots in the Colombian capital, Bogotá. Castro started work as a lawyer, and was intending to stand for a parliamentary seat in the 1952 elections when they were cancelled after General Fulgencio Batista overthrew the government of President Carlos Prio Socarrás in a coup d'état. Castro challenged the decision in court, and when the court rejected his petition he took up arms. On 26 July 1953, Castro led 150 men on an attack on the Moncada Barracks in Santiago de Cuba, the country's second-largest military base, in the hopes of sparking a popular uprising. Half the attackers were killed or captured, and Castro and his brother Raúl were taken prisoner. Castro made an impassioned political defence at the trial, stating defiantly that 'history will absolve me'. They were sentenced to fifteen years' imprisonment, but released in a political amnesty in May 1955.

Castro departed for Mexico, where he recruited another fighting force – the 26th of July Revolutionary Movement. A group of eighty-two men landed on the north coast of Oriente province on 2 December 1956, and all but twelve were immediately killed. The survivors, including Castro, his brother and an Argentine volunteer Che Guevara, retreated to the Sierra Maestra, and from this mountain stronghold they waged an astonishingly successful guerrilla war against the Batista regime. Castro's guerrillas attracted more and more volunteers and achieved spectacular victories against an increasingly demoralized army. Within two years Castro's force of 800 guerrillas had defeated a 30,000-man professional army; Batista fled the country on New Year's Day 1959, and Castro made a victorious entry into Havana. Castro appointed himself commander in chief of the armed forces and premier; he was undisputed leader.

Castro had come to power with the support of most Cubans, promising to restore the 1940 constitution. But once in power, he turned into a committed Marxist-Leninist; he nationalized private commerce and industry, confiscated property owned by non-Cubans, collectivized agriculture and instigated far-reaching welfare and education reforms to benefit the poor. He transformed Cuba into a one-party Communist state and ruthlessly suppressed all political dissent and opposition. Many of the middle class fled the country, some establishing a large, active anti-Castro community in Miami, Florida.

The United States had initially recognized the new government on 7 January 1959, but relations quickly soured as the new Cuban government expropriated American-owned properties and, in

Chronology

1926 Born in Mayari, Cuba, 13 August
1945 Graduated from Colegio Belén, Havana
1950 PhD, University of Havana
1953 Abortive attack on Moncada Barracks
1953–55 Imprisoned
1955 Exile in Mexico
1956 Returns to Cuba, starts armed uprising
1959 Batista driven into exile, Castro takes over
1959–76 Prime Minister
1976– Head of state

A Life For The Revolution

■ *Castro, who was officially 'excommunicated' by the Catholic Church, allowed Pope John Paul to visit Cuba in 1998. Following the visit, Castro reinstated Christmas Day as a national holiday.*

■ *Renowned for his speeches that frequently last for anything up to several hours, Castro perhaps sums himself up best with one of his shortest statements: 'I love power, and I am the revolution,' he said in 1987.*

■ *In 2003, he became the world's longest-ruling head of government.*

■ *Castro's father, Angel Castro y Argiz, had two children by his first wife and five more by his cook, Lina Ruiz Gonzalez. Castro and his brother Raúl were two of these five.*

Within two years of taking up arms, Castro's force of 800 guerillas had defeated a 30,000 strong army

February 1960, announced a trade pact with the Soviet Union to barter Russian oil for Cuban sugar. Cuba in effect became a Soviet satellite and, in the Cold War climate of the 1960s, the US broke diplomatic relations and imposed a trade embargo. The two countries have been at loggerheads ever since and have several times nearly come to blows – notably over the CIA-backed Bay of Pigs invasion in 1961, and the so-called Cuban missile crisis in 1962 when Washington faced down Moscow and forced the Russians to withdraw nuclear warheads from the island. In recent years, mass emigration from Cuba to the US mainland has fuelled further tension between the two countries.

The bearded, cigar-chomping Castro became an international symbol of Communist revolution, and his anti-US rhetoric his calling card, but his attempts to spread Marxist revolutions to other parts of Latin America failed. Che Guevara, one of his most trusted lieutenants, died trying to foment a peasant uprising in Bolivia, and the left-wing guerrilla movements that he supported on the continent were one by one snuffed out. Cuban forces served as proxies for the Soviet Union in various Third World conflicts, notably in the Angolan civil war.

Although there were spectacular advances in health and education, Communism failed to bring prosperity to Cuba, and the island became increasingly dependent on the Soviet Union. The Soviet Union's collapse in 1990 increased economic hardship and set off a new wave of illegal emigration and, although economic necessity forced Castro to permit a partial return to free enterprise, it left Castro's Cuba as the last Communist country in the western hemisphere.

NELSON MANDELA

Nelson Rolihlahla Mandela (1918–) became the international symbol of the struggle to free South Africa from apartheid, and the country's first black president. A leading figure in the African National Congress civil rights group, he served twenty-seven years in jail before being freed in 1990 after President F. W. de Klerk bowed to international pressure and agreed to end apartheid.

NELSON ROLIHLAHLA MANDELA – the middle name means 'troublemaker' – was the son of a Thembu tribal chief and, thus, to some extent shielded from the poverty inflicted on most of his fellow black South Africans by the country's racial segregationalist policy known as apartheid. Born in the Umtata province of the Transkei, now the Eastern Cape Province, in 1918, at the age of seven he was the first of his family to attend school.

After secondary education at Healdtown School, Mandela went on to University College of Fort Hare, then South Africa's only seat of higher education for blacks, to read for a Bachelor of Arts degree. By his early twenties, though, Mandela was becoming increasingly politicized, influenced in particular by Walter Sisulu, one of the brightest young thinkers in the African National Congress (ANC). Mandela joined the organization in 1942 and, with Sisulu, Oliver Tambo and others, played a key role in launching the ANC Youth League with the aim of broadening and radicalizing the ANC's support base. His growing political radicalism cost him his place at Fort Hare, and he was obliged to complete his degree by correspondence, living in Johannesburg, working towards legal qualifications.

When the National Party won the 1948 elections on an apartheid platform, the Youth League's leadership, Mandela included, drew up an action programme advocating boycotts, strikes, civil disobedience and non-cooperation in pursuit of full citizenship and direct parliamentary representation for all South Africans, regardless of race. The programme was adopted as ANC policy in 1949, when Sisulu became its secretary general, Mandela joining him on the National Executive Committee the following year.

In 1952 the ANC launched a mass disobedience campaign and Mandela travelled the country organizing support, which earned him his first serious brush with the law and a six-month suspended prison sentence. The same year, he opened a legal practice in Johannesburg, in partnership with Oliver Tambo.

The late 1950s saw more brushes with the law and Mandela's arrest, banning and imprisonment, plus a treason charge, on which he was eventually acquitted in 1961. The Sharpeville Massacre of 1960, when sixty-seven blacks were shot dead during an anti-apartheid demonstration, had led to the banning of the ANC.

As the struggle for democratic freedoms intensified, the ANC concluded in 1961 that armed struggle was its only realistic option and established Umkhonto we Sizwe (Spear of the Nation), as an

CHRONOLOGY

1918	Born in Umtata district, Transkei, 18 July
1942	Joins civil rights group the African National Congress
1943	Graduates from Fort Hare University College
1944	Helps found ANC Youth League
1952	Qualifies as lawyer, opens own law office in Johannesburg
1956	Arrested and charged with high treason, acquitted 1961
1962	Rearrested, sentenced to five years in jail
1964	Convicted of treason and sabotage, sentenced to life imprisonment
1990	Released from jail, ban on ANC lifted
1993	Awarded Nobel Peace Prize, jointly with President F. W. de Klerk
1994	Elected President in South Africa's first fully democratic general elections
1999	Retires from public life

Speech From The Dock

■ *At his trial at Rivonia, which lasted from October 1963 to June 1964, Mandela spelled out his creed: 'I have fought against white domination, and I have fought against black domination. I have cherished the ideal of a democratic and free society in which all persons live together in harmony and with equal opportunities. It is an ideal which I hope to live for and to achieve. But if needs be, it is an ideal for which I am prepared to die.'*

■ *Mandela's wife Winnie did much to keep the ANC cause alive and transform her husband into the world's most famous political prisoner. But after his release, the couple separated and finally divorced in 1996.*

■ *Mandela was married again on his 80th birthday, in July 1998, to Graca Machel, widow of the first president of Mozambique.*

'I have cherished the ideal of a democratic and free society in which all persons live together in harmony'

armed nucleus, with Mandela as its commander. His successful evasion of the police during this period had earned him the nickname the Black Pimpernel. But in 1962 his luck ran out and he was arrested and jailed for five years for illegally leaving the country to rally support. Two years later he was charged with treason and sabotage, and sentenced to life imprisonment.

Mandela was incarcerated at the notorious Robben Island prison off Cape Town, along with several other key ANC leaders. But over his eighteen years there his international renown grew and pressure for an end to the apartheid system intensified. In 1982 he was moved to a maximum security jail near Cape Town, in much improved conditions. After meetings with a number of international statesmen and 'feelers' from the apartheid regime, Mandela entered into direct talks with the government in 1988 and the following year had his first meeting with President P. W. Botha. When F. W. de Klerk became president later that year, he released Walter Sisulu and other prominent ANC leaders from jail as he began dismantling the apartheid structure. Mandela met de Klerk in December, and two months later, on 11 February 1990, he was a free man.

The next four years saw the steady eradication of decades of repression, alongside preparations for South Africa's first fully democratic elections. Mandela and de Klerk received international recognition for the peaceful transformation when they shared the 1993 Nobel Peace Prize, and in May 1994, with an overwhelming majority, Nelson Mandela became the country's first black president.

Mandela was president for five years, and both during his years in office and in retirement he worked tirelessly as an international ambassador for peace and justice.

Shaka Zulu

Shaka Zulu (1787–1828) was a warrior chief who created a powerful fighting force to wipe out his enemies and establish southern Africa's Zulu Empire.

SHAKA WAS BORN in 1787, the illegitimate son of Senzangakona, a chief of the then little-known Zulu tribe, and Nandi, an orphaned princess of the Langeni clan. Senzangakona repudiated Nandi, and she and Shaka went to live in exile with the Langeni, where both mother and son were treated as virtual outcasts. The Langeni drove Nandi and her son out and they found shelter with the Mtetwa. From about 1802, Shaka joined the Mtetwa army and quickly distinguished himself as a fearless and skilled fighter. He excelled in single combat, using shield and spear, and over six years rose to high rank in the Mtetwa army. On the death of Shaka's father in 1816, the Mtetwa chieftain, Dingiswayo, gave him military assistance to win back his rightful inheritance as chief of the Zulus.

Shaka had enormous ambitions for a tribe that then numbered little more than 1,500. He aimed to rule all of southern Africa and he set about building a powerful Zulu army. He established military towns and provided his army with the best training and provisions, and the strictest discipline. His soldiers were required to remain celibate, and violation of the rule was punished by death. Any soldier who showed fear in battle was instantly killed. He divided the army into regiments or impi and, like the Romans, he incorporated defeated tribes into their ranks. He also introduced women's regiments. His men could march fifty miles in a day.

Shaka revolutionized the Zulu army's weaponry and its military tactics. He perfected complex battle formations to outflank and confuse his enemies, notably the 'buffalo' formation, when the 'horns' encircled the opposing army. It had been customary for Zulu warriors to throw their spears and then withdraw. Shaka changed their approach to battle, and designed a stabbing spear, which forced his men to engage the enemy in close combat.

Chronology

1787	Born
1802	Shaka joins the Mtetwa army
1816	Becomes chief of the Zulu on death of his father
1817	Begins expansion of Zulu Empire
1820	Start of the Mfecane
1827	Death of his mother
1828	Murdered by his half-brothers, 22 September

He fought bloody wars, which normally ended with the total annihilation of his enemies, uprooting thousands, and killing at least a million. He turned first on the Langeni, to avenge his childhood humiliation, impaling their leaders on the stakes of their kraals, and next he destroyed the Butelezi. After the Mtetwa chief Dingiswayo died in 1817, there was no stopping Shaka. He cleaned up the coastal areas and from 1820 set about systematically wiping out all the rival tribes on the Natal plateau – an extermination called the Mfecane or 'Crushing'. The Zulu Empire eventually stretched from the Cape to Tanzania.

Shaka first came into contact with Europeans in Natal in 1824, and he gave them tracts of land. He was treated for a wound by a visiting Englishman. Shaka seems to have gone totally mad following the death of his mother in 1827. In his grief, he slaughtered 7,000 Zulus, and no crops were planted for a year, and milk – a Zulu staple – was banned. Shaka was murdered by his half-brothers in 1828. They stabbed him to death and threw his body into an empty grain pot.

Shaka perfected complex battle formations, most notably the 'buffalo' formation of 'head' and 'horns'

The Mfecane

■ The uprooted people, victims of the Mfecane, migrated as far north as modern Tanzania and as far south as Cape Province. The devastation was so complete that the Boers passed through uninhabited empty land when they crossed Natal on their Great Trek in 1830.
■ Shaka's name, though now hallowed, was originally an insult – 'iShaka' was an intestinal parasite thought to be responsible for menstrual irregularities and said, by Zulu elders, to be the true cause of Nandi's pregnancy.
■ Zulu power endured; fifty years after his death Shaka's army beat British regulars in the Zulu War.

Chiang Kai-shek

Chiang Kai-shek (1887–1975). Statesman and military leader who unified China after the overthrow of the Manchu dynasty and led his country to victory against Japan, only to lose it four years later to the Communists. He established Nationalist China on the island of Taiwan.

Born into a modestly prosperous merchant family in a remote farm village in the eastern province of Chekiang, Chiang attended a military college in Paoting, in North China, and was sent to the Military Staff College in Tokyo from 1907 to 1911. The future Chinese revolutionary leader Sun Yat-sen was one of his classmates. He served in the Japanese army, and the discipline of Japanese soldiers, and their ability to endure hardship, left a lasting impression.

When revolution stirred in 1911, Chiang returned to Shanghai and took part in the overthrow of the imperial government, and establishment in 1912 of the Republic of China. In 1918, he joined Sun's Kuomintang, the Nationalists who were fighting China's warlords for control of the country. He became Sun's military aide, and Sun sent him to the USSR in 1923 to seek Soviet assistance for the beleaguered Nationalist government. On his return he was appointed commandant of the newly created Whampoa Military Academy.

After Sun's death in 1925, Chiang took over as commander in chief of the Nationalist army, and emerged as the strongman of the party. He launched the Northern Expedition to crush the warlords of the North and led a victorious Nationalist army into Hankou, Shanghai and Nanjing. In a dramatic reversal he broke with the Communists in 1927, triggering a long and ultimately fatal civil war. Chiang quickly gained full control of the Kuomintang, and by 1928 he had taken Beijing and established himself at the head of the Nationalist government at Nanjing and as generalissimo of all the Chinese Nationalist Forces.

Chiang was kidnapped by a rival Nationalist general in 1936 and forced to terminate the civil war in order to establish a united front against the Japanese, who had seized Manchuria in 1931 and who looked poised for all-out assault on China. Full-scale war with Japan broke out in 1937, but even then the truce between Nationalists and Communists never really held. Chiang moved his capital to Chongqing after the Japanese overran Nanjing, and, as the Sino-Japanese war merged with World War II, he started to play on the world stage. Nationalist China came to be seen as a bulwark against Japan, and the monk-like general, dressed in unadorned fatigues, started to hobnob with Roosevelt, Stalin and Churchill. In 1942 he was named supreme commander of the Allied forces in China, and the following year he represented China at the Cairo Conference. The Allies, however, never entirely trusted him, always suspecting that he was more interested in his struggle against the Communists than in war against Japan.

Chiang's international stature was bolstered by his beautiful third wife. After dumping the first two, he had married Mei-ling Song, the US-educated daughter of a prominent Shanghai publishing tycoon, in 1927, and had adopted her Christian faith. Mei-ling had a brilliant talent for public relations, and she was largely responsible for transforming Chiang's image abroad.

Chronology

1887	Born in Fenghua, Chekiang province, 31 October
1907	Enters Tokyo's Military Staff College
1911	Returns to China on outbreak of revolution
1917	Military aide to Sun Yat-sen
1926	Takes over as military chief of Kuomintang
1927	Marries Mei-ling Song; breaks with Communists
1928	Defeats regional warlords; unifies China
1943	Attends Cairo Conference
1945	World War II ends
1946–49	Final phase of Chinese civil war
1949	Chiang Kai-shek flees mainland to Taiwan
1975	Dies in Taipei, 5 April

Chiang ruled Taiwan as a benevolent dictator until his death in 1975

Mei-ling Song

- *Mei-ling Song was one of the most influential women of the twentieth century. Her father was a Chinese Methodist minister and businessman. Educated in the US, graduating from Wellesley College in English literature and philosophy in 1917. She met Chiang in 1920 and they only married after he agreed to convert from Buddhism to Christianity. A power behind the general's throne, in 1943 she became the first Chinese national and only the second woman to address a joint session of the US House and Senate.*
- *'The only thing oriental about me', Mei-ling once said, 'is my face.'*
- *Following her husband's death, she returned to the US, where she died on 23 October 2003, aged 105.*

But power bred complacency and corruption, and China was still predominantly feudal. Chiang had ruthlessly crushed the warlords but he had not dismantled their fiefdoms. The peasants, who made up 90 per cent of the population, still had no stake in the country, and ultimately Chiang had no vision for them. He had dallied in the war and allowed his army to ossify. With the war ended, Chiang failed to achieve a settlement with the Communists and the civil war resumed. In four years of bitter fighting, in which at least five million were killed, Chiang was driven out of China by a battle-hardened army led by Mao Zedong.

Chiang withdrew to Taiwan, which he ruled as a benign Fascist dictator until his death in 1975. His last years were overshadowed by the decision of his former close allies, Japan and the United States, to move towards recognizing mainland Communist China, but his legacy is a prosperous island that has developed some semblance of genuine democracy.

Aung San Suu Kyi

Aung San Suu Kyi (1945–), Myanmar's leader in captivity, is an international symbol of peaceful opposition to oppression. She has spent, on and off, some ten years in detention or under house arrest for leading the opposition to her country's military rulers, and her tenacity and courage have earned her world-wide admiration. She was awarded the Nobel Peace Prize in 1991

Suu Kyi was the daughter of Burma's national leader Aung San, who led his country's struggle for independence from Britain. He was assassinated in 1947 when she was just two years old. She was educated in Burma and India, where her mother was Burmese ambassador in the early 1960s. After studying politics at Delhi University, she moved to Oxford University for three years and graduated in 1967 with a degree in PPE (politics, philosophy and economics). It was there that she met and later married an Oxford academic, Michael Aris. She embarked on an international career with the United Nations in New York, moving in various governmental and research roles to Bhutan, India and Japan, before settling back in Oxford to raise her two sons. She would doubtless have remained there had her mother not fallen ill.

Suu Kyi returned to Myanmar (then Burma) to nurse her mother in 1988 to find her country in turmoil; a popular uprising against the military that had seized power in 1962 was being ruthlessly suppressed. Thousands died, and Suu Kyi rose to the challenge. 'I could not, as my father's daughter, remain indifferent to what was going on,' she said at her first mass rally of half a million people in front of Yangon's famous Shwedagon Pagoda. 'This national crisis could in fact be called the second struggle for independence.'

She founded an opposition party, the National League for Democracy, in 1988, and was arrested in 1989 for allegedly inciting violence. The following year, 1990, her National League for Democracy won a landslide victory in elections, capturing 82 per cent of the vote. But the military, calling itself the State Law and Order Restoration Council, refused to hand over power. The Burmese generals set about crushing all resistance and imposed a new harsh regime on Suu Kyi. She was barred from receiving visitors, not even her sons and husband, and held in solitary confinement. When awarded the Nobel Peace Prize in 1991, her sons picked it up on her behalf. The judges called her 'one of the most extraordinary examples of civil courage in Asia'.

She was released in 1995, but kept under strict surveillance, and then rearrested and confined to her house again in September 2000. Her husband had died from cancer in 1999, having not seen her for three years. She was offered the chance to travel to England for his funeral, but she refused, knowing the military would not allow her back into Myanmar. He had been refused a visa to visit her. Suu Kyi was again released in May 2002, and immediately resumed campaigning for the National League for Democracy, only to be placed under house arrest at her lakeside home in Yangon once more in September 2003, after undergoing major surgery.

Chronology

1945	Born in Rangoon (now Yangon), 19 June
1947	General Aung San, Suu Kyi's father, assassinated
1948	Burma gains independence
1962	General Ne Win seizes power
1967	Graduates from Oxford University
1988	Returns to Burma to care for her mother
1988	Forms National League for Democracy
1989	Placed under house arrest
1990	National League wins 82 per cent of vote
1991	Wins Nobel Peace Prize
1995	Freed from house arrest
1999	Her husband Michael Aris dies
2000–06	Intermittent house arrest

'Myanmar' has systematically resisted international calls to release Suu Kyi and restore democracy.

Medal of Freedom

- *Suu Kyi models her struggle for the restoration of democracy on the ways of Mahatma Gandhi, and above all on his commitment to non-violence as a means of achieving one's political ends. She always wears a flower in her hair in public.*
- *In 2000, US President Bill Clinton conferred the Presidential Medal of Freedom, America's highest civilian honour, on Suu Kyi, for her commitment to democracy.*
- *Under house arrest, Suu Kyi says she keeps herself busy by studying and exercising. She meditates, practises her French and Japanese, and plays the piano.*
- *Myanmar, as the military renamed Burma, has systematically resisted international calls to release Suu Kyi and restore democracy.*

SPARTACUS

Spartacus (c120–71 BC) was a Roman slave and gladiator, born in Thrace, who led a major rebellion against Rome.

A THRACIAN BY BIRTH, Spartacus served in the Roman army but somehow ran foul of authority – possibly he deserted – and he and his wife were sold into slavery. They were taken to the slave-market in Rome and were both bought by Lentulus Batiates, who ran a school for gladiators in Capua. Gladiators were trained to fight in the arena to entertain the Romans, many of them to the death.

Once in Capua, Spartacus determined to break out. 'If we must fight, we might as well fight for our freedom', he was reported to have said. Using spits and chopping knives seized from the kitchens, seventy-eight gladiators fought their way out on the streets and into open country, where they defeated a small force sent to capture them. They now had weapons and they established a camp on top of Mount Vesuvius, inside the crater of the dormant volcano.

An army of 3,000 men now marched from Rome and surrounded him. But the gladiators, using ropes that they had twisted from vines to lower themselves down an impregnable cliff face, took them by surprise and captured the entire Roman force. The Senate in Rome hurriedly dispatched two more forces to subdue the slaves, but both were routed. A legend was born, and more and more slaves flocked to join Spartacus; by 72 BC, less than a year after the escape from Capua, Spartacus was commanding an army of 70,000 men. Most of Rome's armies were fighting abroad, so the regular troops in Italy were outnumbered by the rebels.

Spartacus could now roam the length and breadth of Italy and he set his heart on breaking out over the Alps to freedom. But he couldn't persuade the Gauls and Germans who had joined his forces to follow him. Meanwhile, Rome elected a new general to lead a force against Spartacus – Marcus Licinius Crassus. A rich man, he seems to have been one of the few high-ranking men in Rome willing to risk his reputation against a bunch of slaves.

Crassus raised an army of six legions. He sent his lieutenant Mummius on ahead with two legions to harass the slaves and with strict orders not to fight a pitched battle. But Mummius disobeyed and was routed. Crassus sentenced the defeated legions to be decimated – lots were drawn for one in every ten surviving soldiers to be put to the sword.

Spartacus moved south, where he made an unsuccessful bid to escape to Sicily. Crassus closed in on him, and was joined by Pompey's army which had just returned to Italy from Spain. Early in 71 BC, Spartacus decided to risk fighting a decisive battle against the Romans. He knew it would be winner-take-all and famously killed his own horse before the fighting started, saying that if he won the day he would get a better horse and if he lost he would have no need of a mount. At Petelia in Lucania, the Romans prevailed and Spartacus was first wounded and then killed. All the rebel slaves perished, except for 6,000 who were captured and crucified along the road from Capua to Rome.

CHRONOLOGY

120 BC	Estimated date of Spartacus's birth
73 BC	Spartacus leads rebellion of gladiators
72 BC	Gladiators defeat Roman forces
71 BC	Spartacus defeated and killed

An army of 3,000 marched from Rome; Spartacus took them by surprise and captured them all

Revolutionary Hero

■ *Spartacus is often hailed as a champion of the masses and a social revolutionary. In fact there is no evidence that he wanted anything except his freedom and to return home. Nonetheless, his name was frequently invoked by revolutionaries – most notably the German Communist Spartakus League, led by Rosa Luxemburg and Karl Liebknecht, who were both killed in an abortive uprising against the German government in 1919.*

■ *Just as the original gladiators stirred the crowd's imagination in the the Roman amphitheatres, so do rather gentler representations of their prowess today. Spartacus' rebellion against Rome inspired a 1960 Hollywood blockbuster, named simply* Spartacus *and directed by Stanley Kubrick and starring Kirk Douglas as Spartacus, and a 1968 Russian ballet, with music composed by Aram Khachaturian.*

MAXIMILIEN ROBESPIERRE

Maximilien François Marie Isidore de Robespierre (1758–94) was one of the main leaders of the 1789 French Revolution and the principal architect of the 'Terror' which eventually destroyed him. No figure in the French Revolution arouses so much controversy.

BORN INTO A FAMILY of modest means of French and Irish descent in the small northern town of Arras, Robespierre won a scholarship to the Louis-le-Grand College in Paris, and later studied law at the University of Paris. He returned to his native town to practise as a lawyer and judge. He was outspoken and at times radical on social issues, but he earned a reputation for honesty. Always frugal and dressed simply, he was later to be known as 'the incorruptible'.

Elected to the Estates General, the National Assembly that was convened on the eve of the French Revolution in May 1789, Robespierre, a skilled and tireless orator, quickly emerged as one of the radicals. By 1790, he was leader of the Jacobins, a political club which advocated unlimited democracy and the removal of the monarchy, and he had become a popular hero of the Paris mob.

After the downfall of the monarchy in 1792, Robespierre was elected first deputy for Paris to the new National Convention. He played a decisive part in the trial of King Louis XVI, speaking eleven times and arguing that the king had to die in order for France to live. The king was publicly executed in January 1793. In July 1793, Robespierre was elected a member of the National Convention's chief executive body, the Committee of Public Safety. The first committee (April–July 1793) was dominated by Georges Danton, also a lawyer, and the second (July 1793 – July 1794) by Robespierre. The committees assumed total power, and established their grip over France through a network of shadow committees in every department and commune. France was in turmoil, facing counter-revolution at home – uprisings in the Vendée and elsewhere – and the threat of invasion from Prussia and Austria. The committee responded by ordering the death of the opponents of the revolution – both real and imaginary. Thus began the 'Reign of Terror', with Robespierre its chief instigator. He replaced Danton in July 1793 and became virtual dictator of France. Danton and his associates went to the guillotine the following April, for questioning the purposes of the Terror. The uprising in the Vendée, the most serious challenge to the revolution in the provinces, was put down with unremitting harshness – drowning and mass executions: modern Europe's first genocide.

The Reign of Terror was a deliberate instrument of policy, designed to create a climate of fear and uncertainty. In a sea of spies and petty regulations, overseen by the Revolutionary Tribunal which fed its victims to the guillotine, nobody felt safe. What drove Robespierre to it has endlessly fascinated historians. He seems to have been impelled by a genuine sense of duty; far from being a simple fanatic, he fought enemies on both the extreme left and the moderate right. He was cold, reserved and solitary, but his integrity was never in question.

Robespierre's undoing began with his insistence on a decree proclaiming the cult of the Supreme Being as an official religion – Robespierre's homage to the ideas of the writer Jean Jacques Rousseau. This antagonized both Roman Catholics and atheists. In June 1794 Robespierre was elected

CHRONOLOGY

1758	Born in Arras, 6 May
1769	Begins studies in Paris at Louis-le-Grand College
1781	Receives law degree
1782	Sets up law practice in Arras
1789	Elected to the Estates General
1791	Appointed public prosecutor
1792	Elected to new National Convention
1793	Execution of King Louis XVI
1793–94	Committees of Public Safety
1794	Declared an outlaw, guillotined on 28 July

AN EVIL REPUTATION

- *Robespierre was vilified after the revolution as a bloodthirsty dictator. But dispassionate historians have found in him as much a radical social reformer, who became blindly subservient to violence. His social ideals were advanced for their time: he sought the levelling out of extremes of wealth, an increase in small property ownership, and work and education for all.*
- *Robespierre's relationship with the moderate Danton has been the subject of many plays, films and books. One of the best known is Danton's Death, by German dramatist Georg Büchner (1835).*
- *Robespierre went to his death stoically, but he let out a terrible cry on the scaffold when the executioner ripped off the bandage that had been put round his wounded jaw.*

A cold, solitary man, Robespierre's personal integrity was never questioned

president of the National Convention and the Reign of Terror intensified. But the seemingly wanton killing suddenly seemed less justified as a string of military victories removed the imminent danger of foreign invasion. Robespierre, who had withdrawn from the daily fray, suddenly looked vulnerable.

Conspirators barred Robespierre from speaking at the National Convention on 27 July, and as he tried to rally support in the city he was declared an outlaw. Wounded by a pistol shot to the jaw, he was seized and hastily put on trial in accordance with the fast-track system he had himself implemented. Robespierre was condemned to death and he was guillotined together with his two close associates and nineteen supporters the following day.

GIUSEPPE GARIBALDI

Giuseppe Garibaldi (1807–82), a nationalist leader and guerrilla fighter who helped create the modern state of Italy, was a swashbuckling adventurer whose exploits made him a hero on two continents, Europe and South America.

GARIBALDI WAS the self-educated son of a fisherman from Nice, who started life as a humble merchant seaman. His defining achievement was to lead a guerrilla army to free Italy from foreign occupation; in addition he packed in fourteen years fighting battles in South America, was offered a Union command by US President Abraham Lincoln in the American Civil War and took part in the 1870–71 Franco-Prussian war.

Garibaldi's legendary crusade to liberate southern Italy started in May 1860 when he commandeered two old paddle steamers in Genoa and led a volunteer force of 1,070 guerrilla 'Redshirts' to victory against 12,000 regular soldiers in Sicily.

Three months later he crossed the Straits of Messina to the Italian mainland, routing the armies of the Bourbon monarch on the banks of the Volturno River on 26 October 1860 to capture Naples and win the whole of the south for the new kingdom of Italy.

Italy as a nation did not exist when Garibaldi was born. It was divided into warring states, dukedoms, principalities and territories ruled by the popes in Rome, and it was also dominated by its two powerful neighbours – France and Austria.

Inspired by the early Italian nationalists, Garibaldi, by now a merchant sea captain and serving in the Piedmontese navy, embarked on his long revolutionary career by taking part in a mutiny that was intended to provoke an uprising against the Austrians in 1834.

The uprising failed: Garibaldi was sentenced to death *in absentia* and escaped to South America, where he lived from 1836 to 1848, taking part in a number of uprisings in Brazil and fighting for Uruguay in its war of independence with Argentina.

CHRONOLOGY

1807 Born in Nice on 4 July
1834 Sentenced to death for Piedmont uprising
1834–48 South America
1848–49 Revolution and failure of Rome republic
1859 Defeats Austrians in Alps
1860 Conquest of Sicily and Naples
1871 Wins Battle of Dijon with French
1874 Elected to Italian Parliament
1882 Dies in island of Caprera on 2 June

Garibaldi raced back to Europe at the outbreak of the 1848 revolutions to fight for the Risorgimento, or resurrection of Italy, and together with Giuseppe Mazzini he established a republic in Rome before it was crushed by French troops in 1849. His Brazilian wife, Anita, who had fought alongside him, died during the campaign, in which Garibaldi refused to accept defeat and displayed exemplary courage and outstanding leadership. He got away, first to Tangier, then to America, where he became an American citizen, and finally to Peru where, for a time, he plied his original trade as a ship's captain.

Garibaldi came back to Europe in 1854, and four years later joined yet another attempt to reunify Italy. This one succeeded – thanks largely to Garibaldi's extraordinary military leadership. In South America, he had become a master of guerrilla warfare, capable of beating professional forces by hit-and-run and ambush.

He defeated the Austrians in the Alps in 1859, and set out for the south with his famous 'Thousand'. After the fall of Naples, and impatient to complete the reunification of Italy, Garibaldi launched two further abortive military expeditions

Garibaldi became a master of guerrilla warfare, beating professional forces by hit-and-run and ambush

The Redshirts

- Garibaldi's fighters were famous for their red shirts. It was in Uruguay that he first dressed his men in red shirts, obtained from a factory in Montevideo which had intended to export them to the slaughter houses of Argentina.
- Garibaldi's memoirs, Autobiography of Giuseppe Garibaldi, were published in 1887 and had far-reaching impact, inspiring, among others, the movement for independence in India.
- In addition to being hailed as a hero and the 'sword' of Italian reunification in his own country, Garibaldi is honoured with a statue in New York City. He brought London to a standstill when he made a triumphal visit to Britain in 1864.

– to seize Venice and Rome, being wounded and captured in the process. International politics eventually forced the Austrians to cede Venice and the French to withdraw from Rome, and Italy became a unified and free country again in 1870.

Garibaldi went to war one more time, fighting alongside the French against the Prussians in 1871, and earning himself a seat in France's National Assembly.

He was also elected to Italy's Parliament in 1874. He lived out his old age on Caprera as a highly respected statesman on both sides of the Atlantic and a grand old man of national revolution – the 'hero of two worlds'.

Vladimir Lenin

Vladimir Lenin (1870–1924) was one of the world's greatest revolutionary leaders and the founder of the first Marxist State, the Soviet Union. He became a universal symbol of a communist ideology that spawned revolutionary movements around the world.

VLADIMIR ILYICH ULYANOV was born into a privileged class in 19th century Russia. His father, Ilya, an Inspector for Elementary Schools was married to Maria Alexandrovna, daughter of a wealthy Jewish physician. Lenin was one of six children; he was hard working at school and enjoyed outdoor sports. His youth was shattered in 1887 when his older brother Alexander was arrested and hanged for plotting to assassinate Tsar Alexander – an event which set Lenin on the road to revolution.

Lenin enrolled at Kazan University in the same year but he was quickly expelled for illegal opposition activities, and exiled to his grandfather's estate in the village of Kokushkino. In exile, he started reading European revolutionary writers, notably Karl Marx, and he became a self-professed Marxist. After qualifying as a lawyer, he moved to St Petersburg in 1893 where he plunged into underground opposition to the Tsarist regime.

Lenin helped set up a Marxist workers' organisation in St Petersburg for which he was jailed for 15 months, along with his wife-to-be Nadezhda Krupskaya, before being sent into exile for three years to Siberia. Released in 1900, he fled abroad where he joined fellow revolutionaries in starting a newspaper, *Iskra* (The Spark) and in 1902 published his seminal work *What Is To Be Done?*

Lenin had by now come round to believing that revolution would only succeed if it were led by a small professional group – in effect controlled from the top. His insistence on professional revolutionary cadres split the main opposition grouping, the Russian Social Democratic Labour Party. Two powerful factions emerged at the party's 1903 Congress, which was held in London – the Mensheviks (Russian for minority) who opposed Lenin and the Bolsheviks (Russian for majority) who supported him by a small majority.

Lenin was abroad when revolution erupted in 1905; he returned home after it had lost momentum and in its repressive aftermath he again went into exile. The Mensheviks and Bolsheviks bickered for years over the failure of the 1905 revolution and split irrevocably in 1912. Lenin,

Chronology

1870	Born in Simbirsk, on the River Volga, 22 April
1887	Lenin's brother Alexander executed in May
1895	Arrested in St Petersburg
1897	First exile
1898	Marries Nadezhda Krupskaya
1899	Second exile in Siberia
1900	Release of Lenin and publication of *Iskra*
1902	Publication of *What Is To Be Done?*
1905	Outbreak of First Russian Revolution
1917	February, Russian Revolution overthrows Tsar; October, Bolsheviks instigate second Revolution
1918	Bolsheviks become Communist Party; outbreak of civil war and execution of royal family
1921	New Economic Policy
1924	Lenin dies in Gorky, 21 January

Rolls-Royce Revolutionary

- *Lenin had a fetish for Rolls-Royces. He owned nine, including the world's only half-track Rolls-Royce, adapted with skis at the front for driving in the snow.*
- *'Bread not war,' was one of Lenin's most famous slogans.*
- *'I'll make them pay for this! I swear it!' Lenin is supposed to have said on learning of his brother's execution.*
- *The post-mortem on Lenin revealed that his brain had shrunk to a quarter of its normal size. His body was embalmed and laid in a crystal coffin in a mausoleum by the Kremlin, where it still lies in state – almost the last symbolic remnant of the Soviet Union.*

'Peace, bread, land and all power to the soviets'

meanwhile, faced hardship in exile. He continued writing, producing his major philosophical work *Materialism and Empirio-Criticism* in 1909. When World War I broke out, he called on workers to unite against it to 'transform the imperialist war into a civil war'. Their duty was to destroy capitalism, not fight each other.

Lenin missed the outbreak of the February 1917 revolution which overthrew the Tsarist regime; he sneaked back into Russia through Germany one month later in a sealed train. Russia was in the hands of a weak provisional bourgeois government, led by Alexander Kerensky, and her army was still floundering in the war. Lenin seized the moment, and called for outright revolution, and the Bolshevik party emerged from an emergency congress with the slogan: 'All Power to the Soviets'.

A workers' uprising in July failed and Lenin spent August and September in Finland pressing his case for armed insurrection in the capital. It finally broke out on 25 October – 'The October Revolution' – and a few days later Lenin was elected Chairman of the People's Commissars – de facto head of government.

Lenin gradually, but cautiously, consolidated the power of the new Soviet State. He ended the war with Germany, accepting punitive terms, and started to implement what had up until then just been a dream on paper – the communist state. It began with mass transfers of land to the disgruntled peasantry, who had borne the brunt of the war, and a decree of nationalisation of industry. Lenin's overriding concern, however, was to stay in power and the infant Soviet state had first to contend with a brutal civil war, which lasted from 1918-21, and devastating famine, which killed millions.

After the war, Lenin had to compromise to ensure the survival of communism, and issued a New Economic Policy which aimed to restore a degree of market economy. But he suffered the first of three strokes in May 1922 and thereafter lost direct control of government. A master strategist, he did not live long enough to see his dream turn into a nightmare under his successor Joseph Stalin.

CHE GUEVARA

Che Guevara (1928–67) was a South American revolutionary leader who helped bring Fidel Castro to power in Cuba, and died in a vain attempt to ignite a peasant rebellion in Bolivia. His death converted him into a global hero of the left, and almost forty years later his iconic image as a bearded revolutionary wearing a beret remains a symbol of protest around the world.

BORN ERNESTO GUEVARA into a middle-class family of Spanish–Irish origin in the Argentine city of Rosario in 1928, Guevara qualified as a doctor in 1953 at the University of Buenos Aires, but never practised. His extensive student travels around the continent had convinced him that revolution was the only remedy to Latin America's social inequalities, and he went instead to Guatemala to join the pro-Communist regime of Jacobo Arbenz Guzmán. When Guzmán was overthrown in a US-backed coup in 1954, Guevara fled to Mexico where he met Fidel Castro and other Cuban exiles. Guevara joined Castro and they trained together at a guerrilla military camp run by a Spanish civil war veteran, where 'Che' came out with top marks.

The rebels invaded Cuba in 1956, landing on a beach in the province of Oriente where they were almost wiped out. The few survivors, including the wounded Guevara, reached the Sierra Maestra from where they built up their guerrilla army. Guevara quickly proved himself to be a resourceful and tenacious leader, and he was given the revolutionary rank of commandante. By the end of 1958 the rebels had driven Cuba's US-backed President Batista into exile. They entered Havana on 2 January 1959 and established a Marxist government.

As President of the National Bank and later Minister of Industry, Guevara played a key role in aligning Cuba's sugar and tobacco export-based economy to the Soviet Bloc after the US imposed a trade blockade. But, although avidly anti-capitalist, he was never entirely at home with Soviet Communism.

CHRONOLOGY

1928	Born in Rosario, Argentina, 14 June
1953	Qualifies as a doctor
1955	Meets Fidel Castro
1956	Disembarks with Castro on Cuba's south coast
1958	President Batista overthrown
1959	President of Cuba's National Bank
1961	Cuban Minister for Industry until 1965
1965	Fails to foment guerrilla uprising in Congo
1967	Shot dead near Vallegrande, Bolivia, 9 October

At heart a revolutionary rather than an administrator, Guevara went on many missions for Castro, some top-secret: to Europe, Russia, Africa, Asia and as far as Beijing. He quit office in 1965 to promote revolution in other countries. A mission to foment an uprising in the Congo failed, and in 1967, while directing a guerrilla movement in Bolivia, he was wounded in a clash with Bolivian government troops, captured and executed.

Cuba has promoted 'Che' as a symbol of revolutionary virtues, sacrifice and internationalism inside and outside the country since his death. Many people around the world, however, strongly reject Guevara's advocacy of armed insurrection.

In Cuba Guevara proved himself a resourceful and tenacious leader, quickly attaining the revolutionary rank of Commandante

SOLDIER OF THE REVOLUTION

■ *Guevara edited the rebel newspaper* Cuba Libre *during the war, and after it he wrote* Guerrilla Warfare, Man and Socialism in Cuba *and* Reminiscences of the Cuban Revolutionary War.

■ *'Che was the most complete human being of our age,' said Jean-Paul Sartre. Would he say the same in today's post-Communist, and post 9/11, world?*

■ *Guevara acquired his nickname from his native language; Argentines frequently punctuate their speech with the interjection 'che' – originally an Italian word meaning chum or buddy.*

■ *Che Guevara's remains were brought back to Cuba by followers in 1997, where they were placed in a mausoleum in Santa Clara.*

Lech Walesa

Lech Walesa (1943–) led the Polish workers' revolt in the shipyards in Gdansk that gave birth to the Solidarity free trade union and eventually brought down Communist rule in Poland. A Nobel Peace Prize laureate, he became president of his country.

THE SON OF A CARPENTER, Walesa became an electrician at the huge Lenin shipyards in Gdansk, northern Poland, in 1967. The 1970 food riots in which a number of demonstrators were killed outside the shipyard gates led him to join the underground trade union movement, in effect the illegal opposition to the Communists. He lost his job after taking part in a new wave of worker protests in 1976, and spent the next four years working mainly as an underground activist, and playing cat and mouse with the Polish police.

His moment came in the summer of 1980 when Polish workers, displaying a new confidence in their opposition to the deeply unpopular Soviet-backed Communists following the election of Polish Pope John Paul II, staged strikes across the country. Walesa clambered over the fence and took control of the sit-in protest at the Lenin shipyard, and he was soon leading an inter-factory strike committee, which threw down the gauntlet to the beleaguered Communist government in Warsaw. The committee, naming itself Solidarity, demanded the right to form a free trade union and the right to strike – freedoms unheard of in the East Bloc where the ruling Communist Party was meant to control everything. Walesa, with his hallmark walrus moustache, became a global hero overnight. He was brash, tough and charming, and ably supported by other more intellectual activists, and during tough negotiations, and backed by a national strike, they wore down the Communists. The Solidarity Free Trade Union was born on 31 August 1980 and under Walesa's leadership over the next sixteen months its membership grew to some ten million. Solidarity had become a mass protest against Communist rule, threatening the very foundations of Soviet control over eastern Europe.

Pressured by Moscow, the Communists struck back on 13 December 1981, imposed martial law and suspended Solidarity. Walesa and his top aides were arrested, and he spent eleven months in detention. Solidarity went underground with Walesa still in charge, and the protests continued. Walesa was awarded the Nobel Peace Prize in 1983, but, fearing that he would be unable to return, he sent his wife Danuta to Oslo to receive it. A new wave of unrest in 1988, and the glasnost liberalization in Moscow, forced the Communists back to negotiating with Walesa. Solidarity was relegalized and won all the free seats in partial parliamentary elections in 1989. The following year, in December 1990, Walesa was elected President of Poland in a landslide victory.

Walesa was less successful in the largely ceremonial role of President. He was frustrated by his lack of power and indulged in some erratic behaviour, and his plain speech and confrontational style, combined with opposition to the new abortion law, lost him re-election in 1995. He briefly returned to the shipyard – more as a gesture of protest – and ran again for President in 2000. This time he gained less than 1 per cent of the vote, and he announced afterwards that he was quitting politics.

He was a great symbol of protest and a great leader of protest, but in the end he was too much the impatient revolutionary, and neither subtle nor intelligent enough to be a great statesman.

Chronology

1943	Born in Popowo, near Wroclawek, 29 September
1980	Leads workers' strikes, founds Solidarity
1981	Polish Communists impose martial law
1983	Awarded Nobel Peace Prize
1990	Elected President of Poland
1995	Loses presidential election; returns to shipyard
2000	Again loses presidential election; quits politics

A symbol of protest, ultimately Walesa was too much the impatient revolutionary to play the statesman

Following the Pope

■ *Lech Walesa always paid tribute to the role of Pope John Paul in Poland's march to freedom. The pope's visit in 1979 had shown ordinary Poles that there were still millions of believers who rejected the officially atheist Communists, and this gave them the confidence to launch the nation-wide strikes the following summer.*

■ *When Walesa signed the free trade union agreement with the Communists, he used a pen with a big picture of the pope.*

■ *The Polish workers' underground movement KOR also played a major part in fomenting and organizing the 1980 strikes.*

Marco Polo

Marco Polo (1254–1324), a Venetian merchant and adventurer, spent twenty-four years journeying through Asia, reaching beyond Mongolia to China. His accounts of his travels to the Far East inspired and paved the way for the great voyages of discovery.

BORN INTO A PROSPEROUS merchant family, Marco Polo grew up in Venice. He was just six when his father Niccolò and uncle Matteo set off in the footsteps of other Europeans to find new markets in the East – on a journey that would take them to the court of the great Mongol emperor Kublai Khan, in his new capital Khanbalik, now the site of Beijing. They returned to Venice nine years later with tales of undreamed-of wealth and splendour, and with a petition from the Great Khan to the Pope to send 100 missionaries to convert his Mongol tribesmen.

Furnished with letters and gifts from the Pope, and accompanied by two Dominican friars who soon left them, Niccolò and Matteo set out again for the East in 1271. They also took along Niccolò's seventeen-year-old boy Marco. They would be travelling for a quarter of a century. They passed through Armenia, Persia, Afghanistan, over the Pamirs and all along the Silk Road, crossing the vast Mongolian steppes and the Gobi Desert, to China, finally arriving in 1275 at the winter court of the Great Khan in Khanbalik. They had been travelling for three and a half years and were 5,600 miles from home.

Marco, a gifted linguist and master of four languages, became a favourite with the Khan and was appointed to high posts in his administration. He served at the Khan's court and was sent on a number of special missions in China, Burma and Indonesia, reaching some places which Europeans would not see again until the nineteenth century. He became a member of Kublai Khan's privy council and for three years he served as the Khan's representative in the city of Yangzhou. Marco was especially enthralled by the Khan's new city, and its palace – the greatest, he said, that ever was. He also noted some distinct eastern achievements – paper currency, coal and the imperial post.

Chronology

1254	Born, most probably in Venice
1271	Sets out for the East with his father and uncle
1275	Arrives at the court of Kublai Khan
1295	Returns to Venice
1298	Captured by Genoese, dictates book on his travels
1299	Released from captivity, returns to Venice
1324	Dies in Venice, 9 January

The Polo party stayed in the Khan's court for seventeen years, and amassed great wealth in jewels and gold. They were anxious to leave, fearful of what would happen when the Khan died. The Khan initially would not let them go, but eventually they arranged to accompany a Mongol princess to Persia, and set off for home in 1292. A two-year sea voyage across the South China Sea and the Indian Ocean took them to Hormuz, from where they travelled overland to Constantinople and finally to Venice, where relatives and friends had long given them up for dead.

Three years after Marco returned to Venice, he was captured by the Genoese while commanding a Venetian galley and spent a year in a Genoese prison. It was there that he dictated the account of his voyage. 'I believe it was God's will that we should come back, so that men might know the things that are in the world,' Marco related. 'No other man has explored so much of the world.'

Released from prison in 1299, he returned to Venice, where he married, had three daughters and lived comfortably until he died in 1324, aged 70.

On his deathbed Marco Polo would remark: 'I have not told the half of what I have seen'

A Traveller's Account

- Marco Polo dictated the account of his adventures in Asia to a fellow prisoner, Rusticiano of Pisa, who was a well-known writer of romances. The Travels of Marco Polo, first published as Divisament dou Monde (Description of the World), became a medieval best-seller, and it is arguably the most influential travel book in history.
- The book was also known as Il Milione (The Million), a probable reference to the nickname Marco acquired on his return to Venice – he was frequently heard boasting about the 'millions' of this and that he had seen – or to people's disbelief at his accounts.
- Some sceptics suggested he never went to China at all; there are no Chinese records of his journey. On his deathbed he was asked to recant his 'lies', but said only: 'I haven't told the half of what I saw.'
- The book had an incalculable influence on future explorers, not least on Christopher Columbus, who sailed west from Europe in the belief that he would arrive in the Far East described by Marco Polo.

Christopher Columbus

Christopher Columbus (1451–1506) was a Genoese-born merchant adventurer who sailed west across the Atlantic in search of a route to China and arrived in the Caribbean Sea to open the way to America, which he is popularly said to have discovered.

THE SON OF A SPANISH weaver and Italian mother, Columbus was born and brought up in the seafaring city-state of Genoa, and as a young man he went to sea on trading voyages. In 1476, he moved to Portugal, where his brother Bartholomew was working as a cartographer, and he married there in 1479. This was a time of great maritime expansion – Portuguese ships were gradually moving down the coast of Africa, pushing out the boundaries of the known world, and Columbus sailed with them on several West African voyages. Fired by information he had acquired during his sea trips and by the charts that he now voraciously studied, Columbus began to believe that he could find a way to the fabled riches of the East, that Marco Polo and others had described, by sailing west across the Atlantic Ocean. On the advice of a royal commission, King John II of Portugal refused to back his planned venture – largely because Portuguese sailors were on the point of finding a sea route to Asia via the Horn of Africa.

A First-Class Navigator

■ *Columbus was known as Cristoforo Colombo in his native Italy and Cristóbal Colón in his adopted Spain. His reputation has come under fire in modern times. He has been portrayed as a ruthless and greedy imperialist, a naïve entrepreneur and an incompetent administrator. But it is impossible to overestimate the power of his vision and his nautical achievements, above all his brilliant navigation and seamanship – four voyages of discovery across the Atlantic in twelve years, in an age when a Channel crossing between France and England was an adventure.*

■ *Columbus continued voyaging after death. His remains were interred in Seville and then transferred to Santo Domingo, and (almost certainly) moved to Havana before being finally returned to Seville in 1899.*

Chronology

1451 Born in Genoa, between August and October
1476 Settles and marries in Portugal
1484 Conceives plan for the 'Enterprise of the Indies'
1485 Moves to Spain
1492 Sets out for Indies and 'discovers' America
1493 Returns to Spain
1493–96 Second voyage
1498–1500 Third voyage
1502–04 Fourth voyage
1506 Dies in Valladolid, Spain, 20 May

Columbus, displaying the determination of a man with a mission, moved to Spain in 1485, with his Spanish mistress, and sought help from Queen Isabella and King Ferdinand. They at first also spurned his plan, after it had also been dismissed by a Spanish royal commission, but the tide of history turned spectacularly in Columbus's favour. In 1492, the last Moorish stronghold in Spain, Granada, fell to Ferdinand and Isabella. Buoyed by their decisive victory over the 'infidel' and lured by the potential strategic and economic gains, they agreed to sponsor the expedition.

Columbus negotiated a great deal; he was to be viceroy of all the territories he found, and one-tenth of all the precious metals in these lands would be his. He set out on 3 August 1492 from the southern Spanish port of Palos with three ships – the *Santa María*, a decked 35-metre square-rigger, and two smaller partly undecked caravels, the *Pinta* and *Niña*. Although others had almost certainly gone before them – the Vikings and possibly Breton fishermen – in terms of exploration the voyage was a bold leap into the unknown. After many desperate days, they sighted land and rowed ashore on 12 October, most probably at Guanahaní, a tiny island in the

Although others had almost certainly gone before him, for Columbus the Atlantic voyage was a giant leap into the unknown

Bahamas, which Columbus claimed and renamed San Salvador. The expedition later landed on Cuba and the island of Hispaniola, where they left behind thirty-nine men to establish the first European garrison in the New World. It was built from the wreckage of the *Santa María*, which had foundered on rocks off the coast.

The fate of the settlement, La Navidad, characterizes the rest of Columbus's ventures in the Caribbean. His first contacts with the natives of the islands had been peaceful, but the killing and looting of natives started soon after, and the garrison was wiped out in retaliation after he left.

Columbus returned to Spain in March 1493 in triumph and with great honours; he was now Admiral of the Ocean Sea. He led three further expeditions to the Caribbean. The second voyage, from 1493 to 1495, was a huge undertaking. It established the first permanent European settlements in the New World, La Isabella and Santo Domingo in what is now the Dominican Republic, but ended in bloodshed with Columbus defeating a native force and shipping a large number back to Spain as slaves

Columbus surveyed other islands, from Jamaica to Antigua, but still believed that he was on or near the mainland of Cathay – a conviction he clung to even after two more voyages in which he sailed as far as Venezuela and Panama. His last voyages were marked by dissension and rebellion, and only Queen Isabella in Spain saved Columbus from disgrace.

He died far from the sea, in Valladolid in central Spain, in 1506.

Ferdinand Magellan

Ferdinand Magellan (1480–1521), Hispano-Portuguese navigator and explorer, was the first European to cross the Pacific Ocean, and led the first circumnavigation of the globe. He proved beyond doubt that the world was round and that the Pacific and Atlantic were separate oceans.

THE SON OF PEDRO Rui de Magalhães, a minor noble and mayor of his town, Magellan was brought up in the royal court in Lisbon, one of the great centres of the voyages of discovery that were opening up new frontiers for Europe. He went to sea as a young man, and sailed and fought with the Portuguese expeditions sent to Africa and India in the early 1500s to wrest control of the Arabian Sea and establish trading ports around the Indian Ocean. Magellan also took part in Portugal's 1511 capture of the Malayan port of Malacca – the gateway to trade in the wealth of the East, from where the Portuguese pushed on to the Moluccas, or Spice Islands. Magellan returned home a captain in 1512, and the following year he was severely wounded fighting in Morocco, leaving him with a permanent limp.

About this time, he fell out with the king of Portugal. King Emanuel refused his request for higher pay and, more significantly, would not listen to Magellan's plan to sail west round the tip of South America to find an alternative route to the Spice Islands. Undaunted, Magellan turned to Portugal's rival neighbour and offered his services to the young King Charles I of Spain. His plan was attractive to the Spanish because, under terms of the Treaty of Tordesillas, the then known world had been divided into two spheres: everything east of a line of demarcation belonged to Portugal, and everything to the west to Spain. If Magellan could find a western route around South America, then the spice-rich islands would be open to Spain.

Magellan went fully native. He took Spanish nationality, married the daughter of an influential official in Seville, fathered a child and set sail in September 1519 in command of five Spanish ships and some 250 men. After crossing the Atlantic, the fleet made its way down the South American coast and into uncharted waters. The fleet initially tried to find a passage through the wide River Plate estuary, and then headed south and wintered for six months in southern Patagonia, where Magellan quelled a mutiny by executing its leaders and abandoning one of the chief conspirators on shore: the equivalent then of leaving a man on the moon.

After losing one of the ships, the fleet rounded

Chronology

1480	Born at Sabrosa, northern Portugal
1505	Joins Portuguese expedition to India
1511	Takes part in Portuguese capture of Malacca
1512	Wounded in Portuguese expedition to Morocco
1519	Sails west for Indies with Spanish expedition
1520	Navigates Strait of Magellan to Pacific
1521	Killed on Mactan Island, Philippines, 27 April

Monte Video!

- *The Uruguayan capital Montevideo acquired its name from Magellan's voyage. The hill on which it was built came into sight as his ship probed the River Plate estuary. 'Monte video' (I see a hill), Magellan shouted.*
- *Sailing through the Magellan Strait that is named after him, Magellan's crew sighted fires burning on the shore. They were lit by native hunters, and the Spanish sailors called the place Tierra del Fuego – Land of Fire.*
- *When Magellan's fleet emerged into open water, his men were so relieved to find calm sea that they named the ocean ahead of them the Mare Pacifico, the Pacific Ocean.*
- *Magellan's name in Portuguese is Fernão de Magalhães; in Spanish, Fernando de Magallanes.*
- *An Italian crew member Antonio Pigafetta kept a diary of the entire voyage around the world – a key source of our information on this epic journey.*

It took Magellan thirty-eight days of battling against surging tides and gales to work his way through the strait which now bears his name

the southern tip of the continent on 21 October 1520 and entered the passage that is now named the Strait of Magellan. It took thirty-eight days of battling against surging tides and westerly gales to work a way through the treacherous strait; the crew of the *San Antonio* deserted and returned to Spain.

They logged 330 miles – less than 10 miles a day – till they finally emerged into open sea and the Pacific. Like Columbus when he first made landfall in the Caribbean thirty years before, they had no idea where they were – and certainly had no idea that the ocean ahead of them was so vast. Magellan steered north and eventually west, heading into the empty Pacific. With most of the expedition's provisions on their way back to Spain on the mutinous *San Antonio*, Magellan now summoned all his strengths of leadership and courage to drive the fleet on. His men, racked with scurvy and thirst, were reduced to chewing boiled leather and eating rats before they reached Guam on 6 March 1521, their first land for ninety-nine days.

Magellan sailed on to the Philippines, becoming the first European to reach the islands, and then foolishly engaged in a local war on behalf of the ruler of Cebu. He was killed by a poisoned arrow while attacking the island of Mactan.

Two of his surviving ships continued to the Spice Islands, where they loaded up with valuable cargo, and one of them, the *Victoria*, completed the circumnavigation of the globe round the Cape of Good Hope, and berthed back in Seville on 9 September 1522. Her cargo of spices alone paid for the expedition, but she had just eighteen European and four Indian survivors.

Hernán Cortés

Hernán Cortés (1485–1547) was a Spanish explorer who led a tiny army that conquered the mighty Aztec Empire in Mexico. His military daring ensured an astonishing victory that inspired others to invade lands in search of riches throughout Central and South America.

CORTÉS WAS BORN in Medellín, in Extremadura, Spain, to a humble family. He studied law at the University of Salamanca but left without completing his studies, and decided, like many other adventurous young Spaniards at the time, to seek his fortune in the New World. Cortés was nineteen when in 1504 he sailed for the island of Hispaniola (present-day Santo Domingo), where he was granted land and Indian slaves as well as being appointed a notary. In 1511, he took part in the conquest of Cuba under the command of Diego Velázquez, an influential soldier who became governor of Cuba. Cortés was twice elected mayor of the capital, Santiago de Cuba.

In 1518, Cortés convinced Velázquez to appoint him to lead an expedition to the Mexican mainland, which had only recently been discovered. In February 1519 Cortés set sail with eleven ships from Cuba with an army of 600 men and sixteen horses. He landed on the Yucatan Peninsula and conquered the town of Tabasco. The primitive Indians standing on the coastline thought the Spanish ships were 'floating mountains' and were terrified by the sight of white and bearded men. Cortés's arrival coincided with the prophesied return of Quetzalcoatl, an Aztec god. The strange men, their horses and weapons overawed the natives, and Cortés exploited their belief that he was a reincarnation of their god, so that they received him and his party amicably.

The Tabascans told Cortés about the rich and dazzling Aztec Empire and its great warrior-emperor Montezuma. They gave the Spaniards food and women, one of whom, Malinche, was baptized as Marina and became Cortés's mistress. Her skills as a guide and interpreter, and her guile, were crucial to the expedition.

The Spaniards moved north from Tabasco, and Cortés established the fortified port of Vera Cruz. Here, in an act of bold determination, Cortés had his entire fleet sunk apart from one ship; his men now had to follow him or die.

The Aztecs were powerful overlords but they did nothing to assimilate their subject provinces. Cortés ruthlessly exploited this dissension within the Aztec Empire. He formed alliances with the different peoples who resented and feared their Aztec overlords, notably the Tlaxcalans, and gained thousands of local allies.

Ignoring the threats he had received from Montezuma, Cortés led his army and his native allies into the capital, Tenochtitlán, a city built on

Chronology

1485	Born in Medellín, Extremadura
1504	Sails to the New World
1511	Joins Diego Velázquez in the conquest of Cuba
1519	Cortés leads expedition to Mexico
1521	Aztecs conquered
1524	Leads expedition to Honduras
1528	Sails back to Spain
1530	Returns to Mexico
1540	Retires to Spain
1547	Dies in Seville, Spain, 2 December

A Ruthless Conquest

- *When Cortés and his Spaniards arrived in Mexico the Indians, who had never seen horses before, thought that the horse and rider were one creature.*
- *Verse from* Flowers and Songs of Sorrow *(written by a post-conquest Aztec poet): 'Nothing but flowers and songs of sorrow are left in Mexico and Tlatelolco where once we saw warriors and wise men.'*
- *At the time of his trial in Spain, Cortés pushed through the crowds to speak to King Charles V, angrily telling him, 'I am the man who has gained you more provinces than your father left you towns.'*

At Vera Cruz, Cortés had his entire fleet sunk, except for a single ship; his men now had to follow him or die

floating islands, which is now modern-day Mexico City, on 8 November 1519. Montezuma welcomed the Spanish, but Cortés, anticipating his ulterior intentions, took him hostage and made him swear loyalty to the king of Spain. Meanwhile, Governor Velázquez, envious of Cortés's success, had sent a small army to Mexico under Narváez to recall Cortés for insubordination. Cortés left Pedro de Alvarado in charge of Tenochtitlán while he went to meet Narváez's army, which was three times greater than his own. Creeping into the Spanish camp at night, Cortés captured Narváez, and forced his troops to enlist in Cortés' own army.

He returned to chaos in the Aztec capital Alvarado's small garrison had been attacked. He had retaliated by murdering hundreds of Aztecs during a festival, sparking a bloody revolt. Montezuma was killed – probably stoned to death, though accounts of his death vary – and the Spanish and their allies were driven across the causeway out of the city on the night of 30 July 1520 ('Night of Sorrows'). But Cortés rallied his retreating army, smashed an Aztec counter-attack and some months later returned to besiege the city. This time he used brigantines to control the lake on which the city was built and, after much bloody fighting, Tenochtitlán finally fell to his gunpowder, horses and steel on 13 August 1521; the Aztecs' heroic struggle was over.

Mexico City was built on the ruins of the former Aztec capital and the colonization of Mexico proceeded swiftly. Cortés was now the absolute ruler of vast lands and he was appointed governor and captain general of New Spain, as Mexico was then called.

But his great power was the beginning of his downfall; the Spanish court was fearful that he would set himself up as an independent ruler, and he had made powerful enemies, notably Velázquez, who mounted a political campaign against him in Spain. Cortés hit back with five letters to the Spanish king, Charles V.

He continued to lead expeditions in his later life, but none were as successful as the conquest of the Aztecs. He sailed back to Spain in 1528 to defend himself before the king against accusations of cruelty to the natives, but returned to Mexico in 1530 and retired to his estates outside Mexico City. When a viceroy was appointed to govern Mexico in 1540, the disillusioned Cortés moved back to Spain where he died in 1547.

James Cook

Captain James Cook (1728–79) was an explorer who made three great ocean voyages that transformed the known world by putting Australia, New Zealand and Antarctica, and vast tracts of the Pacific, onto the map.

The son of a farm labourer from the Yorkshire village of Marton, Cook left school aged 12 and was apprenticed to a haberdasher in the harbour-town of Staithes. Yorkshire's rugged cliff-bound coast called him to the sea, and in 1746 Cook moved to nearby Whitby to work for a coal shipper named John Walker. He spent 11 years in the service of this enlightened Quaker, honing his seamanship, navigating colliers up and down England's treacherous east coast and to Norwegian, Baltic and Irish ports. By 27 he had risen to first mate, and he enlisted in the Royal Navy as an able seaman. Quickly marked for promotion, he was master by the age of 29.

After seeing action in the Bay of Biscay, Cook was dispatched to Canada where he was given the dangerous task of surveying the St Lawrence River. Braving often hostile natives, Cook successfully charted the channel up which the British fleet ferried General Wolfe and his men in 1759 to storm the Heights of Abraham and retake the city of Quebec from the French. Three years later Cook took part in the recapture of Newfoundland, and was commissioned to survey Canada's east coast. He produced a paper on the solar eclipse he observed off the coast of Newfoundland in 1766, and this gave him his big break.

Impressed by the paper and by his reputation as a skilled navigator, the Admiralty and the Royal Society decided to send Lieutenant Cook on an expedition to the South Pacific to make further astronomical observations and to determine once and for all whether *Terra Australis* existed. Only parts of the great South Land had been prospected, and no one was sure of its extent, nor were they certain that it was a continent.

Cook set sail on 25 August 1768 in the *Endeavour*, a converted Whitby collier, with some 85 men, including a party of scientists, among them Joseph Banks. After stopping in Tahiti in the spring of 1769, Cook sailed south in search of the unknown continent, reaching New Zealand six weeks later. He made contact, for the most part friendly, with the Maoris and circumnavigated and charted both the North and South Islands (the straits between them bear his name), and at Queen Charlotte's Sound Cook formally took possession of the islands on behalf of King George III.

Leaving New Zealand, the *Endeavour* tracked north, and 19 days later Cook made his first sighting of the great island continent of Australia. He sailed up the east coast and finally anchored in Botany Bay. He once again took a party ashore and hoisted the Union Flag to claim the land, which he named New South Wales. He had gained vast new territories without shedding a drop of blood, although the expedition came close to disaster when the *Endeavour* ran onto a reef on the way home.

Back in England, Cook was promoted to commander and he set out on a second voyage in

Chronology

1728	Born at Marton, Yorkshire, 27 October
1736	Family settles in Great Ayton
1744	Cook starts work in Staithes
1746	Cook moves south to Whitby: finds employment with Captain John Walker
1755	Joins the Royal Navy as an ordinary seaman
1759	Takes part in surveying the St Lawrence River in Canada
1760-67	Surveys the islands of Newfoundland, St. Pierre and Miquelon off the east coast of Canada
1768-71	First Voyage round the world in the *Endeavour*
1772-75	Second Voyage round the world in the ships *Resolution* and *Adventure*
1776-80	Third Voyage round the world in the ships *Resolution* and *Discovery*
1779	Killed in Hawaii, 14 February

'I had ambitions not only to go farther than any man had been before, but as far as it was possible for man to go'

1772 with two ships, the *Resolution* and the *Adventure* – this time to explore the seas around Antarctica and 'to complete the discovery of the southern hemisphere'. The second voyage lasted three years, during which Cook covered 60,000 miles, sweeping the icy southern Atlantic and becoming the first to sail around Antarctica, and filling in large hitherto blank areas of the Pacific Ocean, including the Marquesas and Tonga Islands. This voyage established the map of the world as we know it today, and the record of his sailing in the frozen Antarctic led the way for the great Polar explorers of the next centuries.

Cook's third and last expedition was to search for the north passage – a sea-way across the top of the world that would link the Pacific and the Atlantic. With the *Resolution* and *Discovery*, the newly promoted Captain Cook set out in 1776, sailing via Australia and New Zealand before striking into the north Pacific and the uncharted waters beyond the Bering Straits. His way was barred by a wall of ice at Icy Cape, and after surveying north-east Siberia, Cook returned to the warm south Pacific. His two ships anchored at Kealakekura Bay in Hawaii in January 1779. He was killed there a few weeks later in a skirmish with islanders after the theft of a boat.

Cook's Broth

■ *Cook's attention to hygiene and diet were revolutionary – and saved lives. As a preventive to scurvy, then the biggest killer on long sea voyages, he forced his men to down his 'broth'. It was made from scurvy grass, carrot marmalade, sauerkraut, syrup of lemon and other vegetable ingredients. It was probably disgusting, but it worked.*

■ *The naturalist Joseph Banks, enthused by the new plants and flowers that he had discovered ashore, persuaded Cook to name their first anchorage in Australia Botany Bay. Banks had somewhat exaggerated his description of the surrounding countryside as the first convicts to arrive there 19 years later discovered: the 'meadows' were in reality swamps.*

Robert Peary

American Polar explorer, credited with being the first man to the North Pole. The most obsessed of all the Arctic explorers, Peary inspired his small team into an astonishing four-day 'dash for the Pole' that would see them reach the top of the world first.

Robert Peary was born in Cresson, Pennsylvania in 1856. When he was two years old his father died, leaving the young Robert to be brought up by his mother. A restless, adventurous childhood followed, with Robert far more at home in the great outdoors than sitting indoors. At the age of twenty-four, Peary joined the US Navy as a surveyor, and accepted a post in Nicaragua on a canal project. It was while he was in Nicaragua – where the wilderness that had originally attracted him appears to have been too tame – that Peary picked up a book on the Arctic and his imagination became fired with the idea of Polar exploration.

In 1886, on leave from the navy, he undertook his first expedition, to Greenland, with the stated aim of crossing at its widest point. Although the attempt was a failure – Peary actually travelled less than 100 miles before being forced to retreat – the experience confirmed Peary's growing obsession with the Arctic, and with achievement: 'I must have fame!' he wrote in a letter to his mother whilst in Greenland. The Arctic was where Peary intended to find his fame, as the first man to reach the North Pole.

This obsession also had a darker side: on hearing of Norwegian explorer Fridtjof Nansen's successful crossing of Greenland in 1888, Peary was incensed, raving about Nansen's 'treachery', and 'forestalling' (a favourite word of Peary's) of his plans, even though Nansen had planned his expedition long before Peary had ever heard of Greenland. Fergus Fleming, in his outstanding account of the quest for the North Pole *Ninety Degrees North*, calls Peary 'the most driven, possibly the most successful and probably the most unpleasant man in the annals of polar exploration', and it is hard, reading the accounts of Peary's relationships with the men of his expeditions, to argue with this verdict.

Disagreeable though Peary undoubtedly was, there is no denying his toughness: on his second expedition in 1891, Peary refused to turn back for home even after breaking his leg on the outbound voyage, stubbornly insisting he be carried onto the ice on a plank. Also with Peary on this expedition were Dr Frederick Cook, whose 1908 claim to have been first to the Pole would lead to a bitter and lasting controversy (there is today a Frederick Cook Society, whose aim is to prove their hero's claim to the Pole), and Matthew Henson, Peary's African-American assistant, a man who, chiefly on account of his colour, has been afforded little space in the annals of Arctic exploration.

The expedition reached the northern coast of Greenland (although not its northernmost point, as Peary mistakenly believed at the time) and proved that Greenland was indeed an island. Peary would return from this expedition with two huge iron-bearing meteorites, sacred to the Inuit, as well as six Inuit themselves.

Between 1887 and 1906, Peary made several more expeditions to the Arctic, spending a total of nine of the next sixteen years in polar regions.

Peary's 1906 expedition would achieve a furthest North of 87° 6', only 170 or so miles away from his ultimate goal of the Pole. *Nearest the Pole*, Peary's

Chronology

1856	Born at Cresson, Pennsylvania 6 May
1881	Joins the US Navy as surveryor
1885	Becomes obsessed with the idea of the North Pole and Arctic exploration
1886	First expedition to Greenland
1891	Second Greenland expedition: Peary and Henson reach northern coast of Greenland
1906	Reaches a furthest North of 87° 6'; publishes an account of his travels, *Nearest the Pole*
1909	Peary's team becomes the first to the North Pole on 6 April
1911	Retires from Navy a rear-admiral
1920	Dies in Washington, 20 February

'The fates and all hell are against me, but I will conquer yet'

account of the expedition was published in 1907; by this time, however, the American public, perhaps having had their fill of 'Peary Fails Again' headlines, were losing interest in the Arctic, and the book did not sell well. More worryingly for Peary, he found it increasingly difficult to raise funds for his next expedition, despite undertaking a series of his famous lectures up and down the country. At this stage, Peary's prospects of reaching the Pole appeared bleak. Ironically, it was the announcement by Cook that he was on Greenland, and would be mounting a push for the Pole, which seems to have stirred the public's imagination once more, and funds were soon forthcoming from amongst others the widow of Senator Morris Jesup, a long-standing backer of Peary after whom he had named a northerly cape of Greenland.

On 6 July 1908 Peary set out once again for Greenland, aboard the *Roosevelt*, a ship built to his own specifications and named after the US President, who personally came to the docks to wish Peary bon voyage. Calling in at the Greenland port Etah, the expedition moved swiftly on by sea to Cape Sheridan on Ellesmere Island, and from there by sledge to Cape Columbia, a journey of around ninety miles. It was from here that Peary mounted his final 'dash for the Pole'. Four days and 120 miles later, by Peary's account, he and his little party stood on the northernmost point on the planet: ninety degrees north. He had won his race.

A Controversial Position

■ *Although Peary's claim to be first to the North Pole was accepted at the time, inconsistencies in his account of his achievement have since cast doubt on whether Peary in fact reached the Pole. To have travelled an average of thirty miles a day is a feat which has never been repeated, not even by modern expeditions equipped with snowmobiles. When the natural obstacles such as leads – open stretches of water in the ice – and pressure ridges are factored in, Peary's account begins to seem little short of fantastical. The fact that Peary took no longitude readings, making it impossible for him to tell if he was heading due north from Cape Columbia, also suggests that he had no way of knowing if he had reached the North Pole or not.*

■ *The question of whether Peary actually reached the North Pole remains open. It seems clear that if he did not, he came within an ace of his goal; closer than anyone until Kusnetsov's expedition of 1948.*

Roald Amundsen

Roald Amundsen (1872–1928) was a Norwegian explorer, who led the first successful expedition to the South Pole. He was also the first to make a sea voyage through the Northwest Passage, and one of the pioneers of Arctic aviation.

THE SON OF A SHIPOWNER, Amundsen briefly studied medicine, but adventure was in his blood and he gave up thoughts of a conventional career and went to sea as a young man. In 1897 he joined a Belgian expedition on the *Belgica*, which was trapped in ice for thirteen months and became the first boat to winter in Antarctica. The crew survived on seal meat. Six years later, in 1903, Amundsen acquired his own boat, a 47-ton sloop *Gjöa*, and with a seven-man crew became the first to sail through the Northwest Passage. The voyage through the treacherous ice-bound route between mainland Canada and the Arctic islands took almost three years and ended in 1905 in San Francisco, where Amundsen presented the *Gjöa* to the city.

The frozen wastes of the Northwest Passage whetted Amundsen's appetite for polar exploration and made him world-famous. He now turned his mind to the conquest of the North Pole, but abandoned his plans to drift across the polar icecap on the *Fram* when news reached him that American explorer Robert Peary had staked his claims to have reached the North Pole first. Amundsen decided to sail south instead. Aware that British explorer Robert Falcon Scott was already ahead of him in what would become a race to be the first to the South Pole, he set out in utmost secrecy. He did not even inform his team on the *Fram*, who believed they were heading for the North Pole, until they were well on their way. Amundsen did, however, send a telegram to Scott announcing his intentions – making sure that it was cabled after he was beyond the point of recall.

Amundsen was now a highly experienced polar traveller. He established a winter base in the Bay of Whales, on the edge of the Ross Ice Shelf and 60 miles (96 kilometres) closer to the South Pole than Scott's base at McMurdo Sound. He prepared for the coming expedition by laying food depots; unlike Scott, he used Greenland sled dogs to pull his loads. Scott relied on tractorized sledges and ponies, both of which failed him.

After wintering at his base, Amundsen set out in September – early in the season – and was driven back by bad weather. He tried again the following month, leaving camp on 20 October with four companions, fifty-two dogs and four sledges. They arrived at the South Pole at 3 pm on Friday 14 December, spent three days there and returned safely to base on 25 January. Scott and his party, meanwhile, reached the South Pole on 17 January; forced to man-haul their sledges through atrocious weather, they all perished on their return journey.

Amundsen was more fortunate in the weather he encountered, but in the end he prevailed because of his knowledge of polar conditions, his meticulous attention to detail, and his extreme physical endurance. A giant 6-foot man, he was tough on himself, and an exacting leader. He was also heavily in debt, another compelling motivation

Chronology

1872 Born in Borge, near Oslo, 16 July
1897 Winters in Antarctica on the *Belgica*
1903–05 Navigates the Northwest Passage on the *Gjöa*
1911 Reaches South Pole, 14 December
1920 Completes Northeast Passage
1926 Becomes possibly the first man to see the North Pole
1928 Killed in plane crash near Spitsbergen

On hearing that Peary had staked his claim to the North Pole, Amundsen decided to head south

for him to achieve a spectacular success.

After the South Pole, Amundsen embarked on one final polar journey, when he sailed the *Maud* round the top of Siberia to Alaska in 1918–20, to become only the second person to navigate the Northeast Passage.

Amundsen later took up Arctic aviation, and in May 1926 he flew an Italian airship, the *Norge*, across the North Pole on a seventy-hour flight, the first from Europe to North America via the pole. He shared the flight with the *Norge's* Italian designer Umberto Nobile, and with the American aviator Lincoln Ellsworth. Nobile and Amundsen fell out over whose country should claim the honour for the first trans-polar flight. In a twist of fate, Amundsen came out of retirement two years later, in 1928, to help search for Nobile, whose new airship *Italia* had crashed during a polar flight. Nobile was eventually rescued but Amundsen was last heard from on 28 June. 'If you only knew how splendid it is up there, that's where I want to die,' he had said. He achieved his wish.

A Dog's Life

- *Amundsen said his ninety-seven Greenland huskies were crucial to his success. 'The dogs are the most important thing for us,' he said. 'The whole outcome of the expedition depends on them.'*
- *During the expedition, they were systematically culled to provide food for the surviving pack. Some twenty-four dogs were shot at what became known as Butcher's Shop at the top of the Axel Heiberg Glacier before the final push for the South Pole, where six more were shot. A total of eleven dogs returned to base.*
- *The telegram to Scott was correct but terse: 'Beg leave inform you proceeding Antarctic, Amundsen'.*

Ernest Shackleton

Sir Ernest Henry Shackleton (1874–1922) was an Irish polar explorer, who came within 97 miles of being the first to the South Pole and who sailed across the Antarctic Ocean in an open boat to lead all his men back to safety after they had lost their ship.

BORN IN KILKEA, County Kildare, and educated at Dulwich College in London, Shackleton enlisted in the merchant navy in 1890, and sailed to and from the Far East and America to earn his master's certificate in 1898. He then became a Union Star officer and also enlisted in the Royal Navy Reserve. He joined Robert Falcon Scott's *Discovery* expedition as third lieutenant, in 1901–03, and took part with Scott and Edward Wilson in a sledge journey over the Ross Ice Shelf to latitude 82°16′S – the furthest south anyone had yet journeyed. He returned home early and sick, but with his heart set on becoming the first man to reach the South Pole.

Shackleton went back to Antarctica in 1907–09, this time as leader of the *Nimrod* expedition, and a sledging party led by Shackleton reached latitude 88°23′S, just 97 miles (156 kilometres) short of the South Pole. Another of the expedition's team reached the Magnetic South Pole. Both parties had survived extreme hardship, above all hunger. 'Difficulties are just things to overcome, after all,' Shackleton wrote in his diary. Ever ready to share hardship, he was popular with his men, who called him affectionately 'the Boss'. He was a hero back home and was knighted on his return to England.

After months of strenuous fund raising and picking fifty-six volunteers, Shackleton set out again for the south in August 1914, in the shadow of the oncoming world war. The plan was to make the first crossing of Antarctica, from a base on the Weddell Sea via the South Pole to McMurdo Sound, but the expedition ship *Endurance* ran into unusually heavy ice and drifted for ten months before being crushed in the pack ice. The ship disappeared beneath the ice, leaving Shackleton and his men at the 'bottom' of the world drifting on ice floes with everything they had salvaged. After five months on the floes, and as the ice beneath them was cracking up, Shackleton led his men into the boats they had saved from the *Endurance*, and the party eventually made a safe landfall in Elephant Island in the South Shetlands.

From there, Shackleton embarked on one of the most dangerous and daring sea crossings. Together with five others, he sailed the sturdiest of the surviving whaleboats, the *James Caird*, over 800 miles of icy, stormy seas to South Georgia. Once landed, the party had to make the first crossing of the mountainous snow-capped island to raise help from the whaling station on its northern coast. Shackleton then led four relief expeditions before he succeeded in rescuing his men on Elephant Island. His lasting achievement was that they all came back alive.

An Open Boat

- *The open sea voyage took fourteen days; they had fought through icebergs and hurricane winds, and had survived hunger, cold and thirst, and a South Atlantic roller wave which Shackleton described as the biggest he had seen in twenty-six years at sea.*
- *They landed 17 miles from Stromness whaling station. Shackleton left two of his men behind and with the other two set out over South Georgia's glaciers, ice walls and mountains to reach help.*
- *After three failed attempts, Shackleton went with the Chilean steamer* Yelcho *to rescue his men on Elephant Island. They were all alive, having survived 105 days.*

Chronology

1874 Born in Kilkea, County Kildare, 15 February
1890 Joins merchant navy
1901–03 Member of Robert Scott's *Discovery* expedition
1907–08 Leads *Nimrod* Antarctic expedition
1914–16 Leads *Endurance* Antarctic expedition
1922 Dies at Grytviken, South Georgia, 5 January

'Difficulties are, after all, just things to overcome'

Andrew Carnegie

Andrew Carnegie (1836–1919) was a Scottish-born industrialist who became 'the richest man in the world'. He built up and dominated the American steel industry, but gave away 90 per cent of his wealth, maintaining that a man who dies rich, dies disgraced.

ANDREW CARNEGIE was born in Dunfermline, Scotland, into a poor family. His father, a hand-loom weaver, had been hit by the introduction of the power loom and general economic decline in Scotland, and in 1848 the family emigrated to Allegheny, Pennsylvania (now part of Pittsburgh).

Carnegie began working as a bobbin boy in a cotton factory, but even aged twelve he realized the value of education. He taught himself to read and write and attended night school. He became a messenger aged fourteen in a telegraph office, but thanks to his keen memory he was soon promoted as a telegraph operator. By 1853 he was chosen by Thomas Scott, the superintendent of the Pennsylvania Railroad Company, as his personal assistant and telegrapher, and soon displayed initiative and a natural inventiveness.

In 1856 he made the first of his investments, using a bank loan, in Woodruff Sleeping Cars. This was so successful that within two years Carnegie was earning more than three times his salary. He followed this success with other industrial investments in the Keystone Bridge Company, Union Iron Mills, Pittsburgh Locomotive Works and an oilfield. During the Civil War he supervised communications for the Union army, then travelled to Europe selling railroad securities, and by the age of thirty was a rich man.

Carnegie recognized the commercial importance of the iron and steel industries, and he visited steel plants in Europe. In 1865 he gave up the railroad, of which he himself became a superintendent, and became manager of one of his investments, the Keystone Bridge Company. In 1872 he founded the J. Edgar Thomson Steel Works, which later became the Carnegie Steel Company. Carnegie introduced technological innovations such as the Bessemer steelmaking process which he had seen in Britain, as well as reducing costs and furthering efficiency.

Chronology

1836	Born Dunfermline, Scotland, 25 November
1848	Family moves to Allegheny, Pa., USA
1853	Becomes personal assistant to Thomas Scott, at Pennsylvania Railroad Co
1859	Succeeds Scott as superintendent of Pittsburgh division of Pennsylvania Railroad Co
1860s	Makes shrewd investments in industrial companies; investigates steel manufacture
1865	Manages Keystone Bridge Company
1872–73	Founds J. Edgar Thomson Steel Works
1889	Consolidates businesses into Carnegie Steel Company
1900	Profits of Carnegie Steel reach $40,000,000. His share is $25,000,000
1901	Retires and pursues philanthropic interests
1919	Dies in Lenox, Massachusetts, 11 August

He was creative, and a pioneer of vertical integration. This meant his company controlled all stages of manufacture: buying the raw materials (coke-fields and iron ore deposits), as well as the means of transport (railroads and ships). He encouraged the promotion of his employees, once commenting that J. P. Morgan, another business entrepreneur, 'buys his partners, I grow mine'. Carnegie was seen as a caring employer until he broke a strike with armed Pinkerton guards, resulting in the deaths of twenty of his men.

By 1889 his Carnegie Steel Company dominated the American steel market. Even during a depression and strike in 1892 Carnegie's company remained profitable. He sold it to J. P. Morgan for $480 million in 1901, and devoted the rest of his life to philanthropic causes. He set up charitable foundations to benefit his birthplace, Dunfermline,

'It is the mind that makes the body rich'

as well as distributing money for the expansion of Scottish universities, and the building of libraries, theatres and child-welfare centres. Carnegie institutes, foundations and corporations were founded in Pittsburgh, Washington and New York. The present International Court of Justice building in The Hague was built as the Peace Palace with funds donated by Carnegie. This multi-millionaire with an extraordinary social conscience gave $62 million to British and colonial institutions and the bulk of his wealth – $350 million – to beneficiaries in the United States.

THE VALUE OF EDUCATION

- *Carnegie enjoyed promoting his ideas in print. In a book of essays,* The Gospel of Wealth *(1900), he wrote, 'I have known millionaires starve for lack of the nutriment which alone can sustain all that is human in man, and I know workmen, and many so-called poor men, who revel in luxuries beyond the power of those millionaires to reach. It is the mind that makes the body rich.'*
- *He believed that education was vital. He never forgot freely using a small endowed library in Pittsburgh, and this motivated his world-wide library-building campaign. Over 1,700 libraries owe their existence to Carnegie.*
- *On completion of their deal, J.P. Morgan congratulated Carnegie on being 'the richest man in the world'.*
- *Carnegie and his wife, Louise Whitfield, had homes in New York, Lenox, Massachusetts, and until World War I they regularly visited their Scottish home, Skibo Castle, which they bought in 1897.*
- *Carnegie Hall, the historic concert hall in New York, which opened in 1891 and was formerly home of the New York Philharmonic Orchestra, is named after him.*

John D. Rockefeller

John D. Rockefeller (1839–1937) was America's first oil tycoon. He created a monopoly and made a fortune from his Standard Oil Company, providing cheap fuel for the masses, and then gave millions to charity.

JOHN D. (DAVISON) ROCKEFELLER was born in 1839 in Richford, NY to a family of German descent. The family moved to the growing city of Cleveland in the Midwest of America when Rockefeller was thirteen. He left school at sixteen and, after a three-month business course, he began work as a bookkeeper in Cleveland. In 1859, he set up his first business as a commission merchant in grains and other goods. He worked hard, lived simply and saved money, taking after his pious mother who taught him to have a deep love of God, rather than after his unreliable father, nicknamed 'Devil Bill', and he became an active member of the Baptist Church.

Meanwhile, in 1859, the first oil well had been drilled in Titusville in western Pennsylvania, giving birth to the petroleum industry. Cleveland became a major refining centre and Rockefeller soon spotted the potential. Oil became his business. In 1863, he built a refinery in Cleveland, and within two years it was the largest in the area. He bought out his partners, and his stake in the industry expanded rapidly as demand for kerosene for lighting grew. In 1870 he formed the Standard Oil Company, at first with his brother and then with two colleagues. Oil needed transporting, and Rockefeller beat his rivals by obtaining competitive rates from the rival rail companies, then combined different companies into the Southern Improvement Company in an aggressive move to starve out his remaining competitors.

By 1872, he was powerful and rich enough to swoop on them, and he swallowed up twenty-two of his twenty-six competitors in the so-called 'Cleveland Massacre'. Through his new holding company, Standard Oil, Rockefeller gradually gained control over the whole industry – production, refining, storage and shipping. He thought big and played big, and was also cunning. In 1881, Standard Oil's stock and its affiliates were formed into the first US 'trust' with a board of nine trustees. By 1883 Standard Oil had a near total monopoly of the American oil market – owning 75 per cent of it and controlling almost 90 per cent. Congress, alarmed, initiated an investigation, and in 1890 passed the Sherman Antitrust Act to deal specifically with monopolies like Rockefeller's, but

Chronology

1839	Born Richford, NY, 8 July
1853	Family moves to Cleveland
1859	First business based on commissions
1863	Builds first oil refinery near Cleveland
1870	Takes over Standard Oil Company
1871	Standard Oil controls most refineries in Cleveland
1881	Establishes first business 'trust' under board of nine trustees
1882	Standard Oil controls 90 per cent of US oil business
1890	US Congress passes anti-monopoly Sherman Antitrust Act
1891	Trust dissolved, but board of nine remains in control of operations of affiliated companies
1896	Begins to give money and time to charities
1899	Brings together affiliated companies in holding company Standard Oil Company (New Jersey)
1911	Holding company declared illegal under terms of Sherman Antitrust Act; Rockefeller retires
1937	Dies at Ormond Beach, Florida, 23 May

'I have always regarded it as a religious duty to get all I could and to give all I could'

A Monopoly Capitalist

■ *Rockefeller was quite open about his intention: 'to kill competitive capitalism in favour of a new monopoly capitalism'.*

■ *Rockefeller married Laura Spelman, in 1864. They had five children, four daughters and a son John, born in 1874, who took over his father's charitable interests.*

■ *He said: 'I have always regarded it as a religious duty to get all I could and to give all I could.'*

■ *He had homes in New York, on the Hudson River and in Florida, where in retirement he played golf daily and gave new dimes to children he met.*

■ *Rockefeller admired his contemporary Andrew Carnegie, the steel magnate, to whom he wrote, 'You have given away more money than any man living.' The same could be said of Rockefeller, whose name became synonymous with enormous wealth.*

his trust had no paperwork, and its illegality could, therefore, not be proved.

Where Congress had failed, the State of Ohio partially succeeded. The trustees of Standard Oil (Ohio) were ordered to dissolve, reinventing themselves as a 'holding' company and changing the name to Standard Oil (New Jersey) in 1898. With the motor car fuelling ever bigger profits, in 1911 the Supreme Court finally ordered the break-up of the New Jersey parent. The thirty-eight companies it controlled were separated into individual firms.

Rockefeller remained president of Standard Oil until 1911, but retired from day-to-day management of the company in 1896, and devoted the rest of his life to giving away his money. Avoiding publicity, as he had in business, he set up the Rockefeller Institute for Medical Research, the General Education Board and the Rockefeller Foundation. He also provided matching funds to help found the University of Chicago, and in 1928 set up a child welfare trust in memory of his wife. Rockefeller died in Florida, aged ninety-seven.

HENRY FORD

Henry Ford (1863–1947) was one of the driving forces behind the birth of the motor car industry and consumer society. He pioneered the mass production of vehicles, and established a company that has rolled out cars, vans and trucks across the globe for more than 100 years.

BORN TO A PROSPEROUS Irish immigrant farmer near Dearborn in Michigan, Ford left school at sixteen. Handy with machinery, he went to work as an apprentice in the machine shops in nearby Detroit. After three years in various jobs, he returned to his father's farm. He continued tinkering with machinery, built a farm locomotive and also worked part time for Westinghouse Engine Company.

In 1891, he moved back to Detroit with his young wife, Clara Bryant, and started work as an engineer for Edison Light Company. His job was to keep the city's electricity service running, and it gave him time to enrol in classes in mechanical drawing, bookkeeping and business at a local university and also to build a gasoline engine, in 1893, and his first car – the Quadricycle – in 1896. The car so impressed his father's friend, W. C. Maybury, the Mayor of Detroit, that the mayor sponsored a second and encouraged backers to fund the Detroit Automobile Company. It went bust within a year, but the same backers funded a successor company, the Henry Ford Company, for which Ford built several successful racing cars. The company was renamed the Cadillac Automobile Company, using Ford's designs, but with a different engine – so effectively the first Cadillac was actually a Ford.

With the help of local Detroit investors, Ford established the Ford Motor Company in 1903. He was determined to mass-produce cars that were affordable rather than just playthings for the rich, and he began production of the Model T Ford in 1908, proclaiming: 'I will build a motor car for the great multitude.' Although not the first to use standardized parts and assembly-line techniques, Ford was by far the most successful in automating production, and by 1914 his Highland Park plant in Michigan had incorporated the first moving assembly line. The world's first automatic conveyor belt could turn out a car every 93 minutes, an enormous improvement over the 728 minutes required for manual assembly. Eventually the development of mass production slashed the manufacture of a Model T to just 24 seconds – significantly reducing the cost of each vehicle.

CHRONOLOGY

1863	Born in Dearborn, Michigan, 30 July
1891	Chief engineer at Edison plant in Detroit
1896	Builds his first car – the Quadricycle
1889	Works with Detroit Automobile Company
1903	Ford Motor Company founded
1908	Model T Ford starts production
1918	Runs for Senate
1927	Opens new plant at River Rouge
1947	Dies in Dearborn, Michigan, 7 April

Demand soared, and by 1927 he had sold fifteen million 'Tin Lizzies'. They were famously 'available in any colour, as long as it's black'. Profits also soared, and on the back of them Ford early on battled through the courts and bought out his original shareholders so that he could run his vast motor corporation himself. Not only a successful innovator in manufacturing, Ford was also a marketing pioneer. He invented the dealer-franchise system to sell and service his cars. By 1912, there were 7,000 Ford dealers across the country. Gas stations and better roads followed, and suburbs sprang up; Ford's common car transformed the American way of life.

He revolutionized the auto industry by paying high wages – he introduced a minimum $5-a-day

'You may have any colour you like, as long as it's black'

wage in 1914 and decreased the daily shift to eight hours – but he was resolutely opposed to organized labour. Court action and a strike at his new purpose-built main plant at River Rouge, Michigan, however, finally forced him to recognize the labour unions in 1941. River Rouge was by then a manufacturing giant, producing everything from the steel and wooden floorboards for the cars to the rubber for the wheels. That same inflexibility kept him from bringing out a new model until 1927, a delay which cost Ford dearly in what had become an increasingly competitive market.

Using his stature as an industrial leader, Ford led a peace mission to Europe during World War I. After the war, he ran unsuccessfully for the Senate. In addition to manufacturing cars, Ford also bought a railway, built aeroplanes, owned coal mines and timber plantations to supply his plants, published a newspaper and built a hospital in Detroit. He retired in 1945 and died two years later, leaving the largest share of his holdings in the Ford Motor Company to the Ford Foundation.

Ford and Anti-Semitism

■ *Ford was rarely out of the headlines, and he seemed eager to court controversy. 'History is more or less bunk,' he said in a libel case against the* Chicago Tribune, *which had called him 'an ignorant idealist' for his pacifism.*

■ *In addition to his pacifism, Ford was also a convinced anti-Semite. In 1918 he bought a newspaper, the* Dearborn Independent, *in which he kept up a barrage of vitriolic attacks on Jews, articles which were later published as* The International Jew: The World's Foremost Problem. *He kept a photo of Adolf Hitler on his desk in later years, and he was the only American cited in Hitler's* Mein Kampf. *He was awarded the Grand Cross of the German Order by Hitler.*

Akio Morita

Akio Morita (1921–99) created a global corporation, becoming a billionaire and an icon of modern management, but jokingly claimed his greatest achievement was inventing a word in English – Walkman.

TO MANY OUTSIDE JAPAN, Morita epitomized its astonishing post-war economic recovery, a compliment implicitly endorsed in his autobiography's title – *Made in Japan* (1986). But Morita was anything but a typical Japanese 'salaryman'. Japanese executives are cautious, consensual and notoriously poor communicators with foreigners. Morita was none of these things – although he was a workaholic.

Groomed from childhood to take over a sake-brewing business fourteen generations old, instead Morita struck out on his own. Excelling in physics, he served briefly with the Japanese navy's Wartime Research Committee, where he met Masaru Ibuka. In May 1946 they set up business in a bombed-out radio repair shop on borrowed capital of less than 500 dollars. Ibuka, thirty-eight, concentrated on research and product development, Morita, twenty-five, on finance, personnel and marketing. Their first task, in common with most Japanese industry, was to reverse the image of their country as a producer of shoddy, imitative products and to build a reputation for excellence and innovation.

In 1950 they produced Japan's first magnetic tape and tape recorder. In 1957 they launched the world's first mass-produced pocket-sized transistor radio. Just too big for standard shirt pockets, it was sold by salesmen wearing special shirts with slightly larger pockets.

The pocket-radio, fundamental to Morita's strategy, reversed normal business logic. Instead of finding out what the public needed and making it, he made products never thought of, such as a tape-player without a recording function. Morita saw people lugging hefty domestic radios outdoors and intuited the niche for a device to play music and leave the listener free to do something else – the Walkman.

Morita's global ambitions were underlined by changing a well-established and respected company name to one easy for foreigners. Sony, coined as a combination of Latin 'sonus' (sound) and the slang 'sonny', was to imply youthfulness and informality. To emphasize his point domestically, Morita had Sony written in the katakana Japanese script normally used for writing foreign words and names. By dropping 'Kogyo' (Engineering) from the name he prepared the way for diversification into music, entertainment and finance.

In 1960 Sony Corporation of America was established in the USA, and Morita moved there to build his own sales network. In the same year Sony launched the world's first all-transistor TV. In 1961 Morita became the first Japanese entrepreneur to raise capital abroad rather than rely on Japanese banks.

His 1966 book *Never Mind School Records* challenged orthodox Japanese reliance on

Chronology

1921	Born in industrial Nagoya, Japan's third-largest city
1944	Graduates in physics, Osaka Imperial University
1946	Founds Tokyo Tsushin Kogyo KK (Tokyo Telecommunications Engineering Corporation)
1957	Introduces world's first mass-produced pocket radio
1958	Changes company name to Sony Corporation
1963	Moves to USA
1971	Sony becomes the first Japanese company on New York Stock Exchange
1979	Launches Walkman
1989	Launches 3.5-inch floppy disk
1992	Served on Trilateral Commission to ease trade frictions
1993	Confined to a wheelchair after a stroke
1999	Dies of pneumonia

'We don't believe in market research for a new product unknown to the public. So we don't do any'

conventional educational achievement and stressed flexible thinking.

Sony's continuing flow of innovative products included the removable car radio, the miniature TV, the first home VCR, the Trinitron colour TV system and the 3.5-inch floppy disk. There were failures. Sony's technically superior Betamax system lost out to VHS. The 1989 buy-out of Columbia Pictures disappointed expectations. Morita's co-authorship of *The Japan That Can Say No* (1989) proved embarrassing when its criticisms of US corporate sluggishness back-fired. In 1993, on the day Morita's appointment as chairman of the Keidanren (Japan Federation of Economic Organizations) was to be announced, he suffered a stroke which ended his business career.

INTERNATIONAL ACCLAIM

- *Numbering Kissinger and Zubin Mehta among his friends, honoured by a dozen countries, Morita became a model of the internationalized Japanese. Time magazine listed him as one of its 100 most important people of the twentieth century and the only non-American among its business leaders.*
- *In the words of Japanese management guru Kenichi Ohmae, Morita 'made Sony a trusted name everywhere, because a company without borders is one without limit'.*
- *'Curiosity is the key to creativity.'*
- *'We don't believe in market research for a new product unknown to the public. So we never do any.'*

Bill Gates

Bill Gates (1955–), a computer whiz and one of the world's richest men, built the Microsoft Corporation into a software empire that provides the operating system on just about every personal computer in the world.

Born William Henry Gates in comfortable surroundings in Seattle in 1955 to a father who was an attorney and to a schoolteacher mother, Gates developed an interest in computers at the comparatively late age of thirteen when he began programming on a primitive ASR-33 teletype unit while at Lakeside preparatory school. By seventeen he had sold his first program – a scheduling system for the school for $4,200. It was at Lakeside that Gates met Paul Allen, a student two years his senior who shared his interest in computing. 'Of course, in those days we were just goofing around, or so we thought,' Gates wrote in his book *The Road Ahead.*

In 1973, he entered Harvard, where in between all-night poker sessions he developed a version of the programming language BASIC, but he dropped out after two years to devote himself to the company that he and Allen founded. The company was Microsoft.

The pair bought a microcomputer software program, rewrote it and licensed it to computer giant IBM. In a stroke of genius or good fortune, Microsoft retained the rights to the software – the MS-DOS system, which sat at the heart of almost all personal computers – and Gates, recognizing the potential of software in the coming age of the personal computer, launched Microsoft into big-time business on the back of it.

In 1986, Gates successfully floated his company on the NASDAQ exchange and as the price of the stock soared he found himself, aged thirty-one, the youngest self-made billionaire in the world. Microsoft Windows followed, and Gates cleaned up as the system became industry standard for personal computers world-wide.

Chronology

1955	Born in Seattle, 28 October
1973	Enters Harvard; drops out two years later
1975	Co-founds Microsoft with Paul Allen
1980	Develops MS-DOS
1986	Floats Microsoft on NASDAQ
1994	Marries Melinda French
2000	Resigns as chief executive of Microsoft, remains chairman and chief software architect

His net worth, based mainly on his holdings in Microsoft, peaked during the dotcom boom at $144 billion and has slumped as low as $30 billion; there are websites which track its daily fluctuations. Original investors who bought 100 shares at the initial offering price of $21 saw their stake rise to over $500,000.

Microsoft came late to the Internet revolution, but caught up with and destroyed its competitors. It initially lagged behind Netscape in developing a browser for accessing the World Wide Web, but quickly created its Internet Explorer that now dominates the market.

Like earlier industrial 'titans' in America, such as oil magnate John D. Rockefeller, Gates ran into

The Gates Foundation

- *The Bill and Melinda Gates Foundation funds global health projects and programmes on poverty reduction, literacy and learning. Created in 2000, it has endowments of some $26 billion.*
- *In addition to computers and software, Gates is interested in biotechnology. He sits on the board of ICOS, a company that specializes in protein-based and small molecule therapeutics, and he is an investor in a number of other biotechnology companies.*
- *Paul Allen left Microsoft management in 1983 when he was diagnosed with Hodgkin's disease, but he kept his stake in the company.*

Microsoft came late to the Internet revolution, but caught up with and destroyed its competitors

difficulty with the US government in the late 1990s in a protracted anti-trust battle. The three-and-a-half-year tussle prompted Gates to step down as chief executive, but he remained chief software architect and chairman of Microsoft. During the anti-trust trial, Gates refused to answer opposing lawyers' questions directly, prompting the judge in the case to label him a 'Napoleon'. Critics say Gates is a corporate bully, and that Microsoft is an 'evil empire' that exploits its monopoly power, but he cultivates the image of a corporate visionary and philanthropist. He is an avid reader and plays bridge, chess and golf. He has a penchant for jumping over chairs, and an unconscious habit of rocking back and forth in them.

'I think I am having more fun than anybody I know,' Gates says. 'My job forces me to take risks, learn new things all the time. It's a dream come true.'

In 1994, the sandy-haired, bespectacled billionaire married one of his marketing directors, Melinda French. They have three children and live on the edge of Lake Washington near Seattle in a self-styled dream mansion with a swimming pool, cinema and parking for thirty vehicles. The high-tech mansion took seven years to build and cost some $100 million.